Francis A. Drexel
LIBRARY

Books For College Libraries
Third Edition

Core Collection

SAINT JOSEPH'S UNIVERSITY

Functioning of
the Multinational
Corporation

Pergamon Titles of Related Interest

Davis Managing and Organizing Multinational Corporations
Feld Multinational Corporations and U.N. Politics
Grieves Transnationalism in World Politics and Business
McHale/Hughes/Grundy Evaluating Transnational Programs in
Government and Business

Related Journals*

Accounting, Organizations and Society
Journal of Enterprise Management
Long Range Planning
Omega

*Free specimen copies available upon request.

PERGAMON POLICY STUDIES ON BUSINESS

Functioning of the Multinational Corporation
A Global Comparative Study

Edited by
Anant R. Negandhi

HD
62.4
·F86
1980

Pergamon Press
NEW YORK • OXFORD • TORONTO • SYDNEY • PARIS • FRANKFURT

Pergamon Press Offices:

U.S.A.	Pergamon Press Inc., Maxwell House, Fairview Park, Elmsford, New York 10523, U.S.A.
U.K.	Pergamon Press Ltd., Headington Hill Hall, Oxford OX3 0BW, England
CANADA	Pergamon of Canada, Ltd., Suite 104, 150 Consumers Road, Willowdale, Ontario M2J 1P9, Canada
AUSTRALIA	Pergamon Press (Aust.) Pty. Ltd., P.O. Box 544, Potts Point, NSW 2011, Australia
FRANCE	Pergamon Press SARL, 24 rue des Ecoles, 75240 Paris, Cedex 05, France
FEDERAL REPUBLIC OF GERMANY	Pergamon Press GmbH, Hammerweg 6, Postfach 1305, 6242 Kronberg/Taunus, Federal Republic of Germany

Library of Congress Cataloging in Publication Data

Main entry under title:

Functioning of the multinational corporation.

   (Pergamon policy studies)
   Bibliography: p.
   Includes index.
   1. International business enterprises—Management—Addresses, essays, lectures. 2. Comparative management—Addresses, essays, lectures. I. Negandhi, Anant R.
HD69.I7F84 1980   338.8'8   79-27029
ISBN 0-08-025087-4

Printed in the United States of America

Second Printing, 1982

To

PIA,
a transnational child
whose past, present and future
are all interwoven into one real world.

Contents

Preface

One of the foci of the research program of the International Institute of Management, Science Center Berlin, is on the participation of the private enterprise in measures to overcome societal problems such as regional decay, structural unemployment, decline in competitive capacity of industries, and similar industrial policy issues. The participation from the private sector's side is looked upon as an attractive and promising alternative to the establishment of governmental agencies for the said purpose or, in many cases, as an appropriate complement to public sector organizations.

Given the debate of the last ten years, it seems highly necessary to study the preparedness of multinational corporations to engage in such - national and supranational - industrial policy programs, and also to assess their performance in this respect.

Professor Anant Negandhi, who in 1976 undertook to organize a program segment with the said orientation within the Institute, established a worldwide network of experts in science and administration, in support of this task. From time to time the experts met in order to assess the progress and deliberations of the Institute's MNC research. The present volume makes public a number of papers on the issue which were delivered at one of those meetings.

The International Institute of Management wants to express its sincerest thanks to Professor Anant Negandhi, the members of this cooperating team, and in particular the contributors to this volume. It is our hope that the publication will shed light on the functioning of Multinational Corporations in industrialized as well as developing countries.

Berlin, Autumn 1979 Walter H. Goldberg
Professor of Business Administration
Fellow, International Institute of
Management
Science Center Berlin

ix

I

Introduction

1 Multinational Corporations: Issues, Context, and Strategies
Anant R. Negandhi

Energy shortages, inflation, unemployment, and slowdown in economic and industrial activities in most of the industrialized countries have become the "real" news issues both at national and international levels. Only a few years ago, the critics and advocators of the multinationals (MNCs) were arguing about the negative and positive impact of MNCs in either creating or resolving the very same issues of unemployment, inflation, and balance of payment problems.

The advocators conceive MNCs as the most powerful engine of progress ever invented by humans, and regard them as "agents of change and progress . . . building . . . a new world economic system – one in which the constraints of geography have yielded to the logic of efficiency" (Kendall, 1974, p. 22). Multinationals were also viewed "as a powerful engine for diffusing the benefits of superior management and technology across national boundaries, thereby improving the world's allocation of resources" (Benoit, 1970, p. 65).

On the other hand, critics blamed the MNCs for exporting the jobs and technology (Goldfinger, 1973), while the leaders of many developing countries accused them of exploiting local labor, charging high royalty payments for supplying obsolete technology, and of using monopolistic power to crush local competition (Turner, 1970; Barnet and Muller, 1974). Provocative titles of the books on MNCs, published during the late '60s and '70s, such as Sovereignty at Bay (Vernon, 1971), The Invisible Empire (Turner, 1970), The American Challenge (Servan-Schreiber, 1968), The European Revenge (Heller and Willat, 1975), The Sovereign State of ITT (Sampson, 1973), Global Reach (Barnet and Mueller, 1975), and The Frightening Angels (Negandhi-Prasad, 1975), to mention just a few, reflect public opinion concerning the role and status of the multinational corporations.

Although the direct attack on multinational corporations has dampened somewhat and talks of accommodations have begun (Franko, 1976), the influence and stake of the MNCs in the world's economy have changed little. If anything, their role and influence have only increased during the last ten years. For example, in 1950, American MNCs accounted for 17 percent of the total sales of United States manufacturers; by 1967, the percentage increased to 42 percent of the total sales, and by 1974, to 62 percent (Vernon, 1977, p. 13). A similar trend is also noticeable with respect to other countries.

Today the multinational enterprises represent one-third of the world's industrial output and, beyond their economic muscle, many countries in the world, especially the developing countries, depend upon their technological, managerial, and entrepreneurial skills for achieving industrial and economic goals. And very often, the goals, objectives, and policies of the MNCs and the nation-states are inconsistent, and unavoidable conflict results.

PURPOSE AND ORIGIN OF THIS VOLUME

This volume outlines and analyzes some of the critical issues and conflicts between MNCs and nation-states. We will first examine the changing world economic scene and how the New International Economic Order may affect the activities of the MNCs. Secondly, we will compare the strategies, policy making, and organizational adaptability of the multinational corporations with the nation-states' policies and demands. Thirdly, we will look briefly at the individuals who manage multinational corporations in terms of their backgrounds, education, training, and outlook.

The volume is an outcome of a recently organized conference on The Functioning of Multinational Corporations: Their Internal and External Modes of Operations, in West Berlin, Germany, under the auspices of the International Institute of Management, Science Center, Berlin. Some 30 academic scholars, business executives, and governmental officials were invited to share their empirically-based studies on various aspects of the functioning of multinational corporations. More specifically, the following topics concerning the operations of the MNCs were examined:

1. Formulation of Codes of Conduct at international, national, and firm levels, focusing on their rationale, implementation processes, successes, and failures.

2. Conflicts and conflicting issues between MNCs and host countries, MNCs and their home countries, and the MNCs' home and host countries, and the modes of resolution used by different types of MNCs and governmental agencies.

3. The processes of adaptations used by different MNCs to cope with the home and host countries' demands and policies.
4. The MNCs' contributions to the home and host countries' economies - such as balance of payment, and employment.
5. Transfer of skills by MNCs - managerial and technological - to the host countries.
6. Internal structures, control and coordination mechanisms used for managing world-wide operations.
7. Management orientations, philosophy, strategies, and policies of MNCs to manage their world-wide operations.
8. Management of subsidiaries.
9. Personnel and industrial relation policies and practices used by MNCs.
10. Impact of the MNCs' operations on the host countries' socio-cultural norms and life styles.

Research-based papers included in this volume analyze many of the above topics.

ECONOMIC DEVELOPMENT DECADE OF THE 1960s

During the 1950s and 1960s, industrialization became the key goal for many newly-born nations of Asia and Africa. It offered a major hope for solving the problems of poverty, insecurity, overpopulation, and preserving the hard-won political freedom. One author was tempted to call this quest for industrial and economic progress "one of the great world crusades of our time" (Bryce, 1960, p. 3). In the same vein, former Brazilian President Kubitschek, (McMillan et al. 1964) echoed the concern of many leaders of developing countries, almost two decades ago, by saying,

> The majority of our people are convinced that if the road to material progress is barred, Brazil will not be able to avoid the choice between development and the wreckage of its democratic institution.

Many political leaders, businesspeople as well as academicians, believed that the foreign private investor and the multinational corporation could play an important role in achieving the goals of industrial and economic development in developing countries.

The open-arm welcome to foreign investors and multinational corporations was accompanied by numerous incentives offered to the MNCs in the form of tax holidays, tariff protection, duty-free imports of capital goods, and similar other facilities which did result in an increase of inflow of private foreign investment into those countries. However, for many known and unknown reasons, the developmental decade failed to realize its lofty promises of industrial and economic growth.

Disappointed with the negative results and encouraged by the successful attempt of the OPEC countries to increase the oil prices fourfold in a single year, the leaders of the so-called "Group of 77" focused on strengthening their collective political powers at international levels. The North-South dialogue and the current discussion for establishing a New International Economic Order reflect this change in strategies.

In his paper, Sauvant identifies the origin of this current discussion of the New International Economic Order and pinpoints the implications of the changing international economic and political realities for the multinational corporations.

It is well recognized by now that the industrial and economic development is not all blessings. Although industrialization could provide employment, reduce poverty, and increase the standard of living, it also brings along pollution, urban unrest, crime congested housing, and disruption to the existing lifestyle of the people.

Kumar, in his paper, seeks to identify the sociocultural impact of multinational investments in the developing countries, and points out the areas where further research is needed.

As stated earlier, multinationals have been accused of exploiting local labor, charging high royalty payments for obsolete technology and patent rights, and using monopolistic power to crush the local competition. The so-called transfer-pricing practices utilized for intra-company sales are believed to be the central mechanism through which MNCs are accomplishing their objectives.

Rugman, in his paper, argues against this widely-held belief and provides the real reasons for transfer-pricing practices - existence of imperfect market conditions, undue constraints imposed by governments on the private enterprise system - and suggests a novel methodology to ascertain the nature and intensity of transfer-pricing practices utilized by the multinational corporations.

STRATEGIES AND POLICIES OF
MULTINATIONAL CORPORATIONS

The fast changing international environments and the increasing demands by the nation-states have obligated the multinationals, to a large extent, to adjust their strategies and policies in order to achieve global rationalization of production and marketing processes. However, organizations, like human beings, resist change, and yet, change is the very essence of international business today.

In the section to follow, we seek to capture some of the dilemma and frustration experienced by the multinationals as they attempt to perfect the act of balancing strategies and policies to achieve two conflicting demands - global rationalization versus adaptation to differing demands made by the home and host countries.

Prahalad and Doz, utilizing their own empirical studies in the developed and developing countries and published data on the trends and methods of intervention of governments, explore the use of a matrix-type of organizational structure and policy-making the MNCs could use to achieve twin objectives of global rationalization and coping with the differing demands of the host countries, as well as the demands of the complexity of the diversified product-lines and advanced technological and engineering problems.

Studies on the strategies, policies, and structures of the multinationals, undertaken during the last ten years or so, amply suggest that the multinational companies, originating from the United States, Western Europe, and Japan, are different in their modes of operation (Stopford and Wells, 1972; Franko, 1976; Yoshino, 1976; and Negandhi and Baliga, 1979).

In spite of differing strategies, policies, and structures utilized by different types of multinationals, the economic and technological imperatives are pushing all large-scale industrial companies around the world to a point of convergence into their modes of operations and responses. Especially when the environment is benign and the market and economic conditions are competitive rather than controlled, different types of multinationals, as well as large scale local firms, do behave and respond in similar manners. Only when the environment is hostile and restrictive, and market and economic forces are under severe constraints imposed by the governments, do different types of multinationals seem to respond differently.

In the two papers by Negandhi and Baliga, and Negandhi, such similarities and differences among American, European, and Japanese multinationals have been observed.

In the West European countries, where the market and economic conditions are relatively free of undue governmental constraints, American, German, and Japanese MNCs seem to opt for global rationalization strategies, while in developing countries, where governmental controls are severe, these three types of multinationals are responding differently. European and Japanese MNCs are opting to adjust their strategies to the host countries' demands and constraints, while American MNCs are still pursuing a global rationalization strategy.

THE COMMUNIST WORLD AND MULTINATIONALS

Though the multinationals originating from the so called free-world countries are not, in the strictest sense, allowed to operate in centralized, state-controlled economies such as the Soviet Union or the East European communist bloc countries, the need of these countries for advanced technologies and market and management know-how has compelled them to buy, borrow, or steal the knowledge possessed by multinationals.

Depending upon the level of industrial and economic development of a given country, as well as the need and objectives of securing advanced technological, market, and management know-how, those countries have shown differential preferences for negotiating with multinationals (such as turnkey operations versus preference for joint venture with some sort of barter arrangement).

Miller sheds light on the differential preferences of the state-controlled economies and pinpoints to the adaptability of American, European, and Japanese multinationals in those countries, while Vambery explores the situation with respect to the shipping industry and suggests ways and means through which both the MNCs and the home countries of the MNCs could cope with the increasing, and sometimes unfair, competition from the state-controlled shipping industry, originating from communist as well as developing countries.

THE MAN IN THE MIDDLE

Caught between the changing international economic and political realities and huge organizational machines are the managers of the MNCs, who are ultimately being held responsible to play and thus either win or lose the complicated international business chess game. As noted earlier, organizations resist change, and consequently, strategies, policies, and resulting structures formulated in the past, when the environment was benign and cooperative, are still being used, and those who are managing the multinationals need extraordinary talents and skills.

In the last three chapters, we briefly outline background, education, training, and outlook of the MNCs' managers.

In Chapter 10, Merwe and Merwe outline background, education, and training of the chief executives of American, European, and Japanese multinational corporations and suggest the nature of future training needs for those managers.

Stening and his colleagues, in Chapter 11, and Matsusaki, in Chapter 12, compare and contrast styles of the managers of the Japanese subsidiaries with those of the Australian and Canadian local managers, respectively.

In the last chapter, we have attempted to echo some concerns of the academicians, businessmen, and governmental decision-makers with respect to the issues and topics discussed in the proceeding chapters, pinpointing, in the process, the gap in our knowledge about the functioning of multinational corporations, and suggesting an agenda for research for international business scholars.

REFERENCES

Barnet, Richard J., and Muller, Donald. 1974. Global Reach: The Power of Multinational Corporations. New York: Simon and Schuster.

Benoit, Emile. 1970. "The Attack on the Multinationals." Columbia Journal of World Business, November-December, p. 15.

Bryce, Murray D. 1960. Industrial Development. New York: McGraw-Hill.

Franko, L. G. 1976. The European Multinationals. Stanford, Conn.: Greylock Publishers.

Kendall, Donald M. 1974. "The Need for the Multinational Corporation." In John K. Ryans, ed., The Multinational Business World of the 1980's. Kent, Ohio: Center for Business and Economic Research, Kent State University.

Kubitschek. 1964. Brazilian Bulletin. New York: Brazilian Government Trade Bureau, March 1962, p. 4. Quoted in International Enterprises in a Developing Economy, ed. Claude McMillan, Jr. et al., vol. 2. East Lansing, Mich.: Bureau of Business and Economic Research, Michigan State University.

Negandhi, Anant R. and Prasad, Benjamin S. 1975. The Frightening Angels. Kent, Ohio: Kent State University Press.

Negandhi, Anant R., and Baliga, B. R. 1979. Quest For Survival and Growth: A Comparative Study of American, European and Japanese Multinationals. New York: Praeger Publishers.

Sampson, Anthony. 1973. The Sovereign State of ITT. New York: Stein and Day.

Servan-Schreiber, J.J. 1968. The American Challenge. New York: Athenaeum.

Stopford, John, and Wells, Louis T. 1972. Managing the Multinational Enterprise: Organization of the Firm and Ownership of the Subsidiaries. New York: Basic Books, Inc.

Turner, Louis. 1970. Invisible Empires: Multinational Companies in the Modern World. London: Hamish Hamilton Publishers.

Vernon, Raymond. 1971. Sovereignty at Bay: The Multinational Spread of U.S. Enterprises. New York: Basic Books, Inc.

Vernon, Raymond. 1977. Storm Over the Multinationals. Cambridge, Mass. Harvard University Press.

Yoshino, M.Y. 1976. Japan's Multinational Enterprises. Cambridge, Mass. Harvard University Press.

II

Multinationals and Global-Level Issues

2 From Political to Economic Independence: The Historical Context of the New International Economic Order*
Karl P. Sauvant

Only very recently have transnational enterprises (TNEs) become the subject of international discussion. In 1972 the
United Nations Economic and Social Council requested the
Secretary-General, in a unanimously adopted resolution, to
appoint a Group of Eminent Persons to study the role of TNEs
and their impact on the process of development and on international relations. During the fall of 1973, the Group of
Eminent Persons began its deliberations which resulted, in the
spring of 1974, in a report to the Secretary-General which
recommended, inter alia, the establishment of a United Nations
Commission and Centre on Transnational Corporations. The
Secretary-General supported these recommendations and the
General Assembly decided during the same year to create both
institutions.

During 1973, a good part of the economic discussions
within the United Nations centered on TNEs. They were seen
to be at the centre of international economic transactions, they
were understood to be the hinge of the international economic
system.

Beginning in 1974, however, the focus of attention began
to shift away from the individual actors of the systems and
toward the system itself. The debate concerning the establishment of the New International Economic Order (NIEO) is a
debate about the nature of the international economic system,
particularly in its North-South dimension. It deals with the

*This paper was prepared while on a leave of absence at the
Zentrum fuer interdisziplinaere Forschung, University of
Bielefeld, West Germany. The views expressed in it do not
necessarily reflect those of the institutions with which the
author is affiliated.

framework within which international economic transactions take place, the purposes they are meant to serve, the mechanisms that regulate them, and the structures they create.

Curiously enough, however, TNEs are hardly mentioned in the program for the NIEO. (The basic documents of the program for the NIEO are United Nations General Assembly resolutions 3201 [S-VI] "Declaration on the Establishment of a New International Economic Order" and 3202 [S-VI] "Programme of Action on the Establishment of a New International Economic Order," both adopted on May 1, 1974; resolution 3281 [xxix] "Charter of Economic Rights and Duties of State," adopted on December 12, 1974; and resolution 3362 [S-VII] "Development and International Economic Co-operation," adopted on September 16, 1975.) Two reasons appear largely to account for this neglect. The first is that the program addresses itself to governments and not to private actors. The second possible reason is that it has not yet been fully realized that the implementation of the present program requires the active cooperation of TNEs. Naturally, this second observation immediately raises the question of to what extent, under these circumstances, the NIEO program can actually be expected to lead to a truly new order.

Nevertheless, the debate concerning the establishment of the NIEO is of key importance to TNEs because it involves the framework within which their activities are carried out. Rather than sketching out and analyzing the substantive provisions of the program (see Sauvant and Hasenpflug, 1977 and Sauvant, forthcoming), I will focus on the historical context of the NIEO debate. Understanding this context and the origins of the discussions, is important for comprehending why the debate is taking place and the forces that are shaping it.

The present attention given to the North-South issue is mainly the result of the following set of six interrelated factors:

1.   The consolidation of the political independence of the developing countries and the stabilization of the global political-military situation;
2.   the full recognition of the importance of economic development, and the disappointments with the development efforts of the 1960s;
3.   doubts about the prevailing development model;
4.   the emergence of the movement of Non-Aligned Countries as an international pressure group for the reorganization of the international economic system;
5.   the politicization of the development issue; and
6.   the growing assertiveness of the developing countries.

NATIONAL POLITICAL CONSOLIDATION AND INTERNATIONAL POLITICAL-MILITARY STABILIZATION

Most developing countries (DCs) had become independent by the 1960s or liberated themselves from the political domination of their former hegemonial powers. The highest priority of these countries was, naturally, to consolidate their independence. This was all the more important since during the period of the Cold War, pressures were particularly intense to affiliate with one of the two rival superpowers. The 1955 Afro-Asian conference of Bandung was the first major attempt to secure political independence through international cooperation. The foundation of the movement of the non-aligned countries during its first summit in Belgrade in September, 1961, gave this cooperation a stronger and continuing basis. (The documents of the Non-Aligned Countries as well as the Final Communique of the Bandung Conference are contained in Jankowitsch and Sauvant, 1978.) At that time the main objectives of the non-aligned countries were principally of a political nature and reflected the militarily weak and politically threatened position of the individual members of the movement: decolonization, national self-determination, opposition to apartheid, dissolution of the political and military alliances and blocks, peaceful coexistence, dissolutions of military bases on foreign territories, disarmament, recognition of the territorial integrity of all states, noninterference into the internal affairs of states, and the strengthening of the United Nations.

By the beginning of the 1970s, most of these objectives had been achieved or had at least lost their urgency. Most colonies had become independent and most of the new countries had consolidated their sovereignty in its formal political aspects. The global rivalry of the superpowers - and the resulting pressure on the countries of the Third World - had receded and competition seemed to have been channeled into the acceptance of strategic balance, peaceful coexistence and detente. A certain global political-military stability had been achieved.

Although these developments did not resolve the fundamental problems of the East-West conflict, they stabilized the political-military situation sufficiently to allow greater attention to other international problems.

DISAPPOINTMENTS WITH THE DEVELOPMENT RESULTS

For the DCs, questions of economic development began to receive greater attention. After independence, it was widely believed that many of the problems of the DCs were largely a function of their political status. Once independence had been achieved, the DCs would become full and equal members of the international community. And their participation in international developments efforts would soon result, it was hoped, in a considerable improvement in their economic situation.

By the end of the 1960s, these hopes had been shattered. The First United Nations Development Decade, which had been launched with high hopes in 1961, fell short of its objectives; its extension in 1970 was viewed with dampened expectations. The Alliance for Progress, also launched in 1961 and accompanied with similar hopes, quietly faltered. Another regional effort, the First Yaounde of 1963 was replaced by the Second Yaounde Convention and the Arusha Convention (1969), but the expectations associated with them were not fulfilled (in spite of the improved conditions contained in the latter two agreements). The United Nations Conference on Trade and Development (UNCTAD) had a promising start with its first meeting 1964, but did not make considerable progress in its second (1968) and third (1972) meetings and thus only increased the sense of frustration in the developing countries. The same can be said for the Group of 77, formed in 1964 during UNCTAD. (The main purpose of the Group of 77 is to represent the economic interests of the DCs in the day-to-day work of UNCTAD and the United Nations General Assembly and its committees. It meets periodically at the ministerial level in order to prepare the negotiating positions of the developing countries for the UNCTAD conferences. Every developing country, regardless of United Nations membership, automatically belongs to the Group of 77. Yugoslavia was included since the beginning. In addition, the Republic of Korea and the Republic of Vietnam are members and, since the 1976 Manila ministerial meeting, Malta and Romania).

At the end of the decade it became clear that the economic situation of the DCs, aggravated further by unchecked population growth, had remained desperate. For many of them, in fact, the economic situation had worsened in comparison to that of the developed market economies (DMEs). While per capita income (at 1970 prices) in the DMEs increased from about $2,000 to $3,000 in the period from 1960 to 1975, in the DCs it rose by a mere $91 – from $169 to $260. Thus, it appeared, that the international and regional development efforts, or, more generally, the mechanisms of the international economic system, had failed to contain, let alone eliminate, absolute poverty. This was all the more disappointing since the DMEs had experienced unparalleled growth during the 1960s.

Importantly, the disappointments with the functioning of the international economic system came at a time when political-military developments allowed the full realization of the implications of these failures. Increasingly it became apparent that political independence would be a mere chimera unless comple-

mented by a minimum of economic independence, economic
development came to be sought with greater urgency.

DOUBTS ABOUT THE PREVAILING DEVELOPMENT MODEL

The question arose, therefore, whether the continuing difficulties of the DCs might not be, at least partially, a function of
the nature of the international economic system and especially
the mechanisms and structures through which the DCs were
linked with the DMEs. Questions were even asked that put
the development model of the overwhelming majority of the
Third-World nations into doubt. Two of the main characteristics of the prevailing model, in particular, were questioned:
its world-market orientation and its emphasis on GNP growth
rates.
        The key characteristic of the prevailing development mod-
el is that its framework of references is the world economy and
the world market. The close integration of the Third-World
countries into the world economy and their orientation towards
the world market is expected to trigger, and then to maintain,
the development process. While this integration involves a
whole range of transactions - such as technology, consumption
patterns, skills, and capital - trade has traditionally been
regarded as the most important among them. Trade is the
"engine" of development. The operative assumptions are that
the industrial states continue to grow; that this growth
translates itself into increased demand for imports from the
developing countries; and that this, in turn, stimulates the
industrial development of the latter. Conversely, if the
economic growth of the industrial countries slows down (such
as through a recession or a deliberate zero-growth policy) or
if this growth does not translate itself into equally increased
demand for goods and services from the Third-World (for
example, because of changing demand patterns or the development of substitutes), then the export-led industrialization
process of the South slows down as well or comes to a halt.
The experiences of the 1960s had put into question the indirect
mechanisms of this approach. In addition, the prevailing
development strategy tended to accentuate the structural
deformation of the economies of many DCs and, furthermore,
increase their dependency on the North. (See especially
Senghaas 1977.)
        These deficiencies contributed to the emergence and rise
of the concept of individual and collective self-reliance. Instead
of looking toward external impulses for growth, the self-
reliance approach looks toward internal impulses, particularly
the creation of a domestic market; transactions (especially
trade) with the DMEs are no longer the engine of development,
but instead have a supplementary function.

The concept of self-reliance had been introduced into the development debate by the President of Tanzania, Mwalima Julius K. Nyerere, in a speech before the 1970 Dar-es-Salaam Preparatory Conference of the Non-Aligned Countries. In the subsequent Third Conference of Heads of State or Government of Non-Aligned Countries at Lusaka in September 1970, the concept became the main plank of the economic program of the Non-Aligned Countries. During later conferences, and through concrete efforts among non-aligned and other developing countries, the concept of individual and collective self-reliance was elaborated further and became the main substantive contribution of the Non-Aligned Countries to the international development debate. (For the relevant documents, see Jankowitsch and Sauvant, 1978.)

The logic of the concept also required a common approach to foreign direct investment and transnational enterprises. This was recognized at the Dar-es-Salaam Preparatory Conference and also found its way into the 1970 Lusaka Summit "Declaration in Non-Alignment and Economic Progress" (Jankowitsch and Sauvant, 1978, p. 86). There, the Non-Aligned Countries pledged themselves "to adopt so far as practicable a common approach to problems and possibilities of investment of private capital in developing countries.

This pledge was followed up by "The Action Programme for Economic Co-operation Among Non-Aligned Countries," at the 1972 Non-Aligned Countries' Foreign Minister Conference with a decision to establish a Committee of Experts on Private Foreign Investment "to draw up a draft set of criteria, techniques and procedures which would make private foreign investment subserve national development objectives and would govern the adoption of a common approach to private investment (Jankowitsch and Sauvant, 1978, p. 454). Such a draft statute was presented to the 1975 Lima Conference of Foreign Ministers of Non-Aligned Countries in the "Plan of Action for Strengthening Co-operation, Solidarity and the Action Capacity of Non-Aligned and other Developing Countries and for Achieving the Establishment of the New International Economic Order" (Jankowitsch and Sauvant, p. 1240). The conference, however, did not, as requested, approve the statute for adoption by the member countries. The ministers merely decided to submit it "to the consideration of their Governments so that they may possibly be inspired by it in the framework of their national policies in this field." But the conference did decide to establish an Information Center of the Non-Aligned Countries on Transnational Corporations.

The self-reliance approach has not become the prevailing development model. This remains an export-led strategy. Still, key economic elements of the approach - mostly under the title "cooperation among developing countries" - have entered into all important international development programs, including the resolutions adopted at the Sixth and Seventh Special Sessions. There they are, because of their domestic (and Third World) market orientation, out of harmony with the overwhelming thrust of the respective programs, which remain world-market oriented. This applies as much for the program of the United Nations as it does for those of the Group of 77 and the Non-Aligned Countries.

Nevertheless, the self-reliance model has clear and important functions. It remains an alternative development strategy which - even if it may be very difficult to implement in its extreme form of "de-linking" the South from the North - can at least provide guidance for the kind of changes that are required to eliminate underdevelopment. Naturally this alternative becomes more attractive as the limitations of the export-led approach becomes apparent and/or the negotiations about the implementation of the NIEO program do not progress.

The most important contribution of the self-reliance discussions for the movement toward the NIEO, however, was that it led the DCs to recognize the political dimensions of development and to examine seriously the international framework of the development effort. This led to a questioning of the purposes of the international economic system and channeled the development discussion into more fundamental directions.

Apart from the world-market orientation of the prevailing development strategy, its quantitative growth emphasis and especially the prevalent practice of measuring development by - and equating it with - the growth of GNP particularly drew criticism and contributed to the rising doubts about the model itself. It was recognized that growth alone does not eliminate poverty since growth rates do not provide information about the quality and distribution of growth. If development involves the qualitative improvement of the standard of living of the entire population, growth cannot simply be equated with development. Hence the basic question was again raised: what kind of improvements are sought for whom? In other words; what is the objective of development?

In response to this question, many turned to the concept of basic needs. Accordingly, development first meant that the needs of the entire population for primary consumption goods (food, clothing, shelter), services (water, health, education, transport) and employment have to be satisfied, and development policy must address itself squarely to this objective. Such a goal orientation also requires growth, but a qualitatively different growth than in the past and most notably a growth that is directly geared towards the 40 percent of the population that has so far been neglected. This model no longer puts faith into an internal trickling-down effect but, instead, focusses on the domestic production and consumption patterns.

THE ROLE OF THE NON-ALIGNED COUNTRIES

Thus, a number of developments converged at the end of the 1960s: most developing countries had obtained and consolidated their political independence. The global political-military situation had stabilized. The countries of the Third World began to pay greater attention to development questions. The regional and international development program had had disappointing results. And doubts began to be raised about the appropriateness of the prevailing development model. By drawing the political consequences from the combination of these processes, the Non-Aligned Countries came to play a crucial role in this situation. Only the non-aligned movement could take this step because it is the only organization of the Third World that could draw political conclusions and lend them the necessary weight in the arena of international discussions.

Since its inception, membership in the non-aligned movement had grown consistently. At the first summit meeting in Belgrade in September 1961, 25 countries attended as full members. At the fifth summit in Colombo in August 1976, the number had increased to 85. In addition, a number of observers and guest countries participated in the movement. In 1976, three-quarters of the members of the Group of 77 were also members of the non-aligned movement. If observers are added, the percentage increases to 90. Thus, the non-aligned movement had succeeded in mobilizing most of the nations of the Third World.

Furthermore, the movement set up a highly-structured organization. Before the 1970 Lusaka Summit, the movement's organizational structure consisted only of the summit conferences (held at irregular intervals) and the preparatory conferences of foreign ministers. Since 1970, several organizational layers emerged which reached down to the level of seminars and symposia. The importance of these increased institutionalized contacts lay in the fact that they created horizontal lines of communication (i.e., lines of communications that are independent from the former colonial powers); they led to intensified contacts; and they allowed the Non-Aligned Countries to exchange information, define their interests, and coordinate their policies - and all that in a framework that is characterized by a stronger political awareness than that of the Group of 77. (The Non-Aligned Countries perceive themselves in fact as playing a "catalyst role" in the Group of 77.) The non-aligned movement provides, therefore, the organizational infrastructure for effective cooperation.

The organizational development of the movement went hand in hand with a shift in its programmatic emphasis. Before the 1970 Lusaka summit, the Non-Aligned Countries had mainly a political perspective - witness their principal objectives listed earlier. At the Lusaka summit, development questions received, for the first time, considerable attention. This shift developed further at the 1972 Georgetown foreign ministers conference and was ratified during the 1973 Algiers summit: the movement included the development issue among its principal objectives. The economic program adopted at Algiers called already for fundamental reforms of the international economic system; it was, in fact, the basis of the resolutions adopted several months later during the Sixth Special Session. The concrete contents of the economic program of the Non-Aligned Countries reaches back to the early 1950s and is largely based on the developmental concepts elaborated under Raul Prebisch in the Economic Commission for Latin America. Through UNCTAD's establishment in 1964 - Prebisch was its first Secretary-General - these concepts found a broader audience and subsequently became the basis of the work of the Group of 77 and the formulation of the strategies for the United Nations Development Decades. For a detailed analysis of the evolution of the non-aligned movement (and especially the emergence of the development issue) see "The Origins of the New International Economic Order: The Role of the Non-Aligned Countries" (Sauvant, forthcoming).

After the Algiers summit, the overwhelming share of the organized activities of the Non-Aligned Countries and, in fact, the dynamic of the movement, shifted toward economic matters. Within a few years, the non-aligned movement had transformed itself from an informal club of like-minded heads of state or government into a highly organized international pressure group for the reorganization of the international economic system.

THE POLITICIZATION OF THE DEVELOPMENT ISSUE

This transformation of the non-aligned movement had a crucial effect on the way in which development matters were perceived, presented and pursued. During the 1960s - and as late as UNCTAD III (1972) - questions of economic development were essentially regarded as "low politics": they were left to the ministers of economics, finance, and planning. Attempts to politicize these issues - for example the Group of 77's Charter of Algiers (1967), which had been adopted in preparation for UNCTAD II - therefore failed. With the beginning of the 1970s, however, this attitude changed and development questions became "high politics": they were elevated from the level of heads of departments to the level of heads of state or government. The development issues had become politicized.

It is not important that many of the concrete suggestions had already been presented earlier in one form or another. It is perhaps not even important that basic changes were desired. What was important, however, is that the movement of the Non-Aligned Countries, as the political coalition of the Third World, embraced these suggestions and supported them with its entire political weight. The decisive factor was not the novelty of the ideas but their political relevance and the political support that was given to them.

The Algiers summit had made the development issue a priority item on the agenda of the Non-Aligned Countries. From there it was only a small step until it would become a priority item on the international agenda. But the scheduling of the Non-Aligned Countries - which had requested at Algiers that a special session of the United Nations General Assembly on development questions be convened in 1975 (the later Seventh Special Session) - was derailed when one month after the summit war broke out between Israel and the Arab states.

THE GROWING ASSERTIVENESS OF THE THIRD WORLD

With their growing appreciation of the importance of economic matters, the DCs became increasingly aware of their bargaining power. Limited as this bargaining power is, it lies basically in the economic sphere and depends on the ability of the Third World to maintain a minimum of solidarity. Primary products play a key role.

This role has two aspects. The first concerns the generation of financial resources for development and the full integration of the production of raw materials into the domestic economy. Since primary commodities are of primary importance for the development process of most developing countries, they have to be fully utilized for this purpose. The greatest efforts are therefore needed to assure that the largest possible share of the value created through their production accrues to the developing countries. Prices, royalties and the like are the means through which this objective can be achieved. In addition, efforts have to be made to capture the indirect (multiplicator) effects created through the processing of raw materials to utilize them for the stimulation of domestic development. Consequently, a larger share of processing has to be located in the producing countries. But since, for historical reasons, raw materials are frequently controlled by TNEs - whose normal preference is to favor transnational vertical linkages over national horizontal ones (e.g., backward and forward linkages in the host economy) - the DCs reserve their right to nationalize these natural resources and the production facilities associated with them if this should become necessary in the interest of national economic development.

The second aspect of the role of primary products concerns their function as bargaining instruments in North-South relations. But the sine qua non for their effective utilization

is cooperation among the exporting countries. Producers'
associations offer the framework for such cooperation. Not
surprisingly, then, the DCs would like to see them legitimized.
    The prototype of a producers' association is, of course,
OPEC. And OPEC also demonstrates how the increased awareness about the importance of economic factors has influenced
the actions of the Third World. Although OPEC had been
established in 1960, it had spent the whole decade of the 1960s
negotiating minor improvements in the division of revenues
which, in the end, resulted in additional government income of
25 million dollars. Between 1970 and 1974, on the other hand,
the income of OPEC increased by about 80 billion dollars.
Moreover, most oil production facilities passed into domestic
ownership.
    The success of OPEC was, in fact, responsible for the
speeding up of the schedule agreed upon at the 1973 Algiers
summit. Following the oil embargo and the quadrupling of oil
prices, the United States invited the major developed oil con-
suming countries to a February 1974 conference in Washington
to deliberate about a coordinated response. In reaction to this
suggestion, the Algerian president, Houari Boumediene, in his
capacity as the president in office of the Movement of the
Non-Aligned Countries, requested the Secretary General of the
United Nations to convene a special session on the problems of
raw materials and development. The Sixth Special Session was
thus called to take place from April 9 to May 2, 1974. It
adopted the "Declaration on the Establishment of a New International Economic Order" and the "Programme of Action on the
Establishment of a New International Economic Order," and
made the restructuring of the international economic system a
priority item on the international agenda.
    Without any doubt, OPEC has been instrumental in achiev-
ing this result. The actions of OPEC forced the developed
countries to listen to the developing ones. Nevertheless, the
word "instrumental" has been chosen deliberately. With the
Algiers summit, the development issue had acquired such sa-
liency and the DCs had reached such a degree of mobilization
and organization that it was only a question of time until this
issue would be forcefully pursued on the international level.
As a matter of fact, the Algiers summit itself had already
called for a special session of the United Nations General Assembly on development.
    This qualification does not intentionally slighten the role
of OPEC. Rather it underlines that the DCs' insistence on the
New International Economic Order is not merely a by-product
of OPEC's success. It is based on detailed and highly structured preparatory work and is carried by a broad consensus
of the Third World. Regardless of OPEC's future role and
regardless of the extent to which the present NIEO program is
sufficient to bring about structural changes, the task of reor-

ganizing the world economic system in its North-South dimension will, therefore, remain on the international agenda.
It will also remain there because the integration of the
DCs as equal partners into the international economic system is
a logical step in the emancipation of these states from colonial
subordination. Inevitably, this will transform the existing
system. The challenge is, therefore, to keep the tensions that
are necessarily associated with such a process at a minimum in
order to make the transformation as smooth as possible. And
this requires the ready and unreserved cooperation of the
industrialized countries in each of the major areas of North-
South interaction: trade and commodities, money and finance,
science and technology, industrialization, and food and agriculture.
In each of these areas, TNEs play a prominent role
(United Nations, 1978) and, hence, will be affected by any
changes introduced by the implementation of the NIEO program. Given the importance of this role and the importance
these areas have for the development process of the Third
World, it is not surprising that attempts are being made to
establish an international regime for transnational enterprises.

REFERENCES

Jankowitsch, Odette, and Sauvant, Karl P., eds. 1978. The
     Third World without Superpowers: The Collected Docu-
     ments of the Non-Aligned Countries. Dobbs Ferry, N.Y.:
     Oceana. 4 vols.

Sauvant, Karl P., ed. forthcoming. The New International
     Economic Order: Changing Priorities on the International
     Agenda. Oxford: Pergamon Press.

Sauvant, Karl P., and Hasenpflug, Hajo, eds. 1977. The
     New International Economic Order: Confrontation or Co-
     operation between North and South? Boulder, Col.:
     Westview Press.

Senghaas, Dieter. 1977. Weltwirtschaftsordnung und Entwick-
     lungshilfe: Pladoyer fur Dissoziation. Frankfurt: Suhr-
     kamp.

United Nations. 1978. Transnational Corporations in World De-
     velopment: A Re-examination. New York: United Na-
     tions.

3 Economics Falls Short: The Need for Studies on the Social and Cultural Impact of Transnational Enterprises
Krishna Kumar

THE NEED FOR STUDIES ON THE SOCIAL AND CULTURAL IMPACT OF TNEs

It is now widely recognized that the development of a nation includes much more than continual increase in the gross national product and its capacity to produce goods and services. The basic premise of the fifties and sixties that economic development invariably contributes to social and cultural development has failed to stand the test of time. The experiences of developing nations, and for that matter of the industrialized countries as well, have shown that undue emphasis on economic growth might not only lead to lop-sided development (if we can call it development) but can come in the way of realization of the desired social and cultural goals. That this belated realization has boosted the public image of those social scientists who study society and culture is besides the point. What is significant is the fact that it puts them in a position to analyze the social and cultural impact of policies and programs of national and international economic organizations not as mere academic exercises but as desired inputs to policy making.

One of the most crucial types of economic organizations which deserve careful consideration in this regard, are the transnational enterprises (TNEs). The critical role which they have been playing in shaping national economies and international economic order is too well-known to need any mention. On a conservative estimate there are more than 10,000 TNEs (Business International, 1976, p. 254). Although the vast majority of them are based in rich, industrialized nations, the developing countries too can now legitimately boast of them. The number of subsidiaries owned by TNEs is about 50,000, which clearly attests to their importance in the movement of factors of production and products across national boundaries. However, despite their decisive importance, little attention has been given by social scientists to their over-all impact on the societies and cultures of the home and host nations. Scholars have treated them as if their effects were confined to economic, and to a limited extent, political fields. Such a state of affairs has two consequences: either those who are called upon to formulate policies both within and toward TNEs totally ignore their social and cultural consequences, or formulate policies on the basis of very impressionistic, limited data. It is therefore suggested here that the time has come when social scientists give up this attitude of "benign neglect" and undertake comprehensive, comparative researches and investigations on this subject.

The purpose of this chapter is to discuss briefly some of the effects of the operations of TNCs on the societies and cultures of host nations. I have also sought to identify, on the basis of available literature, some areas which deserve to be investigated by social scientists. The ideas mentioned are to be taken simply as hypotheses for further exploration rather than valid conclusions or generalizations. My hope is that they may stimulate further discussions on the subject, which might clear some of the existing confusion and pave the way for empirically grounded theorizing. It should be noted that my main concern here is with the TNEs' impact on developing host nations.

Since scholars have offered a wide variety of definitions of TNEs using different criteria-variables, it is necessary to mention that I have followed the United Nation's (U.N. Report, 1973, p. 25) definition which has the widest acceptance. Following this definition, TNEs are treated as the enterprises that "own or control production or service facilities outside the country in which they are based." These enterprises can operate in extractive, agricultural, manufacturing or service sectors and can be private, semi-private or government owned operations. Obviously, this definition excludes all those firms which do not own or control production and service facilities in foreign countries, and yet are involved in substantial foreign operations. The enterprises operating within the confines of national boundaries have been termed National Enterprises (NEs).

SOCIAL IMPACT

Social impact refers to the effects on social structures and processes. Ideally, for analyzing social impact, one should list all major social classes, institutions and processes, and then examine, on the basis of theoretical and empirical grounds, whether they are directly or indirectly affected by the presence of TNEs. However, it is hardly possible to follow such a course, least of all in a brief chapter. Hence, I have confined myself to the discussion of only four areas of TNE's impact, namely entrepreneurs, working class, ethnic stratification and social and economic inequalities, which are widely recognized to be affected by TNEs in developing nations.

Entrepreneurs

Entrepreneurs are the persons who own, control and manage means of production and employ them for gainful economic activity. In classical economic theory, they are the leaders who transform a tradition-bound agrarian order into a prosperous industrial system. It is therefore necessary to briefly examine the effects of TNEs or entrepreneurs in developing nations. I hereby deal with two interrelated issues: a) growth - whether TNEs promote or inhibit the growth of local entrepreneurial class, and b) autonomy - whether the local entrepreneurs in a country having considerable foreign direct investment, exercise autonomy or remain dependent on TNEs.

It is often argued that the growth of a local entrepreneurial class can be inhibited by TNEs in several ways. The most obvious is that LDC's entrepreneurs find it difficult, though not impossible, to compete with them. TNEs possess enormous technological resources and are in a position to introduce new production technologies and products more rapidly and economically than national enterprises. Besides, since they can raise resources nationally and internationally, TNEs do not suffer from the shortage of capital. In contrast, local entrepreneurs generally find it difficult to raise the necessary capital, nor are they in a position to take risks. TNEs also have the advantage of familiar brands, trademarks and patents. Before they establish a manufacturing subsidiary in a LDC, their products are well-known to the potential consumers. The local entrepreneurs, on the other hand, have no such visibility and do not have access to assured markets. They are further hampered by the fact that consumers in LDCs prefer foreign brands over the domestic ones. Thus, the cumulative effect is that, as a result of the operations of TNEs, the position of the local entrepreneur is constantly undermined and potential competitors are discouraged.

Available evidence, thought not entirely reliable, indicates that the growth of TNEs in a sector is often marked by the decline of small, local or family enterprises (ILO, 1976b, p. 16). Brundenius (1972) has shown that the domination of the mining sector by TNEs in Peru has inhibited local entrepreneurs. According to him, the national entrepreneur has been confronted by two unpalatable choices: to collaborate with

TNEs or face extinction by being outcompeted. Weinstein (1976, p. 44) also observes that Japanese joint ventures in the textile industry have been responsible for the closure of a large number of indigenous firms in Indonesia.

I must point out here that the above mentioned inhibiting effects are confined to only sectors in which there is a scope for competition between TNEs and NEs. These do not necessarily occur in the other sectors of the economy. However, there are some undesirable effects on the entrepreneurs in other sectors which cannot be ignored.

Most of LDCs have undergone a period of foreign subjugation which has shaped their self-images and identities and has created a widespread feeling of inferiority and inadequacy. The people have been socialized to look at outsiders for guidance and support. In the post-colonial era, the labels of "underdeveloped," "traditional," or "developing" which have been indiscriminately applied to these nations, have hardly helped to improve their self-images. Under these conditions, the widespread operations of TNEs in LDCs can tend to nourish the prevalent feelings of inferiority and inadequacy instead of eradicating them. Potential entrepreneurs, then, are discouraged because they tend to assume that they cannot be as "efficient," "innovative," or "successful" as the foreigners.

Finally, some social scientists have suggested that TNEs, by virtue of their being "outsiders," are not in a position to remove or control the prevalent institutional impediments to entrepreneurial behavior. They cannot press for the necessary reforms. As Hirschman (1972, p. 44) has pointed out: "The trouble with the foreign investor may well be not that he is so meddlesome but that he is so mousy! It is the foreign investor's mousiness which deprives the policymakers of the guidance, pressures and support they badly need to push through critically required decisions and policies amid a welter of conflicting and antagonistic interests."

On the other hand, there are both logical and empirical grounds for hypothesizing positive effects of TNEs on local entrepreneurship. TNEs have backward, forward and lateral linkages with the economy, though their volume and extent differ in time and place. Hence, TNEs create new entrepreneurs by generating demands for those goods and services used as inputs by them. These local producers or contractors gradually gain expertise and confidence and begin to move to other sectors of the economy as well. Moreover, the goods and services produced by TNEs enter as inputs in other industries. For example, TNEs involvement in steel, chemicals, heavy machinery and tools, electronics, and the like, have opened new opportunities for local entrepreneurs in several sectors. In addition, they create new national and international markets for local products. Above all, TNEs also provide skills, often unknowingly, which are necessary for entrepreneurial behavior.

In the past, foreign direct investment has contributed to the growth of entrepreneurs in several countries. Levkovsky (1966, p. 52) has argued, though not very convincingly, that the British capital in India was responsible for the rise of the Indian bourgeoisie. Vernon (1971, p. 198) has mentioned that the Mexican mining and railway building boom in the nineteenth century helped to establish a new entrepreneurial class composed of traders, bankers, provisioners, contractors and small manufacturers. He has also suggested that the Peruvian boom of the nineteenth century "though centered on some off-shore islands in the Pacific was responsible for bringing a local contractor industry into existence on the mainland - an industry which lived off the public works that the guano boom financed" (Vernon, 1971, p. 198). Case studies of several Asian and Pacific nations also show that the influx of foreign capital led to the creation of petty entrepreneurs in the early part of the twentieth century. Some of the success stories of economic growth in recent years come from nations that register considerable investment by TNEs. Brazil, Hong Kong, Malaysia, Nigeria, Singapore, South Korea, and Taiwan provide good illustrations. In all these countries, an entrepreneurial class has simultaneously grown with the increase in foreign investment. Kerdpibule (1974, p. 26) concluded in his study of the effects of joint ventures in Thailand that they "are positively helping the formation of local entrepreneurship."

I am inclined to believe that the overall impact of TNEs on local entrepreneurs depends upon factors such as the level of industrialization of the host nation, the sectors of the economy in which TNEs operate and the policies of the government. While in a traditional society their impact is generally positive, TNEs can inhibit the potential of entrepreneurs in a country which has already made some progress toward industrialization. Moreover, TNEs' effects can differ from sector to sector depending on the nature of their integration within the economy. In extractive sectors that have relatively few backward or forward linkages, the positive effects are marginal. The case of manufacturing sector is, however, different. Manufacturing subsidiaries, especially when they utilize local inputs, can help to promote local entrepreneurs.

However, the most significant factor is the role of government. The local entrepreneurs in LDCs need special protection and support to compete effectively with TNEs in established or new industries. Therefore, the policies of the government can promote or hamper the growth of local entrepreneurs. If it fails to protect them at an early stage, their growth can be slanted. On the other hand, if it bestows excessive protection and squeezes TNEs away, the country can be deprived of the economic benefits of direct foreign investment.

Another issue, which is basically related to the growth of the entrepreneurial class, concerns the autonomy of entrepreneurs. Dependencia theorists have stressed that because of the operations of TNEs, the entrepreneurial classes which are emerging in LDCs are not independent but dependent. They lack autonomy to play a critical role in the industrialization process - a role played by entrepreneurs in West European and North American nations. Various labels such as "lumpen-bourgeoisie," "compradore classes," or "client classes" have been used to indicate the dependent status of local entrepreneurs (Evans, 1976; Frank, 1972, pp. 425-433; and Johnson, 1972, pp. 71-114).

These social scientists are aware that the dependent status of local entrepreneurs is not necessarily the result of Machiavellian manipulations of TNEs or of the military and political power of their home countries. Rather, it is inherent in the present situation in which local entrepreneurs derive tangible benefits from their alliance with TNEs. As Johnson (1972, p. 105) points out, in Latin America "the new urban based oligarchies and national bourgeoisie, though essentially dependent, even client or compradore classes, profit from the structure of the international system and from their close financial and political relations with multinational corporations and those who hold power internationally."

In the absence of comparative and historical studies, it is indeed difficult to make any valid generalization in this connection. However, the thesis cannot be taken at its face value. As mentioned earlier, there are several factors that condition the overall effects of TNEs on the local entrepreneurship - and these could possibly be also examined in this connection. Besides, the role of surging economic nationalism should not be underestimated in shaping the ideological orientations of entrepreneurs in LDCs (Fayerweather, 1972; and Johnson, 1972). There is little doubt that during the initial phase of industrialization pioneered by foreign capital, the local entrepreneurs are highly dependent on TNEs. The question then is whether they are able to transform this relationship in their favor with the passing of time.

Vernon (1976, pp. 49 - 50) has argued that the dependent status of local entrepreneurs in LDCs has drastically changed during the last three decades. According to him, up until the Second World War, the local businesspeople in Latin America, Asia, and North Africa largely served as "adjuncts and partners of foreign entrepreneurs." The Second World War, Vernon suggests, was a turning point. It made local entrepreneurs in several LDCs self-reliant by cutting off their overseas sources of supply of foreign markets. Since then, the local entrepreneurs have started asserting their independence: "On the whole, one could see the emergence of a new breed of tough local entrepreneurs prepared to make partnerships or do battle with foreign enterprises as their interests demanded" (Vernon, 1976, p. 50).

While one may not concur fully with Vernon's analysis, he does bring to fore a basic sociological insight: as a country treads the path of industrialization, its entrepreneurial class undergoes a process of differentiation. New cleavages and conflicts arise within it. A section of it undoubtedly remains allied to TNEs - and often in a junior position. It generally consists of entrepreneurs who collaborate with TNEs in the sectors requiring sophisticated technology, huge capital invest-ments or access to foreign markets. Some others seek to im-prove their position by challenging the domination of TNEs in the sectors in which technology has already been standardized. They solicit the support of their governments in their regard. In several sectors such as banking, mining, and petroleum, the local entrepreneurs have more or less succeeded in dislodging TNEs. Still others remain unaffected by the operations of TNEs and are therefore indifferent toward them.

The above discussion clearly demonstrates that TNEs affect the growth and orientations of local entrepreneurs in the host LDCs, and that their effects are not always desirable. Perhaps, the same can be said about their impact on the working class.

Working Class

The concept of working class, as used here, refers to that segment of the population employed in extractive, manufactur-ing, agricultural or service sectors of the economy. The contribution of TNEs to the growth of the working class is both direct and indirect. TNEs employ skilled and unskilled workers in their subsidiaries. More importantly, through their backward and forward linkages, they create additional jobs. It is estimated that about two million people are directly employed by TNEs in the LDCs (ILO, 1976A, p. 1).

The available evidence, though fragmentary, unmistakably indicates that TNEs as a rule provide higher wages than national enterprises in LDCs. Their wages are high for all categories of workers. Reuber's (1973) study of direct foreign investment shows that TNEs claim to follow a high wage policy in Asian, Latin American and African countries. A most comprehensive study by ILO (1976b, p. 44) of the wage policy concludes: "In LDCs, the average level of earnings of em-ployees in multinational enterprises far exceeds those of their counterparts in all national firms. This gap is much larger than is found for developed countries (in most cases being above 50 percent) and appears to be related to the stage of economic development."

Wage differentials between NEs and TNEs are the result of several factors: first, TNEs are concentrated in the most modernized sector of the economy. Since they use more so-

phisticated technology, it is reasonable to assume that they
employ a larger percentage of skilled and semi-skilled workers
than NEs, and this is responsible for their high wage bills.
Second, their profit margin is generally higher than those of
NEs, partly because of the economies of scale and mainly because of their semi-monopolistic position. National enterprises
in LDCs are often small firms carrying out a wide range of
production activities with little capital investment. Finally,
TNEs have been known to establish their subsidiaries near
metropolitan areas where wages are relatively high.

The fact that TNEs generally pay better wages have led
some scholars to suggest that they contribute to the emergence
of a labor aristocracy in LDCs. Arrighi (1971) has argued
that management practices and technology introduced by TNEs
in tropical Africa, which has a general shortage of skilled
workers, have led to the creation of a small, semi-skilled but
highly productive and well-paid labor elite. Sunkel (1973)
suggested that the labor force engaged in the transnational
sector occupies a privileged position in Latin America. Sklar
(1975, pp. 205 - 206) has also mentioned the special interest
group orientations of organized mine workers in Zambia. "As
Michael Burawoy says, the Zambian mine workers are 'a labor
elite' or 'aristocracy. . . .' The special interest orientation of
organized mine workers within the Zambian nationalist movement is a well documented historical fact. Recently, Burawoy
and others have shown that the ruling party elicits far less
enthusiasm from mine workers than from other, less advan-
taged sections of the proletariat."

The implicit assumption of the above formulation is that
the elite working class develops an interest in maintaining the
status quo, since it is beneficial or at least is perceived to be
such. While there are occasions for tensions and conflicts
between the labor elites and TNEs, these relate to marginal
benefits rather than to the structural transformation of the
society. Thus, the working class is fragmented and loses its
revolutionary potential. A segment of the labor-elites perceives the opportunities for upward mobility in the system,
and even begins to identify itself with the lower-middle class,
instead of its counterparts in NEs.

In the absence of studies on the socio-political orientations
of workers employed in TNEs, the whole thesis looks highly
speculative. Only the empirical research about the differences
in the attitudes, perceptions and behavior of workers employed
in national and transnational firms can substantiate or refute
it. However, two points can be made in this connection.
First, past experience does not necessarily show that the
workers in TNEs have always sided with TNEs whenever the
latter have come into conflict with the national government.
Often, these workers have demanded outright nationalization of
TNEs. Arrighi (1971, p. 256) is aware of this fact and has

conceded that the labor aristocracy might not be opposed to state ownership and management of the means of production. Second, the very notion of revolutionary potential of the working class springing from their "class consciousness" represents more an article of faith than an empirically observable phenomena in LDCs. Workers are highly fragmented in these nations; ethnic, cultural, political and sectoral cleavages and conflicts rather than wage differentials may then appear to be posing barriers to their mobilization, assuming that such a mobilization is possible. Under these circumstances, the thesis of labor aristocracy seems to have limited analytical value.

Related to the above thesis is the hypothesis that TNEs contribute to the docility of the working class. Undoubtedly, TNEs sometimes exert pressure on the governments of host LDCs for following "labor repressive" policies. Often, though not always, such a pressure is unintended and is rooted in the present situation in which LDCs compete with one another for foreign investment.

The governments of LDCs are undoubtedly sensitive to the fact that one of the main considerations in TNEs' decisions about overseas expansion is the availability of a docile, disciplined working force. As a result, they are tempted to "tame" their working class by curbing trade unions and other activities, which might be construed as "unfavorable" by TNEs.

Some partial confirmation of this hypothesis is provided by the advertisements placed by several Latin American and Asian nations in well-known business magazines stressing the proverbial docility of their workers. Kreye (1977, p. 37) has mentioned that one form of major political incentive provided by the host LDCs is "restrictions on and/or suspension of the political and social rights of the labor force that work in the export processing zones." Goodman (1976, p. 14) has pointed out that "in extreme cases, corporations have demanded guarantees of police action against the formation of unions or the arrest of principal union militants as preconditions for establishing a plant in a host country." However, it should be noted here that such direct pressure is generally not favored by most the TNEs for political and ethical grounds.

Chomsky and Herman (1977) have alluded to the fact that countries such as Brazil, Chile, Dominican Republic, Philippines, South Korea, Thailand and Uruguay, which have received substantial United States aid and direct investment, follow "labor repressive policies." They imply a direct causal relationship between foreign investment and labor-repressive policies. However, I think that it is indeed an over-simplification to attribute the anti-labor policies of several LDCs to the presence of TNEs. Obviously, many LDCs adopt such policies not because of the pressures from TNEs but out of their own ideological and political commitments. The ruling elites in these countries often represent the dominant social and economic strata and are therefore apprehensive about labor movements and trade union activities. A majority of them also believe that the only way in which their underdeveloped economies can make strides toward industrialization is through the accumulation of surplus by hard work and subsistence standards of living.

Thus, the validity of the thesis of labor docility seems questionable. While some TNEs undoubtedly prefer curbs on the political and trade union activities of their employees, others also realize that the best way to ensure industrial peace is not through coercion but by satisfying the economic needs of their employees and providing them suitable channels for expressing their grievances. To that extent, TNEs might promote progressive policies and attitudes toward working classes. However, this remains an empirical issue to be settled on the basis of research.

Ethnic Stratification

LDCs are often faced with the problem of ethnic stratification − a situation in which one or more ethnic groups have come to occupy a dominant position in social, economic or political affairs. Thus, the question can be posed: how does the presence of TNEs affect the existing ethnic stratification? Do they contribute to the maintenance of existing ethnic boundaries, and even consolidate them? Or, do they provide opportunities to deprived groups for upward mobility?

TNEs generally do not have a corporate policy on this issue. As economic bureaucracies, they are neither for nor against any ethnic group (which, of course, does not mean that their executives in host nations are free from ethnic prejudices and stereotypes). What can be safely suggested is that given adequate opportunities, the same TNEs can effectively operate in South Africa, where its policies will discriminate against non-white ethnic groups as well as in Uganda, where the main benefit of its investment might accrue to black ethnic groups. After all, most TNEs do not perceive themselves as crusaders for social or ethnic equality.

There is the possibility that under some situations (such as when some ethnic groups in host nations have close ties with the ethnic groups of home countries), TNEs are likely to favor specific ethnic groups. Several examples can be given. The British TNEs have largely depended upon English expatriates for fulfilling middle- and senior-range positions in the former colonies. Empirical investigation has shown that Japanese firms in Hawaii have demonstrated a marked preference for hiring Japanese-Americans (Heller, 1974, p. 109). Chinese firms in ASEAN countries are generally accused of hiring and collaborating with people of Chinese ancestry. Such cases are

not uncommon. However, with a trend toward the indigeniza-
tion of management and personnel, and a growing sensitivity
for ethnic tensions, only a few TNEs are likely to follow such
policies in the near future.

TNEs impact on ethnic stratification stems not from conscious, deliberate policy, but from a set of structural constraints which are imposed on them. TNEs need employees and
collaborators who have economic resources, technical and entrepreneurial skills, and if possible, access to bureaucratic
and political leadership in the government. In situations
where an ethnic group has monopolistic or quasi-monopolistic
position with regards to these factors, they have little option
other than depending on them. Under these circumstances,
this ethnic group is likely to be the main beneficiary of direct
foreign investment and might even be able to consolidate and
improve its position.

Malaysia provides a good illustration in this regard. In
this country, TNEs have largely entered into collaborative
arrangements with local Chinese firms. Moreover, in these
subsidiaries, the percentage of Chinese employees as compared
to Malays is higher in technical and management positions.
The explanation is not that TNEs like Chinese better than
Malays or Indians, but that Chinese have in the past owned
retail outlets and distribution networks in Malaysia. Therefore, when TNEs begin establishing their manufacturing plants,
they form alliances with the existing Chinese firms. Moreover,
since the Chinese have come to acquire entrepreneurial and
technical skills because of their preeminent position in the
economic affairs of the country, they are in a position to
capitalize on the job opportunities offered by TNEs. A similar
situation, though on a smaller scale, exists in Indonesia.
Perhaps only governmental intervention, as exemplified by the
"Bhumiputra" policies in Malaysia, can establish a more
balanced situation in these nations.

The presence of TNEs can have both stabilizing and
destabilizing effects on ethnic boundaries. This is evident
from the case of South Africa, where TNEs have generally
followed, though perhaps reluctantly, the apartheid policies of
the government (Rogers, 1976; Dehner, 1974; Seidman and
Seidman, 1977; Jackson, 1974; United Church Board, 1977;
Nickel, 1978; Spandau, 1978; and U.N. Report, 1977). Some
of them have not even hesitated from exerting pressures on
home countries for not supporting "economic sanctions" against
South Africa. By all accounts, the huge investments made by
TNEs in South Africa have contributed to its growing economic
power and political stability. However, while the main benefits
accrued to the white minority, it is wrong to infer that Blacks
and Asians did not derive any benefits. In fact, TNEs have
contributed, to a small extent, to the emergence of non-white
middle classes in South Africa (Spandau, 1978, pp. 110-178).

In the face of mounting public pressure and the growing power of Black nations in South Africa, some TNEs are now formulating non-discriminatory policies toward Blacks and Asians. They recently signed a code of fair employment practices, which commits them to eradicating racial discriminations. About 98 TNEs have been signatories to this code, and "task forces - one for each point - are meeting regularly to compare notes and develop new approaches" (Nickel, 1978, p. 70). Thus, TNEs are showing some defiance to the apartheid policies, which can hardly be demonstrated by national firms in South Africa.

It should be stressed here that the past history shows that when plural societies make rapid economic advancement (even without foreign investment), the resulting benefits are not always evenly shared by all the existing ethnic groups. Some, decidedly, profit more than others. Therefore, while the effects of TNEs on ethnic relationships cannot be ignored, it is quite likely that they may not be different from those of NEs in most of the cases.

Social and Economic Inequalities

There now exists a widespread concern for increasing economic inequalities in LDCs. Gini index (a measure of economic disparities) data, whatever its reliability, unmistakenly indicates that economic disparities, instead of being bridged, have actually increased over the last decade in most of the LDCs. The benefits of economic growth registered in many nations have not reached the needy segments of the population. It is sometimes suggested that the TNEs should also share the blame for the present state of affairs. A recent study (Bornschier, et al. 1978, p. 677) notes: "The effect of direct foreign investment and foreign aid has been to increase economic inequality within countries. This effect holds for income inequality, land inequality, and sectoral income inequality."

There are some ways in which the presence of TNEs could contribute to economic disparities in LDCs. First, it has been mentioned that because TNEs pay higher wages, they indirectly promote economic disparities. As suggested earlier, the wages for all the categories of employees - blue collar, white collar and professional - are higher in TNEs as compared to NEs. The argument, despite its intuitive appeal, is not very convincing. Wage differentials between TNEs and NEs are not as significant as to make a critical difference in the existing economic system. Moreover, by no stretch of the imagination can employees of TNEs be regarded as the most affluent strata of LDCs. They constitute the lower, middle and upper middle stratas of LDCs: they are not the owners but the wage earners.

Second, some social scientists have pointed out that whenever TNEs have entered into collaborative arrangements, they have strengthened the position of dominant economic and political groups. Tsuda (1977) has shown that well-known Filipino business groups and figures are the major beneficiaries of the direct foreign investment in the Philippines. With the active support of the government, they have made collaborative arrangements with Japanese TNEs and have enriched themselves. Still, in other countries, local military or political officials have made partnership in the joint ventures established by TNEs and have amassed wealth in addition to political power. Such an alliance has made the existing economic stratification more rigid and has blocked the channels of social mobility.

Third, the presence of TNEs can aggravate regional economic imbalances in LDCs. While NEs and TNEs are likely to determine the location of their plants on the basis of more or less similar criteria, past experience has shown that TNEs prefer metropolitan sites, where an economic infrastructure already exists. Weinstein (1976, p. 400) has reported that within the Southeast Asian countries (with the exception of Singapore), "the concentration of foreign enterprises near the chief metropolitan centers has accentuated the disparity between rural and urban areas."

Sometimes, TNEs are also instrumental in creating enclaves of prosperity amidst poverty, especially in extractive agricultural sectors. The relative affluence of the employees and petty entrepreneurs who flourish around such enclaves offer a sharp contrast to the overall poverty of the surrounding areas.

Finally, TNEs' effects on the consumption patterns and lifestyles cannot be ignored in this connection. TNEs produce a large range of consumer items such as electronics, cosmetics, soft drinks, canned foods and cars, which are within the reach of the majority of the populace in DCs. However, in LDCs, because of the low income levels of the masses and the skewed nature of income distribution, only a small proportion are able to purchase them. This sharpens the gulf between the standard of living of the higher and lower income groups. It makes economic disparities more conspicuous and thus creates relative deprivation in the minds of the deprived.

However, it is wrong to assume that TNEs always contribute to economic inequalities. They have been quite successful in operating in socialistic economies. In such countries, the operations of TNEs do not further disparities of wealth. Moreover, TNEs have formed joint ventures with the state controlled sectors in LDCs, especially in extractive and heavy industries. Under these situations, it is governments rather than TNEs that shape the policies and output of the enterprise. In addition, suitable measures can be taken about the location of plants, wages and salaries paid to the employees, and the nature of products produced, which can control the effects of TNEs in increasing economic disparities even in a free economy.

I have discussed above some of the TNE's effects on two social classes, namely entrepreneurs and workers, and social stratification. However, there remain several other institutions and groups, such as family, national elites, and civilian bureaucracies which can also be affected by the presence of TNEs in the host LDCs.

IMPACT ON CULTURE

I define culture with reference to the symbolic and expressive dimensions of a society. Culture in this sense refers to the prevailing values, ideologies, beliefs, knowledge, language, arts, literature and the like. All these elements of a cultural system can be directly or indirectly affected by TNEs in host nations. However, I confine myself here to their effects on consumption patterns and values, knowledge and skills, and cultural identity.

Consumption Patterns and Values

Perhaps the most obvious effects of TNEs are on consumption. It is now widely recognized that because of their operations, people, or at least elites in LDCs, are becoming accustomed to the goods and services available in DCs. Several scholars have examined the role of TNEs with regard to the use of a specific commodity (Bader, 1976; Greiner, 1975; Jelliffe and Jelliffe, 1971; Ledogar, 1975; and Muller, 1974) or to life styles (Barnet and Muller, 1974; pp. 123 - 147; Sunkel and Fuenzalida, 1976; and Sauvant, 1976).

TNEs generally introduce new products and product innovations in their home nations or in DCs where they have large markets and effective sales organizations. The early consumers often come from the upper socio-economic strata, for they are in a position to take the necessary risks. Others prefer to wait. However, once the product proves successful with the early consumers, the whole scene changes. People with low income levels start using it. It is at this stage that a firm often decides to manufacture the item in LDCs. Since it has been producing it for some time, technical problems in the new environment are perceived to be minimal. Moreover, by this time, a section of potential consumers is also familiar with the product which they might be importing. In LDCs, the early pattern of adoption repeats itself. The upper socio-economic groups are the first users followed by middle and lower middle classes.

The point is that the products are developed by TNEs, not with reference to the needs of host nations, but to those of the home countries. The problem arises because the socio-economic milieu of LDCs is undoubtedly different from that of DCs. Most of the people in the former live in utter poverty and penury; their elementary needs for food, clothing and shelter remain unfulfilled. In all these countries, only a tiny minority can engage in the consumption of goods and gadgets that are commonly used in DCs. Consequently, the social utility of the consumer products manufactured by TNEs remains doubtful.

Several studies can be mentioned here which illustrate the unsuitability of the consumer products of TNEs, not necessarily because of their intrinsic properties but because of the different socio-economic contexts in which they are consumed. Ledogar (1975, pp. 111 - 126) has presented some interesting data about soft drinks in Mexico and Brazil which show that people, especially poor, spend disproportionate amounts of their income on soft drinks produced by TNEs which have very little nutritional value. Several TNEs produce baby foods and aggressively promote them as alternatives to breast feeding in LDCs. However, the majority of their customers are often too poor to purchase them in the required quantities. Nor do they possess adequate refrigeration facilities. The result is that bottle feeding has often contributed to malnutrition, leading to infant diseases and even mortality, especially among the poor in many LDCs (Muller, 1974). Jelliffe (1972), a nutrition expert, has used the expression "commerciogenic malnutrition" to refer to the starvation and death caused by the baby food industry among the poor. Barnet and Muller (1974, p. 183) have cited studies in rural Mexico indicating that subsistence farmers purchase white bread instead of their traditional bread, which costs less and is at the same time rich in protein. Girling (1976, p. 59) has given the example of the breakfast cereals in Jamaica, where most of the people used to consume fish and bananas for their breakfast, which were cheap and plentiful. However, through advertising, the idea has been sold that "breakfast cereals" are better than the traditional foods, with the result being that people now consume Kellogg's products while "large quantities of bananas spoil for want of markets." Ledogar (1975, pp. 6 - 51) has documented the fact that pharmaceutical TNEs in Latin America manufactured and marketed drugs considered unsafe in their home nations. Often the necessary warnings were missing in the case of drugs that had significant side effects.

The above discussion should not give the impression that the consumer products manufactured by TNEs are always of little intrinsic value or are dysfunctional to the conditions of LDCs. This is hardly the case. In many fields, despite shortcomings, TNEs have made useful contributions to the welfare of the people. Pharmaceutical firms, for example, have undoubtedly helped in LDC's fight against common diseases. They have been instrumental in making drugs locally available, which might not have been otherwise possible. However, as the U.N. Report (1973, p. 48) points out: "Indeed, not enough has been done by the multinational corporations themselves or governments to channel corporate production towards satisfying basic consumption needs in nutrition, health and housing."

There is little incentive for TNEs to manufacture products that satisfy the basic physical needs of the majority. To them, it remains more profitable to introduce well-known products, for which they already possess technical know-how rather than investing in altogether different items which might be more suitable to host nations. They know for certain that if allowed to operate, they are likely to create effective demand for their product, whatever its utility. Therefore, it is unrealistic to expect the Coca-Cola company to develop a new drink utilizing local fruits and sell it at a reasonable price, when it has little difficulty in marketing Coca-Cola or other drinks. Moreover, the fact remains that even if TNEs make efforts to invest in consumer foods needed by the majority, it is questionable that it will be a profitable exercise.

TNEs not only promote the consumption of certain goods and services manufactured by them, but also help to diffuse and reproduce the consumption-oriented value system of capitalistic economies. The essence of this value system is that the happiness, fulfillment and development of an individual or collectivity are measured in terms of the quantity and quality of goods and services consumed. Other things being equal, a person who owns and consumes more goods and gadgets is considered happier than the one who possesses less of them. The countries with high per capital consumption are "developed" while those with low consumption are labeled as "underdeveloped." Thus, consumption becomes the measuring rod, the standard for the evaluation of individual and collective happiness.

The issue here is not the desirability of the consumption-oriented value system but the role TNEs play in its production and diffusion in LDCs. Two factors can be mentioned in this connection. First, the very production of mass-consumption goods and services contributes to the emergence of a consumption-oriented value system. The fact is that when consumer goods are produced in a free market economy, they create their own demands. People learn to feel that they are desirable, if not indispensable. For example, until television sets were introduced in LDCs, people were not aware of their need, but they are considered indispensable by middle classes in LDCs. Thus, to the extent TNEs are instrumental in introducing new technologies for producing consumer goods, they tend to create and diffuse a consumption-oriented value system. Second, communication TNEs, that is, those involved in television, news agencies, books, magazines, and advertising also play an important role in the diffusion of consumption-oriented value system to LDCs.

It should not be presumed that the LDCs in the past did not have "subcultures" or social stratas, which subscribed to this value system. Nor are TNEs to be regarded as the only transmitter of consumption values. What is simply stressed is that TNE's role cannot be ignored in this connection.

Knowledge and Skills

There is little data, much less empirical studies, on the subject of the overall impact of TNEs on the knowledge and skills of people in LDCs. Consequently, the only course open is to discuss briefly the ways in which TNEs contribute to, or inhibit, the growth of knowledge and skills in host nations.

TNEs widely recognize the need of extensive training for their employees in LDCs. Increasingly, they are following the concept of treating manpower development as an investment; that is, they capitalize on training costs in the same fashion as expenditures on plants and machinery. There are, of course, significant variations among TNEs depending on the level of industrialization of the host nation, the sectors in which the TNEs operate, the capital or labor utilized, the intensive nature of the technology used and their respective corporate and personnel policies. However, it is safe to assume that the majority of TNEs impart training to their employees and that collectively their contribution is quite significant. The OECD study (1967, p. 23), for example, notes that "of the 48 firms interviewed, 40 of them trained people from developing countries at the home base in 1965. It may be estimated that their total number of trainees was at least 4,500 and may have been as high as 8,000." The report concluded that "even allowing for the fact that this survey includes several of the biggest enterprises of the industrially advanced countries, it may be safely assumed that home based training by private firms as a whole substantially exceeded the amount of officially (the governments of home countries) financed training." These figures do not include the number of employees trained in LDCs by TNEs, which is undoubtedly much higher.

From the host nation point of view, what is most critical is not the skills created within the confines of a subsidiary, but their diffusion to the wider society. In case the skills or knowledge are used only within the specific TNEs, the benefits to the host nation remain marginal and other sectors of the economy are not benefited. There are reasons to believe that this is the situation. Germidis (1976, p. 3) notes that "empirical studies, notably those conducted by the OECD Development Center, have revealed a relatively low mobility in the case of skilled workers, and a practically negligible mobility in the case of senior executives. Moreover, there sometimes exist institutional obstacles to this mobility, created by MNC's themselves, when competing subsidiaries (in Brazil, for example) enter into agreements among themselves to prevent executives leaving any one of them from being recruited by any of the other."

TNEs award contracts to local contractors and manufacturers for specific inputs. Sometimes this involves providing them necessary training and instructions. Such training is also useful in the manufacturing of items not used by TNEs. Corporations such as Heinz, Del Monte and Dole are known to provide necessary information and expertise to independent growers of fruits and vegetables. They also supply other inputs such as seeds, fertilizers, and insecticides.

All available evidence points to the conclusion that TNEs do not undertake significant R & D activities in the LDCs. An investigation carried out by the National Academy of Sciences (1973, pp. 1 - 2) on the research, development and engineering activities of the United States-based TNEs concluded: "Except for the engineering involved in scaling down production techniques for markets of more limited size and in making modest adjustments to consumer tastes, little R D & E has actually been carried out in the LDCs." A more recent study by Creamer (1976, p. 5) came to the same conclusion: "only a negligible share of the U.S. Overseas R & D found its way to the developing countries of the world, about 1.8 percent in 1966 but by 1972, a larger 3.3 percent." Moreover, the intrinsic value to the society of what little R & D TNEs have undertaken in LDCs remains doubtful. For example, Wionczek (1976, p. 145) has found that "most of the limited R & D by M.E. (TNE) subsidiaries in Latin America is directed not only to adapting products to consumer tastes, but also to changing these tastes."

Some TNEs have recently started operating research facilities in a few LDCs. However, they have followed the principle of international specialization, with the result being that facilities do not feed to the national subsidiaries but are directly and vertically related to the R & D wing of the parent company. For example, the research wing of IBM in India did not directly feed its findings and output to the Indian subsidiary, but to the headquarters. Under such conditions, host nations hardly benefit from research and development activities. This "pseudo-decentralized" type of laboratory and research, Germidis (1976, p. 9) suggests "is not slanted to the needs of the local market. It meets first and foremost the imperatives of the policy of recruiting high level staff at salaries marked lower than in the country of origin: in other words, it results in a 'brain drain' in situ and 'occupational training' ultimately acts to the detriment of the developing host nations." Thus, IBM mainly utilized the local talents in India at least at one-fifth of prevalent salaries in industrialized nations.

No discussion of the TNE's impact on knowledge and skills can be complete without the mention of the role of two communication TNEs - transnational news agencies and transnational book publishing firms. In recent years, there has been a growing controversy about the operations of transnational news agencies that provide news all over the world. Since the beginning of the present century, three or four agencies have dominated the world scene. They have been the main suppliers of international and national news to print and visual media as well as to the governmental agencies. Some critics (Matta, 1976; Schiller, 1976; Somavia, 1976; Tunstall, 1977) have suggested that by virtue of their origin and control by DCs, they have been selective in their news coverage and have often articulated the vantage viewpoint of these countries. The result is that the elites in LDCs often learn to interpret the current events from the point of view of DCs. However, a few would deny that despite their limitations, they have been playing a significant part in making people aware of happenings and events in different parts of the world.

Perhaps, more important from our point of view is the contribution of book publishing TNEs which are gradually extending their operations to LDCs. They are bringing out local editions of scientific, technical and general books. As the labor costs are relatively less in LDCs, these TNEs find it economical to bring out cheap editions which can be purchased by students and libraries. Often, governmental aid agencies have subsidized them in publishing cheap editions of well-known works. This has undoubtedly helped to build up the intellectual resources of host LDCs. It should be noted that most of them generally reprint the works of home countries, which has led to the criticism that they perpetuate a kind of intellectual dependency. As a result, they have started seeking manuscripts from local authors as well. In addition, other TNEs, specifically those involved in advertising, accountancy and consultancy, have been responsible for the diffusion of some technical know-how in LDCs.

The above discussion clearly shows that the role which TNEs play in the diffusion of knowledge and skills is much more than is usually covered under the fashionable topic of "technology transfer." The fact that social scientists have ignored it, does not minimize its importance to the host LDCs.

Cultural Identity

Finally, a word about the impact of TNEs on cultural identity. This is indeed an important but neglected area. Although the broad formulation of the dependencia theorists is well-known, little empirical work has been done in this regard. It need hardly be stressed that TNEs not only facilitate the movement of the factors of production and products across national boundaries but also the underlying ideas, philosophies, values and behavior patterns. In fact, some social scientists have theorized that TNEs transmit "business culture" to host nations (Sauvant, 1976; and Sauvant and Mennis, 1977). Besides, communication TNEs are partly responsible for the transnational diffusion of the music, the arts, literature and films of the metropole nations. They also promote consumption patterns and a consumption-oriented value system in the host LDCs. The contribution of the U.S.- and U.K.-based TNEs to the promotion of English in trade and commerce is now widely recognized (Sauvant, 1976a, p. 56).

Such cultural diffusions and reproductions, some social scientists have contended, undermine the cultural identity in LDCs (Kumar, 1976, 1979). The masses and the elites come to idealize the lifestyles, beliefs, value systems, worldviews and the arts of the metropole nations: they begin to accept them uncritically and develop a feeling of inferiority about their own cultural systems. In fact, their own self-images are shaped by the images of them held by people in DCs. Fanon (1965), Freire (1968) and Ryan (1971) have cogently argued that the subjugated people iternalize the values, beliefs and prejudices of the dominant nations. This cultural dependence, it can be pointed out, sheds some light on the ambivalent attitudes of the dominant elites in LDCs toward the operations of TNEs. On the one hand, they want them as transmitters of not only capital and technology but also of "modern" values and behavior patterns. They seem to believe that the values, beliefs and ideologies of DCs are the major causes of their economic and political dominance, and their own nations can progress only when they accept them. On the other hand, they are not comfortable about their dependence. They resent being manipulated by outside economic institutions over which they have little control. Their presence also makes them aware of their own limitations.

While the validity of the above formulation cannot be easily dismissed, one should resist the temptation to reify cultural systems, whether of DCs or LDCs. There is nothing sacrosanct about their elements or processes that they be preserved at all costs. In fact, for their own survival, they should be able to adopt the elements of the other cultural systems and respond to the changing economic, social, and political milieu. Therefore, the intersystemic contact facilitated by

TNEs should not always be construed to be disfunctional to the cultural systems of the host nations. Thus, it is obvious that TNEs have effects on the various elements of the cultural system of the host LDCs. They influence consumption patterns and contribute to the creation and diffusion of a consumption-oriented value system. The general levels of knowledge and skills in a country are also affected by the presence of TNEs. Finally, they also have some impact on the cultural identity of the people. In addition, it can be argued that they might have consequences for the formal educational system (Mazrui, 1976), spread of English language (Sauvant, 1976), and the like.

I shall conclude this chapter by stressing the need for the study of the social and cultural impact of TNEs. The above discussion, though very impressionistic and incomplete, demonstrates that the presence of TNEs can have wide-ranging influences on the social and cultural systems of the host nations - and it is indeed a shortsighted policy focus exclusively on economic dimensions.

REFERENCES

Arrighi, Giovanni. 1971. "International corporations, Labor Aristocrats, and Economic Development in Tropical Africa." In Imperialism and Underdevelopment: A Reader. New York: Monthly Review Press, pp. 220 - 267.

Bader, Michael B. 1976. "Breast-feeding: the Role of Multinational Corporations in Latin America." International Journal of Health Services 6, no. 4: 609 - 626.

Barnet, Richard J., and Muller, Ronald. 1974. Global Reach: The Power of Multinational Corporations. New York: Simon and Schuster, pp. 123 - 210, 363 - 388.

Bornschier, V.; Chase-Dunn, Christopher; and Rubinson, Richard. 1978. "Cross-National Evidence of the Effects of Foreign Investment and Aid on Economic Growth and Inequality: A Survey of Findings and a Reanalysis." American Journal of Sociology 84, no. 3: 651 - 683.

Boyce, J., and Lombard, F. 1976. Colombia's Treatment of Foreign Banks. Washington, D.C.: American Enterprise Institute for Public Policy Research.

Brundenius, Claes. 1972. "The Anatomy of Imperialism: the Case of the Multinational Mining Corporations in Peru." Journal of Peace Research 9, no. 3: 189 - 207.

Business International. 1976. "More Multinationals in the EEC than in the US." Business International 23, no. 32 (August 6): 254.

Chomsky, Noam, and Herman, Edward S. 1977. "Why American Business Supports Third World Facism." Business and Society Review, no. 23 (Fall): 13 - 21.

Creamer, Daniel B. 1976. Overseas Research and Development by United States Multinationals, 1966 - 1975: Estimates of Expenditures and a Statistical Profile. New York: The Conference Board.

Dehner, W. J. 1974. "Multinational Enterprise and Racial Non-discrimination: United States Enforcement of An International Human Right." Harvard International Law Journal 15, no. 1: 71-125.

Evans, Peter B. 1976. "Industrialization and Imperialism Growth and Stagnation On the Periphery." Berkeley Journal of Sociology 20. 113-145.

Fanon, Frantz. 1965. The Wretched of the Earth. New York: Monthly Review Press.

Fayerweather, John. 1972. "Nationalism and the Multinational Firm." In The Multinational Enterprise in Transition, ed. A. Kerpoor and P. Grub, Princeton: Darwin.

Frank, Andre Gunder. 1972. Lumpenbourgeoisie and Lumpendevelopment: Dependence, Class and Politics in Latin America. New York: Monthly Review Press.

Freire, Paulo. 1968. Pedagogy of the Oppressed. New York: The Seabury Press.

Germidis, Dimitri. 1976. Multinational Firms and Vocational Training in Developing Countries. Paris: United Nations Educational, Scientific and Cultural Organization. SHC.76/CONF.635/COL.7.

Girling, Robert. 1976. "Mechanisms of Imperialism: Technology and The Dependent State." Latin American Perspectives 3, no. 4. 54-64.

Goodman, Louis Wolf. 1976. "The Social Organization of Decision Making In the Multinational Corporations." In The Multinational Corporation and Social Change, ed. David Apter and Louis Wolf Goodman. New York: Praeger, pp. 63-95.

Greiner, Ted. 1975. The Promotion of Bottle Feeding by
    Multinational Corporations: How Advertising and the
    Health Professions Have Contributed. Ithaca, N.Y.:
    Program on International Nutrition and Development
    Policy, Cornell University (Cornell International Nutrition
    Monograph Series, no. 2).

Heller, H. Robert. 1974. "The Hawaiian Experience." Colum-
    bia Journal of World Business 9, no. 3. 105 - 110.

Hirschman, Albert O. 1972. "How to Divest in Latin America,
    and Why." In The Multinational Enterprise in Transition:
    Selected Readings and Essays, ed. A. Kapoor and Phillip
    Grub. Princeton, New Jersey: Darwin Press, pp. 445 -
    466.

International Labor Office. 1976A. The Impact of Multi-
    national Enterprises on Employment and Training. Gene-
    va: International Labor Office.

International Labor Office. 1976B. Wages and Working Condi-
    tions in Multinational Enterprises. Geneva: International
    Labor Office.

Jackson, Richard A. (ed.). 1974. Multinational Corporation
    and Social Policy: Special Reference to General Motors in
    South Africa. New York: Praeger.

Jelliffe, D.B. & E.F.P. Jelliffe. 1971. "An Overview."
    American Journal of Clinical Nutrition 24, no. 8. 1013 -
    1024.

Jelliffe, D.B. 1972. "Commerciogenic Malnutrition." Nutri-
    tion Reviews 30, no. 9. 199 - 205.

Johnson, Dale L. 1972. "The National and Progressive
    Bourgeoisie in Chile." In Dependence and Underdevelop-
    ment: Latin America's Political Economy, ed. James D.
    Cockcroft, Andre Gunder Frank and Dale L. Johnson.
    Garden City, N.Y.: Anchor Books, pp. 165 - 217.

Kerdpibule, Udom. 1974. "Thailand's Experience with Multi-
    national Corporations." Mimeographed. Bangkok: De-
    partment of Economics, Kasetsart University.

Kreye, Otto. 1977. "World Market-oriented Industrialization
    of Developing Countries: Free Production Zones and
    World Market Factories." In Die neue internationale Ar-
    beitsteilung. Strukturelle Arbeitslosigkeit in den Indus-
    trielandern und die Industrialisierung der Entwicklungs-

lander, by Folker Frobel, Jurgen Heinrichs and Otto Kreye. Hamburg: Rowohlt Taschenbuch Verlag.

Kumar, Krishna (ed.). 1979. Bonds Without Bondage. Honolulu: University of Hawaii Press.

Kumar, Krishna. 1976. "Some Reflections on Transnational Social Science Networks." Paper presented at Mediating Person's Conference held in Honolulu at the East-West Center, June 21 - July 4, 1976.

Ledogar, Robert J. 1975. Hungry for Profits: U.S. Food and Drug Multinationals in Latin America. New York: IDOC North America.

Levkovsky, A.I. 1966. Capitalism in India: Basic Trends in Its Development. Bombay: Peoples Publishing House.

Matta, Fernando Reyes. 1976. "The Information Bedazzlement of Latin America: A Study of World News in the Region." Development Dialogue. no. 2. 29 - 42.

Mazrui, Ali. 1976. The Impact of Transnational Corporations on Educational Processes and Cultural Change: An African Perspective. Paris: United Nations Educational, Scientific and Cultural Organization. SHC.76/CONF.6 635/COL.9.

Muller, M. 1974. The Baby Killer. London: War on Want Pamphlet.

National Academy of Sciences. 1973. U.S. International Firms and R, D and E in Developing Countries. Washington, D.C.: NAS.

Nickel, Herman. 1978. "The Case for Doing Business in South Africa." Fortune 97, no. 12, June 19. 60 - 74.

OECD. 1967. Pilot Survey on Technical Assistance Extended by Private Enterprise. Paris: OECD.

Reuber, Grant L. 1973. Private Foreign Investment in Development. Oxford: Clarendon Press.

Rogers, B. 1976. "Apartheid for Profit." Business and Society Review. no. 19. 65 - 69.

Ryan, William. 1971. Blaming the Victim. New York: Vintage Books.

Sauvant, Karl P. 1976A. "The Potential of Multinational En-
    terprises as Vehicles for the Transmission of Business
    Culture," Controlling Multinational Enterprises: Prob-
    lems, Strategies, Counterstrategies. Edited by Karl P.
    Sauvant and Farid G. Lavipour. Boulder: Westview
    Press.

Sauvant, Karl P. 1976. "His Master's Voice." CERES 9, no.
    5. 27 - 32.

Sauvant, Karl P. and Mennis, Bernard. 1977. "Puzzling Over
    the Immaculate Conception of Indifference Curves: The
    Transnational Transfer and Creation of Socio-political and
    Economic Preferences." Paper presented at the Second
    German Studies Conference, Indiana University, Bloom-
    ington, April 12 - 17, 1977. Bloomington: Indiana Uni-
    versity.

Schiller, H.I. 1976. Communication and Cultural Domination.
    New York: International Arts and Sciences Press.

Seidman, A. and Seidman, N. 1977. South Africa and the
    U.S. Multinational Corporations. Westport, Conn.: Law-
    rence Hill.

Sklar, Richard L. 1975. Corporate Power in an African
    State: The Political Impact of Multinational Mining Com-
    panies in Zambia. Berkeley: University of California
    Press.

Somavia, Juan. 1976. "The Transnational Power Structure
    and International Information." Development Dialogue.
    no. 2. 15 - 28.

Spandau, Arnt. 1978. Economic Boycott Against South Afri-
    ca - Normative and Factual Issues. Johannesburg: Uni-
    versity of Witwatersrand.

Sunkel, Osvaldo. 1973. "Transnational capitalism and National
    Disintegration, in Latin America." Social and Economic
    Studies 22, no. 1. 132 - 176.

Sunkel, Osvaldo and Faivovich, Edmundo 1976. "The Effects
    of Transnational Corporations on Culture." Paris:
    United Nations Educational, Social, and Cultural Organiza-
    tion (SHC-76/CONF. 635/COL 5).

Tsuda, Ey Mamoru. 1977. "The Social Organization of Trans-
    national Business and Industry: A Study of Japanese
    Capital - Affiliated Joint-ventures in the Philippines."

M.A. thesis submitted to the College of Arts and Sciences, University of the Philippines.

Tunstall, Jeremy. 1977. The Media are American. New York: Columbia University Press.

United Church Board for World Ministries, et al. 1977. "Report to the Eleventh General Synod of the United Church of Christ on 1975 - 1977 Corporate Social Responsibility Actions, with Special Emphasis on Southern Africa." New York: United Church Board.

United Nations. 1977. Activities of TNS's in Southern Africa and the Extent of their Collaboration with the Regimes in the Area. New York: United Nations, Economic and Social Council, Commission on Transnational Corporations.

United Nations Department of Economic and Social Affairs. 1973. Multinational Corporations in World Development. New York: United Nations, ST/ECA/190.

Vernon, Raymond. 1971. Sovereignty at Bay. New York: Basic Books.

Vernon, Raymond. 1976. "Multinational Enterprises in Developing Countries: Issues in Dependency and Interdependence." In The Multinational Corporation and Social Change. Edited by David E. Apter and Louis W. Goodman. New York: Praeger, pp. 40 - 62.

Weinstein, Franklin B. 1976. "Multinational Corporation and the Third World: The Case of Japan and Southeast Asia." International Organization 30, no. 3. 373 - 404.

Wionczek, Miguel. 1976. "Notes on Technology-transfer Through Multinational Enterprises in Latin America." Development and Change 7, no. 2. 135 - 155.

4 Transfer-Pricing Problems and the Multinational Corporations

Alan M. Rugman

INTRODUCTION

This study* examines the use of transfer pricing by multinational firms. After an introduction and review of the theoretical and empirical literature on transfer pricing, it proceeds to discuss possible methods of testing for transfer pricing. One suitable method is to evaluate the impact of transfer pricing on the performance of the multinational firm and its subsidiaries. The empirical work reported here is restricted to a group of multinational mining firms active in the Canadian mineral resource sector. The narrow focus of this empirical analysis was dictated by data availability and time constraints.

The study is potentially useful and is perhaps worthy of some attention at this time since it presents results for an industry case study which differ in major respects from those reported by Vaitsos (1974) and Lall (1973) for another case study – that of the pharmaceutical industry operating in Colombia. Although Vaitsos attempted to extend his analysis to three other industries and three other South American nations, the overwhelming body of his evidence is drawn from the pharmaceutical industry alone. Given the impact of his findings on the subsequent thinking of United Nations agencies and other organizations keen to regulate multinational firms, it is important for policy purposes to have the results of another study with different findings available at this time. Future work on transfer pricing should attempt to extend the analysis

---

*The excellent research assistance of Ruth Kristjanson and David Baril was supported by a grant from the Research and Travel Committee of the University of Winnipeg.

to more industries and other nations, in order to widen our knowledge of this data-deficient subject.

The work in this study uses economic analysis rather than the techniques of managerial, organizational and behavioral theory. Thus, it serves to balance some of the other contributions in this volume, which do adopt such approaches. The multinational enterprise is a complex animal and the academic study of it in the emerging field of international business is one of the few truly interdisciplinary areas of research. Some preliminary remarks are required, therefore, to explain the concentration of this work on the economic aspects of transfer pricing.

The basic premise of this study is that transfer pricing is an efficient response of multinational firms to external constraints, such as effective international tax-rate differentials, currency controls or other government-inspired regulation of foreign direct investment. A managerial approach to transfer pricing could detail the methods by which international tax payments might be minimized, or it could evaluate strategies for the avoidance of currency controls and other restrictions imposed on multinational firms by host nations, such as blocked funds. Therefore the managerial approach and the economic approach are both going in the same direction, namely toward an analysis of the use of transfer pricing as an internal device within the organizational structure of the multinational firm.

Both the economic and the managerial approach to transfer pricing suggest that it is theoretically possible for the multinational firm to manipulate intracorporate pricing. While the managerial approach examines practical methods by which a multinational firm can use transfer pricing to its advantage, it is possible to use economic analysis to carry the issue a stage further. Ultimately the use of transfer pricing must affect the performance of the multinational firm. Performance can be measured in terms of higher profits, increased managerial compensation, greater utility to shareholders, and an increase in the stock market's evaluation of the share prices of the firm. Clearly these (and possibly other) effects of transfer pricing are interrelated, and different studies could choose to examine any one, or more, of these aspects of improved performance.

Here attention is directed mainly toward the profits of multinationals and their subsidiaries. In addition, the risk of earnings is examined. A basic mean-variance portfolio theory model is used to find the effects of transfer pricing on the chosen group of multinational mining firms active in Canada. With these prefatory remarks about the methodology of this study, I now proceed to review the hostile political climate in Canada toward foreign direct investment. There is an implicit assumption in Canadian public policy that since mining multinationals appear to have the power to use transfer pricing, their assumed excess profits should be removed by provincial and federal taxation.

CANADIAN POLICY ON TRANSFER PRICING AND PROFITS

The conflict between multinational enterprise (MNE) and the nation-state is an issue of great current concern in tradition-ally open trading nations such as Canada. In response to a perceived increase in nationalist sentiment, both federal and provincial governments have increased taxation of Canadian petroleum and mining industries.

It is apparently widely believed by nonbusiness members of the public, many academics, and even some legislators, that profits of multinational corporations operating in Canada (and elsewhere) have been, and continue to be, excessively high. That this view is simplistic and factually incorrect has been demonstrated at an aggregate level in a study by Rugman (1976) and at a disaggregate level, for the oil industry in Rugman (1975). The latter confirmed that profits of subsidiary firms in host nations (such as Canada) approximately equal profit rates of the parent firm in the home nation (the United States). The risk of profits was also studied, and it was found that MNEs have less variability in profits than do non MNEs of comparable size. This approach was also tested for Canadian mining corporations (see Rugman, 1977, who found that MNE profit rates are about average, but that risk is higher than for most other sectors).

Despite such work, the attitude persists that there is something abnormal and even immoral about the profits earned by, and general financial operations of, MNEs. Cyclical up-turns in profits indeed yield large percentage increases which are given a high profile in reports by the media. In general, comparable cyclical downturns and company losses are not given the same exposure, thereby creating a false impression of excessive profitability in the mining industry.

THE MNE AND TRANSFER PRICING

A frequent argument made against the MNE is that since it operates internationally, it is uniquely well-endowed to engage in transfer pricing; that is, to manipulate intrafirm input prices to its overall advantage. By such manipulation of input prices, between subsidiary and parent, the MNE is alleged to have the power to avoid payment of full local taxes, thus de-priving the host nation (or province) of some of its legitimate tax revenue. A recent theoretical model by Nieckels (1976) has demonstrated that a MNE can use transfer pricing to increase its profit rate, and this has been confirmed by Booth and Jensen (1977). Empirical work by Lall (1973) and Vaitsos (1974) on Latin America has revealed some evidence of exceptional profits for MNEs in the pharmaceuticals field. These issues are discussed by Adams and Whalley (1977), who bring out the interrelationships between transfer pricing and international tax policy, as first demonstrated by Horst (1971) and Copithorne (1971).

The existing literature on foreign investment, the role of the MNE, and MNE-related tax revenues does not support the popular view that the MNE avoids taxation or fails to contribute to a nation's economic growth. For example, the seminal theoretical article by MacDougall (1960) on the advantages of foreign direct investment has been extended by Corden (1974) to demonstrate that the advantages of free trade and capital flows still persist when the rigid neoclassical assumptions of the MacDougall model are relaxed. Thus, in contrast to the arguments of writers such as Vaitsos (1974), Kierans (1973), Barnet and Muller (1974), and others, there is no theoretical case to be made against foreign direct investment by the MNE on efficiency grounds. The critical view of the MNE by these authors should be contrasted with the more agnostic views of: Johnson (1970), Grubel and Sydneysmith (1975), Vernon (1971, 1977) and Horst (1977). The latter works are based on the correct use of economic analysis, since these writers manage to separate efficiency from distributional questions, in contrast to many writers who confuse them.

The MacDougall model has been tested by Grubel (1974) and Jenkins (1973). They find that there is no social loss in Canada from the activities of MNEs. In fact Grubel argues the opposite case - that the United States suffers a social loss since its MNEs are not subject to double taxation, and thus do not pay tax in the United States once it is paid by a subsidiary in Canada. Evidence in a similar vein has been found by Horst (1977).

Even if the MNE were able to exploit Canadians, it is not clear that excessive profits could be realized at home. Examination of existing tax codes by Musgrave (1969) and others shows that the United States government has the authority to impose "arm's length," that is, market, prices for intracorporate prices. This power of the internal revenue service should be a check against possible transfer-pricing policies of United States-based MNEs. It is, of course, necessary to extend this work by an examination of Canadian tax legislation as it affects the MNE. In any analysis of transfer pricing, it is necessary, therefore, to consider the impact of taxes, tariffs, profit controls, and other regulations which affect the profits of a MNE.

METHODS OF TESTING FOR TRANSFER PRICING

It is basically an empirical question as to whether or not multi-national firms engage in transfer pricing. Unfortunately, little or no data are available on the internal pricing policies of individual firms. Therefore the independent researcher is faced with a difficult task in attempting to measure any alleged divergence between the theoretically appropriate market price for a product or input and the actual price charged in intrafirm accounting. However, there are ways to overcome the problem of lack of data on transfer pricing.

First, it may be possible to engage in several individual firm case studies, using figures disclosed by firms upon personal request. This is not a very practical method, however, unless corporations are willing to set aside the time and resources to answer survey questionnaires, and to prepare detailed accounts.

Second, it is possible to study the world prices of intermediate products at industry level using import and export data. With the use of concentration ratios, the leading firms in an industry group can be identified and the revealed world price can be applied to actual industry-level prices charged by the divisions of the MNE. The foreign trade prices of intermediate inputs can be compared to the world price, with the difference being taken as a proxy measure of the distortion caused by transfer pricing. In this manner dominant corporations in sub-sectors of the mining industry can be tested for transfer-pricing activities. In this approach, it is important to allow for price divergences caused by exchange rate fluctuations, the influence of government barriers to trade (such as tariffs), and other factors outside the control of an individual corporation.

Third, it is possible to use published data on firm and industry profits to test indirectly the effect (or noneffect) of transfer pricing. For example, profit figures for a Canadian subsidiary can be compared with profits of the parent firm. In the absence of transfer pricing it would be expected that profit rates for subsidiary and parent would be approximately equal, given similar patterns of factor costs and government taxation policies. If transfer pricing does exist, then it would be hypothesized that the parent firm's rate of profit would exceed the profit rate of its subsidiary - since the subsidiary must either be under paid for sales for resources to the parent, or forced to pay too much for purchases from the parent firm.

In this paper the third method is pursued, not because it is theoretically superior to the other two, but due to data availability. Given the paucity of objective research on the emotional subject of transfer pricing, such a pioneering approach is necessary as a first step toward a more complete empirical analysis. In the next section, details of the actual research procedure are given and several tables are used to illustrate the performance of mining MNEs and their subsidiaries. Section 6 contains conclusions and policy implications. It is found that the subsidiaries with high returns also experience high levels of (total) risk. Therefore a simple mean-variance version of portfolio theory appears to explain the profits of these MNEs. No evidence is found of transfer pricing.

RESEARCH METHODOLOGY

In summary, it has become apparent that the MNE has the ability to engage in transfer pricing. The recent theoretical work by Horst (1971), Nieckels (1976), Booth and Jensen (1977) and others has demonstrated that a MNE can use its organizational structure to charge nonmarket prices for intermediate inputs, and thereby influence the net revenues earned by its various subsidiaries. The extent to which the MNE uses its own internal market to manipulate intra corporate prices of intermediate goods will be influenced by the taxation policy of national governments.

Transfer prices and tax rates are intimately related. More specifically, the international tax rate differential on an input for the MNE enters into its production process as a cost item along with the normal costs of factors such as labor and capital. If international tax rates were uniform there would be no incentive for transfer pricing, and "arm's length" prices would exist within the MNE. However, the observed exogenous market imperfection of international tax differentials acts as an incentive for transfer pricing. The MNE responds to the market imperfection by manipulation of prices within its internal market and organization. This is an efficient response.

If, in theory, the MNE can engage in transfer pricing, what evidence is there of this activity? There are few empirical studies of transfer pricing except for the widely quoted, but inadequate work of Vaitsos (1974) and Lall (1973). Both authors use data on the pricing of pharmaceuticals by MNEs active in Colombia and other South American nations. This industry is perhaps not representative of MNEs, as suggested by Vernon (1977) and Lessard (1977). The data base is not available for public scrutiny since it was provided by government agencies on a confidential basis. Another problem is that Vaitsos does not address the issue of whether it is appropriate to use official or market-determined foreign exchange rates when calculating international costs and prices.

Nor does he consider in any detail the complex issues of multi-national tax policy and double taxation agreements.

An alternative approach to that of Vaitsos, based on classical microeconomic theory, is followed in this paper. We choose to evaluate the performance of the MNEs active in the Canadian mining industry. The ultimate criterion of economic performance is profitability. Therefore the profits of both parent and subsidiaries are calculated and examined for significant differences. If transfer pricing is being used by the MNE, it should show up in excessive profits of either the parent or one or more of its subsidiaries. However, if profit rates are found to be virtually identical for all parts of the MNE, it is hard to live with the idea that transfer pricing is in operation.

It should be noted that this investigation of profitability examines the breakdown between parent and subsidiary. Naturally a MNE can use any market power it may possess to normalize profits or even set a target profit rate (presumably close to the average for all manufacturing firms). If this procedure is followed, then the MNE manipulates the costs and revenues of various subsidiaries to stabilize the profit rate of the consolidated MNE. The approach followed here permits us to go behind the screen of consolidated balance sheets and potentially stable profits. The profit rates of individual subsidiaries and of the parent are examined for significant differences.

RESULTS AND IMPLICATIONS

This project extends an earlier study by Rugman (1977), in which the fifteen largest multinational corporations active in the Canadian mining industry were identified and their performance analyzed. The profit rates of consolidated MNEs were found; but here, using annual reports and 10-ks, it is possible to assemble new information on the performance of major divisions and lines of business of the mining MNEs. Although it was difficult to develop a long-time series for all of the firms, it was possible to trace back the disaggregated profits for eight of the major firms. Rates of return on revenue, on assets, and a shareholders' equity were then calculated.

The details of the performance measured for profits on revenue, by division, are reported in tables 4.1 to 4.8 for AMAX (1968-77), Falconbridge (1971-77), INCO (1974-77), IMC (1971-77), Noranda (1970-77), Patino (1971-77), JMC (1971-75) and Rio Algom (1963-77). The rates of return on assets and equity give a similar picture, but are not as complete as the return on revenue figures.

It can be observed that there is typically a wide deviation in profit rates between the divisions of a MNE. Some subsidiaries earn very high profits while others have much less than the firm average. Is this evidence of transfer pricing? To examine the disparity in profit rates further, a simple portfolio theory approach is used. The mean profit rate over time and the standard deviation (S.D.) of the profit stream were calculated to represent expected return and total risk respectively. The resulting means and S.D.s can be graphed in risk-return space, although space limitations prevent the reproduction here of such diagrams. Instead table 4.9 summarizes these data.

It is striking to observe the positive relationship between risk and return for all of the eight MNEs. Thus the highly profitable divisions experience the greatest risk, while the less profitable ones have low risk. This is consistent with the implications of portfolio theory and indicates that the subdivisions of the mining MNEs examined are not engaged in any unusual economic activities. Indeed, the internal performance of the MNEs is entirely consistent with portfolio theory, and this may lead to the implication that these MNEs are efficient. These tests, therefore, do not provide any support for transfer pricing among the divisions since transfer pricing is a symptom of market inefficiency.

It is also apparent that the parent (total) firm has a risk-return relationship that is the average of its divisions. Thus the parent is not able to squeeze its subsidiaries in order to realize an excessive profit rate for any level of risk. In conclusion, no evidence is found of transfer pricing in this examination of the performance of major subsidiaries and divisions of MNEs active in Canadian mining.

Clearly further empirical work is required before a definite conclusion can be drawn about the lack of transfer pricing by these MNEs. In this paper, an interesting new approach has been suggested; one which allows the independent researcher to overcome the lack of data on internal pricing by the MNE. It should be noted that governments have greater research facilities and that their internal revenue services have access to company information on intracorporate pricing. Therefore the nation-state is in a strong position to observe and regulate the profits of the MNE, if it is engaging in transfer pricing. The tentative conclusion from this research is that transfer pricing is not reflected in the profit performance of the MNE and its subsidiaries.

Table 4.1. AMAX Rate of Return on Revenue by Line of Business
(percent)

	1977	1976	1975	1974	1973	1972	1971	1970	1969	1968
Molybdenum, Nickel and Specialty Metals	20.6	24.3	16.5	13.8	17.3	21.9	17.6	31.72	32.26	26.85
Base Metals	7.1	9.1	7.9	2.0	11.7	6.3	1.9	4.4	2.6	6.6
Fuels	10.9	14.4	18.4	7.5	5.2	14.3	10.4	8.2	-5.3	-20.0
Iron Ore	28.8	28.9	37.4	37.2	63.3	55.6	59.0	52.0	50.0	N/A
Chemicals	25.0	30.2	43.1	41.8	27.3	25.0	14.8	17.4	4.8	N/A
Consolidated	12.6	13.6	14.1	12.3	12.9	13.0	10.3	12.3	10.0	11.3

Note: Earnings are before tax.
Source: 1977 Annual Report.

Table 4.2.   Falconbridge

	1977	1976	1975	1974	1973	1972	1971
Total (Consolidated)			$ M				
Revenues	382	483	429	458	438	275	211
Op. Profit	7	57	46	98	138	45	33
Ebit	(29)	25	15	69	103	18	13
Y & Mng. Taxes	.06	7	8	34	35	6	(3)
E (net income)	(24)	22	9	39	71	12	18
Assets	828	675	717	729	698	617	658
E/A perc.	-2.85	3.32	1.25	5.40	10.12	1.93	2.77
E/Rev. perc.	-6.18	4.64	2.09	8.60	16.13	4.34	8.64

(i)   Integrated Nickel Operations (Nickel, Copper in Ontario, Manitoba and Norway)

	1977	1976	1975	1974	1973	1972	1971
Revenues	119	210	166	217	205	155	154
Op. Profit	(16)	13	(2)	41	46	22	23
Ebit	(29)	3	(11)	34	35	11	5
Y & Mng. Taxes	(7)	(2)	(5)	17	15	6	(5)
E	(22)	5	(5)	16	19	5	10
Assets	478	341	350	367	335	285	303
E/A	-4.52	1.39	1.54	4.46	5.79	1.80	3.43
E/Rev.	-18.20	2.25	-3.24	7.54	9.50	3.29	6.75

(ii)   Falconbridge Copper Ltd.   (Copper & Zinc in Quebec and Ontario)

	1977	1976	1975	1974	1973	1972	1971
Revenues	108	89	80	65	79	48	34
Operating II	13	9	2	18	36	11	9
Ebit	13	8	2	18	36	10	8
Y & Mng. Taxes	5	3	.9	9	9	1	3
E	8	5	.7	9	28	9	5
Assets	72	61	54	56	59	36	35
E/A	10.62	7.91	1.20	15.64	46.74	26.00	14.01
E/Rev.	7.08	5.45	0.82	13.36	34.80	19.30	14.65

(continued)

Table 4.2. (contd.)

	1977	1976	1975	1974	1973	1972	1971
(iii) Falconbridge Dominicana (Ferronickel in Dominican Republic)							
Revenues	99	116	106	99	91	41	
Operating II	19	30	28	17	38	16	
Ebit	7	17	13	2	21	6	
Y & Mng. Taxes	2	6	4	.9	7	2	
E	5	11	9	2	14	4	
Assets	197	208	209	210	219	202	195
E/A	2.39	5.37	4.44	0.75	6.32	2.00	
E/Rev.	4.75	9.60	8.74	1.59	15.15	9.89	
(iv) Indusmin Ltd. (Industrial Minerals and Metal Castings in Ontario & Quebec)							
Revenues	42	39	22	18	16	13	11
Operating II	4	5	4	3	3	2	.5
Ebit	3	5	3	2	2	1	.5
Y & Mng. Taxes	1	2	1	1	.8	.2	.1
E	2	3	2	1	2	1.3	.5
Assets	37	33	25	20	18	18	18
E/A	5.66	9.07	7.69	6.97	8.98	7.01	2.53
E/Rev.	4.88	7.80	8.61	7.82	10.13	9.44	4.19
(v) Oamites Mining Co. (Copper in Southwest Africa)							
Revenues	11	10	11	14	14	5	
Operating II	(1)	.3	1	3	6	.8	
Ebit	(1)	.3	1	3	5	.5	
Y & Mng. Taxes	(0.2)	.1	(.07)	1	2	.2	
E	(0.5)	.2	1	2	3	.3	
Assets	10	10	9	10	10	8	
E/A	-5.09	1.92	12.23	20.17	30.54	3.21	
E/Rev.	-4.28	1.94	10.39	14.00	23.52	5.80	

(continued)

Table 4.2.   (contd.)

	1977	1976	1975	1974	1973	1972	1971
(vi) Wesfrob Mines Ltd. (Iron and Copper in British Columbia)							
Revenues	8	12	14	12	13	8	15
Operating II	(2)	(.04)	(.7)	2	4	(3)	1.4
Ebit	(2)	(.4)	(.9)	.7	3	(4)	1.5
Y & Mng. Taxes	0	0	.4	.06	.5	.02	.6
E	(2)	(.4)	(1)	.6	2	(4)	.9
Assets	11	12	13	13	15	17	25
E/A	-19.51	-3.01	-9.95	4.91	14.24	-21.44	3.64
E/Rev.	-26.72	-2.88	-9.85	5.16	16.50	-44.15	5.93
(vii) Others							
Revenues	1	.8	16	12	9	8	13
Operating II	(.5)	(.4)	2	.6	(.1)	.5	1.5
Ebit	(.9)	(.8)	2	.5	(.05)	.5	1.7
Y & Mng. Taxes	(.05)	.1	1	.3	.1	.2	.4
E	(.6)	(.9)	2	.7	.6	.4	.8
Assets	42	42	54	52	49	49	58
E/A	-1.44	-2.01	3.83	1.41	1.13	0.86	1.43
E/Rev.	-62.27	-99.3	13.13	6.30	6.51	5.37	6.33
(viii) Aluminex Ltd. (Oil and Gas in Alberta)* (Prior to 1976)							
Revenues			20	14	11	8	6
Operating II			15	10	7	5	4
Ebit			12	8	5	3	2
Y & Mng. Taxes			7	4	2	1	1
E			5	5	3	2	1
Assets			37	33	30	27	26
E/A			13.26	14.79	10.24	6.04	4.83
E/Rev.			25.05	33.88	26.91	20.91	19.56

*Sold in 1976
Source: Annual Reports.

Table 4.3. INCO Parent - Subsidiaries

Time Divisions	1977	1976	1975	1974
Parent				
1) Rev.	892,710	1,172,026	934,901	1,201,366
2) Ebit	106,420	277,501	262,217	494,048
3) Net E	69,428	171,879	155,766	277,659
4) Assets	2,685,747	2,574,490	2,303,606	2,203,443
5) K	1,662,531	1,340,498	1,287,365	1,250,547
6) E/A	2.59	6.68	6.76	22.2
7) E/K	4.18	12.82	12.1	12.6
8) E/Rev.	7.78	14.67	16.66	23.11
Subsidiaries				
1) Rev.	1,060,618	868,256	759,867	483,242
2) Ebit	68,933	69,678	59,880	52,971
3) Net E	30,431	24,879	31,123	20,929
4) A	1,390,017	1,053,821	723,069	596,268
5) K	252,298	221,867	196,988	165,865
6) E/A	2.19	2.36	4.31	3.51
7) E/K	12.06	11.21	15.8	12.62
8) E/Rev.	2.87	2.87	4.1	4.33
Consolidated				
1) R	1,953,328	2,040,282	1,694,768	1,684,608
2) Ebit	175,352	347,179	322,097	547,019
3) Net E	99,859	196,758	186,889	298,588
4) A	4,075,764	3,628,311	3,025,675	2,799,711
5) K	1,914,829	1,562,365	1,484,353	1,416,412
6) E/A	2.45	5.4	6.18	10.66
7) E/K	5.22	12.59	12.59	21.08
8) E/Rev.	5.11	9.64	11.03	17.72

Table 4.4. IMC Rate of Return on Revenue and
Invested Capital by Line of Business

	1977	1976	1975	1974	1973	1972	1971
				Millions US$			
Agriculture							
Revenue	602.7	653.6	748.6	416.7	242.3	210.3	202.4
Earnings (E)	73.4	114.9	131.4	53.6	23.1	21.3	13.5
Invested Cap. (K)	553.6	533.2	530.2	387.7	311.2	N/A	N/A
E/R (percent)	12.2	17.6	17.6	12.9	9.5	10.1	6.7
E/K* (1) (percent)	14.1	22.7	26.1	14.8	8.5	N/A	N/A
Industry							
Revenue	371.2	351.2	433.9	373.9	305.6	275.6	291.9
Earnings	12.6	13.9	18.1	.5	2.3	-0.4	2.0
(K)*	141.6	118.6	87.6	61.2	79.9		
E/R (percent)	3.4	4.0	4.2	0.1	0.8	-0.2	0.7
E/K* (1) (percent)	12.3	14.7	24.6	6.0	6.1		
Chemicals							
Revenue	306.2	255.2	120.4	67.9			
Earnings	27.2	6.4	12.2	3.2			
(K)*							
E/R (percent)	8.9	2.5	10.1	4.7			
E/K* (1) (percent)	8.5	3.9	7.1	5.7			
Consolidated							
Revenue	1280.2	1260.0	1302.9	858.5	547.9	491.2	517.6
Earnings	108.2	135.2	161.7	57.3	25.4	20.3	12.9
(K)*	1036.3	969.0	763.2	563.5	404.3		
E/R (percent)	8.5	10.7	12.4	6.7	4.6	4.1	2.5
E/K* (1) (percent)	12.1	15.5	22.7	11.6	7.9		

Table 4.5. Noranda

	1977	1976	1975	1974	1973	1972	1971	1970
Total					$M			
(Consolidated)								
Revenue	1,387	1,232	1,156	1,147	849	576	462	457
Earnings	67	47	51	155	121	64	61	60
E/Rev. perc.	4.84	3.79	4.37	13.5	14.31	11.17	13.31	13.03
(i) Copper Mining, Smelting & Refining								
Revenue	310	321	294	395	328	214	237	259
Earnings	37	46	32	80	46	45	47	39
E/Rev.	11.97	14.26	11.00	20.29	14.11	20.88	19.63	15.114
(ii) Other Mining & Smelting Operations								
Revenue	420	340	372	339	230	86	40	41
Earnings	31	25	41	67	67	9	4	11
E/Rev.	7.40	7.20	10.98	19.68	29.35	10.34	9.95	27.19
(iii) Total Mining & Metallurgy								
Revenue	729	662	666	734	558	300	277	301
Earnings	55	62	57	134	107	61	62	61
E/Rev.	7.60	9.31	8.52	18.29	19.21	20.31	22.52	20.34
(iv) Manufacturing Operations								
Revenue	704	575	540	564	439	303	236	251
Earnings	31	11	23	39	23	11	5	6
E/Rev.	4.33	1.84	4.31	6.98	5.29	3.75	2.03	2.31
(v) Forest Product Operations								
Revenue	552	490	373	365	254	168	73	168
Earnings	31	19	11	11	15	11	4	2
E/Rev.	5.63	3.92	3.01	3.10	5.91	6.37	4.89	0.95
Also:								
Sales Between Divisions:								
	127	99	85	170	103	72	76	77
Sales by Associated Companies:								
	473	395	338	346	299	122	78	186
Common Costs	50	45	41	30	24	19	10	9

Source: Annual Reports.

Table 4.6. Patino Rate of Return on Revenue by Line of Business

	1977	1976	1975	1974	1973	1972	1971
		US $	- - - 000's - - -			CDN $	
Merchanting in Metals and Ore							
Revenue	1,394.3	1,442.7	1,263.0	1,301.0	713.8	410.3	609.5
Earnings	-1.7	3.1	2.2	13.4	2.8	-0.6	-3.8
E/R perc.	-0.1	0.2	0.2	1.0	0.4	-0.2	-0.6
Tin Smelting							
Revenue	393.9	356.9	308.7	350.0	155.0	131.7	204.8
Earnings	15.9	8.6	6.2	6.8	4.1	3.5	-0.5
E/R perc.	4.0	2.4	2.0	1.9	2.7	2.7	-0.2
Steel Merchanting and Fabricating							
Revenue	47.5	49.4	41.7	67.0	46.2	25.7	7.3
Earnings	-2.8	-0.3	-0.4	4.5	3.5	0.8	0.6
E/R perc.	-5.9	-0.6	-1.0	6.7	7.6	3.1	8.2
Sales of Mineral Production							
Revenue	35.6	25.9	12.6	37.2	27.1	18.9	20.5
Earnings	1.5	1.2	0.5	16.4	9.4	1.5	2.5
E/R perc.	4.2	4.6	4.0	44.1	34.7	7.9	12.2
Other Activities							
Revenue	59.7	49.9	51.1	65.1	20.7	34.6	10.1
Earnings	5.4	3.4	0.1	3.4	2.5	7.4	2.6
E/R perc.	9.1	6.8	0.2	5.2	12.1	21.4	25.7
Consolidated							
Revenue	1931.0	1924.8	1704.0	1781.1	965.0	621.1	852.2
Earnings	18.2	16.0	11.3	45.3	22.6	12.7	1.4
E/R perc.	0.9	0.8	0.7	2.5	2.3	2.0	0.2

Note: Earnings are before taxes and extraordinary items.

Source: Annual Reports.

Table 4.7. Rio Algom Rate of Return on Revenue by Line of Business

	1977	1976	1975	1974	1973	1972	1971	1970	1969	1968	1967	1966	1965	1964	1963
								CDN $ Millions							
Mining															
Revenue	207.5	176.2	148.8	164.8	151.5	63.6	46.9	44.4	45.9	35.3	44.8	44.1	30.0	34.4	43.2
Earnings	77.4	72.2	63.0	81.4	81.4	22.5	13.8	10.2	12.9	6.2	13.6	13.8	10.4	8.7	10.9
E/R (percent)	37.3	41.0	42.2	49.4	53.7	35.4	29.4	23.0	28.1	17.6	30.3	31.3	34.7	25.3	25.2
Steel															
Revenue	279.1	225.3	218.5	225.7	163.4	132.6	121.2	139.1	127.2	110.5	105.0	105.0	96.6	86.3	74.3
Earnings	17.7	7.2	19.3	36.4	14.2	3.5	1.8	9.6	7.6	5.0	3.8	2.7	2.1	1.9	3.7
E/R (percent)	6.3	3.2	8.8	16.1	8.7	2.6	1.5	6.9	6.0	4.5	3.6	2.6	2.2	2.2	5.0
Consolidated															
Revenue	486.6	401.6	367.4	390.6	314.9	187.2	168.0	183.5	175.4	148.3	151.0	148.0	127.3	121.6	118.4
Earnings	83.1	68.9	65.9	104.2	78.7	18.8	11.6	16.9	15.4	8.1	12.5	11.4	9.8	9.5	12.3
E/R (percent)	17.1	17.2	17.9	26.7	25.0	10.0	6.9	9.2	8.8	5.5	8.3	7.7	7.7	7.8	10.4

Note: Earnings before taxes.

Source: Annual Reports.

Table 4.8. JMC

	1975	1974	1973	1972	1971
Total (Consolidated)		(000,000's)			
Revenue	1107	1105	905	799	696
E (before taxes)	70	87	86	83	78
E/R (percent)	6.30	7.88	9.52	10.36	11.19
Thermal Insulations					
Revenue	323	294	245	196	174
Earnings	23	15	25	23	21
E/R (percent)	7.15	5.19	10.15	11.79	12.02
Pipe Products and Systems					
Revenue	192	232	164	147	127
Earnings	(4)	23	6	14	13
E/R (percent)	-1.98	10.11	3.53	9.44	10.62
Roofing Products					
Revenue	170	168	135	115	92
Earnings	17	18	16	14	11
E/R (percent)	10.22	10.78	11.76	12.37	12.14
General Building Products					
Revenue	166	173	167	163	142
Earnings	2	7	13	11	10
E/R (percent)	1.44	4.29	7.97	6.74	6.93
Mining and Minerals					
Revenue	141	118	97	90	81
Earnings	21	22	17	18	19
E/R (percent)	14.97	19.07	17.82	20.21	23.80
Industrial and Other Products					
Revenue	114	121	97	88	80
Earnings	11	7	5	3	3
E/R (percent)	9.53	5.98	4.64	3.02	3.63

Table 4.9.   Rate of Return on Revenues

Firm	Division/Subsidiary	Mean	S.D.
AMAX	(1968-1977)		
	Base Metals	5.95	3.24
	Fuels	10.41	7.26
	Molybdenum, Nickel etc.	22.28	6.40
	Chemicals	24.36	14.43
	Iron Ore	45.79	13.00
	Consolidated	12.2	1.3
Falconbridge	(1971-1977)		
	Indusmin	7.55	2.23
	Domininia	8.29	4.67
	Oamites	8.56	9.73
	Copper	13.64	11.22
	Integrated Nickel	1.13	9.50
	Desfrob	- 8.00	21.03
	Total	5.47	6.86
INCO	(1974-1977)		
	Subsidiaries	3.54	0.78
	Parent	15.56	6.31
	Total	10.88	5.22
IMC	(1971-1977)		
	Industry	1.67	2.12
	Chemicals (1974-1977)	6.55	3.56
	Agriculture	12.37	4.1
	Consolidated	7.1	3.6
	Foreign Subsidiaries 1974-1977	9.22	1.94
Noranda	(by subsidiary) (1966-1972)		
	Pamour Porcupine	19.39	8.74
	Empresa Minera	20.09	8.68
	Orchan Mines	25.61	4.42
	Kerr Addison	30.86	5.63
	Empresa Fluorspar	67.51	30.63
	Consolidated	12.81	1.41

(continued)

Table 4.9   (continued)

Firm	Division/Subsidiary	Mean	S.D.
Noranda	(by industrial division) (1970-1977)		
	Manufacturing	3.86	1.78
	Forest Products	4.22	1.83
	Other Mining	15.26	8.93
	Total Mining	15.76	6.17
	Copper Mining, Smelting Refining	15.91	3.86
	Consolidated	9.82	4.63
Patino	(1971-1977)		
	Metals and Ore	0.13	0.51
	Tin Smelting	2.21	1.28
	Steel	3.11	8.22
	Other Activities	11.44	9.18
	Mineral Sales	15.96	16.49
	Consolidated	1.3	0.9
Rio Algom	(1963-1977)		
	Steel	5.4	3.8
	Mining	33.6	9.9
	Consolidated	12.4	6.7
JMC	(1971-1975)		
	Industrial	4.63	3.53
	General Building Products	5.47	2.63
	Pipe Systems	6.34	5.46
	Thermal Insulators	9.26	2.99
	Roofing Products	11.45	0.92
	Mining and Minerals	19.14	3.30
	Consolidated	9.05	1.97

REFERENCES

Adams, J. D. R. and Whalley, J. 1977. The International Taxation of Multinational Enterprises in Developed Countries. London: A.B.P.

Barnet, R. J. and Muller, Ronald. 1974. Global Reach: The Power of the Multinational Corporation. New York: Simon and Schuster.

Booth, E. J. R. and Jensen, O. W. 1977. "Transfer Prices in the Global Corporation under Internal and External Constraints." Canadian Journal of Economics X (Aug. 1977), pp. 434-446.

Burns, R. M. 1976. Conflict and Its Resolution in the Administration of Mineral Resources in Canada. Kingston, Ontario: Centre for Resource Studies, Queen's University.

Copithorne, L. W. 1971. "International Corporate Transfer Prices and Government Policy." Canadian Journal of Economics IV (1971), pp. 324-341.

Corden, W. M. 1974. Trade Policy and Economic Welfare. Oxford: Oxford University Press.

Dunning, John H. (ed.). 1972. International Investment: Selected Readings. Harmondsworth: Penguin.

Dunning, John H. (ed.). 1974. Economic Analysis and the Multinational Enterprise. London: Allen & Unwin.

Grubel, Herbert G. 1974. "Taxation and the Rates of Return from Some U. S. Asset Holdings Abroad." Journal of Political Economy 82, no. 3 (May-June 1974): 469-488.

Grubel, Herbert G. and Sydneysmith, S. 1975. "The Taxation of Windfall Gains on Stocks of Natural Resources." Canadian Public Policy 1, no. 1 (Winter 1975): 13-29.

Horst, Thomas. 1971. "The Theory of the Multinational Firm: Optimal Behaviour Under Different Tariff and Tax Rates." Journal of Political Economy (1971), pp. 1059-1072.

Horst, Thomas. 1977. "American Taxation of Multinational Corporations." American Economic Review (June 1977), pp. 376-389.

Jenkins, Glenn P. 1973. "The Measurement of Rates of Return and Taxation from Private Capital in Canada." Discussion paper no. 282, Harvard University.

Johnson, Harry G. 1970. "The Efficiency and Welfare Implications of the International Corporation." In The International Corporation, edited by C. P. Kindleberger. Cambridge: M.I.T. Press, pp. 35-56.

Kierans, E. 1973. Report on Natural Resources Policy in Manitoba. Government of Manitoba.

Kindleberger, Charles P. 1968. American Business Abroad. New Haven, Conn.: Yale University Press.

Krause, Lawrence and Dam, Kenneth. 1964. Federal Tax Treatment of Foreign Income. Washington, D.C.: Brookings Institution.

Lall, Sanjaya. 1973. "Transfer Pricing by Multinational Manufacturing Firms." Oxford Bulletin of Economics and Statistics (August 1975), pp. 173-195.

Lessard, Donald R. 1977. "Transfer Prices, Taxes, and Financial Markets: Implications of Internal Financial Transfers Within the Multinational Firm." Sloan School working paper 919-77, April 1977, M.I.T.

MacDougall, G. D. A. 1960. "The Benefits and Costs of Private Investment from Abroad: A Theoretical Approach." Economic Record 36 (1960): 13-35.

Murray, John D. 1976. "Tax Differentials and Foreign Direct Investment Flows: The Canadian-U.S. Experience." Mimeographed. Department of Economics, University of British Columbia.

Musgrave, Peggy B. 1969. United States Taxation of Foreign Investment Income: Issue and Arguments. Cambridge, Mass.: Harvard Law School International Program.

Nieckels, Lars. 1976. Transfer Pricing in Multinational Firms. Stockholm: Almqvist and Wicksell.

Rugman, Alan. 1975. "Risk and Return in the Petroleum Industry." Paper delivered to the Academy of International Business, Dallas, Texas, December 1975; Chapter 9 in International Diversification and the Multinational Enterprise. Lexington: D. C. Heath, 1979.

Rugman, Alan. 1976. "Risk Reduction by International Diver-
    sification." Journal of International Business Studies
    (Fall 1976), pp. 75-80.

Rugman, Alan. 1977. Risk and Return in the Canadian Min-
    ing Industry. Kingston, Centre for Resource Studies,
    Queen's University.

Thunell, Lars H. 1977. Political Risks in International Busi-
    ness: Investment Behaviour of Multinational Corporations.
    New York: Praeger.

Vernon, Raymond. 1971. Sovereignty at Bay: The Multi-
    national Spread of U.S. Enterprises. New York: Basic
    Books.

Vernon, Raymond. 1977. Storm over the Multinationals.
    London: Macmillan.

Vaitsos, Constantine. 1974. Intercountry Income Distribution
    and Transnational Enterprise. Oxford: Oxford Univer-
    sity Press.

III

Strategies, Policy Making, and Organizational Adaptability of Multinational Corporations

5 Strategic Management of Diversified Multinational Corporations

C.K. Prahalad
Yves Doz

Over the last ten years, two interrelated issues have engaged the attention of managers in diversified (multibusiness) multinationals (DMNCs). The first is the need to create an administrative system that can cope with the complexities of managing multiple businesses in a multinational setting. The administrative complexities of a DMNC strategy result from the complex nature and relationships of businesses in the DMNC portfolio (an internal source of complexity) as well as from the nature of pressures and demands imposed on those businesses by the competitive and governmental environments (an external source of complexity). The second is the increasing competition for capital and markets which has forced DMNCs to be selective in the opportunities they want to pursue and to focus their resources - whether capital, technology, or management. Current corporate concern with methodologies for categorizing businesses for the purpose of resource allocation and the current willingness to divest or prune portfolios for strategic reasons are indicators of the perceived need to be selective and focussed in committing corporate resources. It is our objective in this paper to present a conceptual framework for examining the interaction of the two factors - the need for strategic clarity (selectivity and focus on resource commitments) and the need for administrative capacity for the complex task of managing a DMNC.

A number of well-known DMNCs, such as Dow Corning, Union Carbide, or Philips, have adopted a global matrix form of management to cope with their complexities. The management of these companies perceive the matrix as a way to combine selectivity and strategic clarity for various businesses with the ability to manage interdependencies between businesses. As the matrix also represents the most complex form of management and encompasses the most sophisticated administrative systems used by DMNCs, we will develop our analysis around the problems of managing DMNCs which operate in a matrix mode. In this introduction, we shall first suggest a possible framework to consider strategic management in a matrix, then present the overall structure of this paper, and finally introduce our methodology.

A FRAMEWORK TO CONSIDER STRATEGIC MANAGEMENT IN THE MATRIX MODE

While almost all writers on matrix organization agree that it is a distinct and a totally different type of organizational form from the more conventional, functional, line-staff and product or area forms of organization, they invariably describe a matrix with concepts used to study and manage the traditional forms. As a result, descriptions of a matrix are couched in terms such as the following: "Multiple command system and related support systems" (Davis and Lawrence, 1977), "dual authority relationship and power balance" (Galbraith, 1971), "Unity of Command vs. Balance of Power" (Davis, 1975), a "Web of Relationships" (Mee, 1964), "a structure with alternative authority figures to the position based authority figures in the hierarchy" (Argyris, 1967), or "a business organized by both resources and programs which are integrated by means of coordination functions" (Corey and Star, 1971). Notice that the words used are: command system, authority, hierarchy, coordination, integration, balance of power, duality, web of relationships, and so forth. We do not have, as yet, a conceptual framework for describing organizations broad enough to encompass distinct organizational modes - functional, divisional, and matrix. In fact, we have found it useful to separate the matrix from more traditional forms clearly, and to develop a separate framework for describing and managing matrix organizations based on the following premises:

1. Traditional organizational forms reflect a strong strategic orientation of the firm, at a given point in time and as such are unidimensional (for example, a worldwide product organization reflects a strategy of global rationalization, a la Motorola, or an area organization reflects a strategy of area and regional responsiveness a la CPC International). Such structures reflect the commitment of top management to develop a competitive posture and a pattern of resource commitments (strategy) and the location of the power to commit such resources in the structure (authority). As a result, over time the pattern of information flow within the organization as well as the understanding of the "relevant" environment (cognitive orientation) of the key executives also change.

2. A move to a matrix or multidimensional organizational form indicates an unwillingness or an inability on the part of top management to make a one-time strategic commitment to a strategy of rationalization (product mode), or regional responsiveness (area mode). The reason for adopting a matrix form may be environmental pressures (such as host governmental pressures), complexity of businesses (such as interdependence among businesses or a strategy of related diversification), need for high levels of information processing (such as advanced and complex technologies), scarce organizational resources (such as engineering design), leading to a desire for multiple foci in strategic management. This leads to the demand on the organization to be responsive to product, area and functional perspectives and interests.

The two premises outlined above lead to the following propositions. In a matrix organization, for a strategy to be implemented, top management must influence

a) the perception of the "relevant environment," or the cognitive orientation of key executives,

b) the competitive posture that the organization will adopt in its businesses given the perception of the relevant environment, or the strategic orientation,

c) the pattern of resource allocation decisions that are consistent with the strategic orientation by suitably altering the locus of relative power to commit resources, and

d) the development of support systems like administrative procedures to match the three mentioned above. This we call the administrative mode.

In other words, in a matrix, strategic change calls for managing the four subprocesses outlined above. Conversely, in a unidimensional structure like the product group structure, the four subprocesses are all aligned with the formal organizational hierarchy. For example, if one knew who the "boss is," in a product group structure, one also knew what the relevant environment was (that is, other global competitors), the strategy to compete (that is, worldwide rationalization) and who had the power to commit corporate resources (such as the product group managers). There is no compelling need conceptually to disaggregate the organization into its component subprocesses. In a unidimensional organizational form, the administrative support capabilities and the locus of power reside with the same person; the cognitive and strategic orientations are aligned and the resource commitments follow hierarchical arrangements.

The matrix form by design reflects not a strong "commitment to" but only a "preference for" a certain strategic orientation as different components of the organization can legitimately perceive the "relevant environment" and the "competitive posture" differently. They may also compete with each other to gain control over resources or to enhance their influence in the "resource allocation process" leading to power conflicts. The administrative support systems can also reflect this continuing competition for influence within by a lack of focus or an overload of information. Most often this condition is seen "as a pathology" by researchers and practitioners (Davis and Lawrence, 1977).

The subprocess in matrix organization that has attracted the most academic attention is the process of influence or what appears to be a constant power imbalance.

As the current literature does not disaggregate the organization into the four subprocesses and orientations (and it was unnecessary for understanding the traditional unidimensional structures), and as the concept of authority or influence was a critical concept in the conventional organizational theory, the matrix with a dual focus (product and area or product and function) was conceived of as a system to share equal power or influence. Power asymmetry was then postulated as a pathology. Power asymmetry might reflect, at a given point in time, either the shifting criticalities - strategic and operational - in a given business, some best addressed by area managers and others best addressed by product managers, or the personalities of key executives or both. Matrix managers can also shift the balance of power by identification, redefinition and prioritizing of strategic and operational contingencies they face by changing the cognitive and strategic orientations of the business. In fact, our work has suggested that in order to gain strategic focus in a matrix, top managers have to create and manage this asymmetry in power; that equal power between area and product dimensions is not conducive to strategic management (Prahalad, 1976). We should think in terms of "matrices with product emphasis" and "matrices with area emphasis."

Figure 5.1 is a schematic representation of typical product, area, and matrix organizations. Notice that the scheme makes a distinction between the "ideal version" of the matrix as conceived of in the literature and "ideal versions" of the matrix, as required for strategic management purposes.

In summary, in order to understand strategic management in the matrix mode, we suggest starting with the following propositions:

1. A matrix is more than mere structure. It is a form of managerial behavior, a style of decision making, and a structural arrangement. It is an administrative system.
2. A matrix represents a blending of the four orientations - cognitive, strategic, power, and authority. It is important to consider these orientations separately in order to understand a matrix.
3. The locus of each of these orientations in the matrix can be managed. This implies that the locus of power or the basis for resource allocation can also be managed.

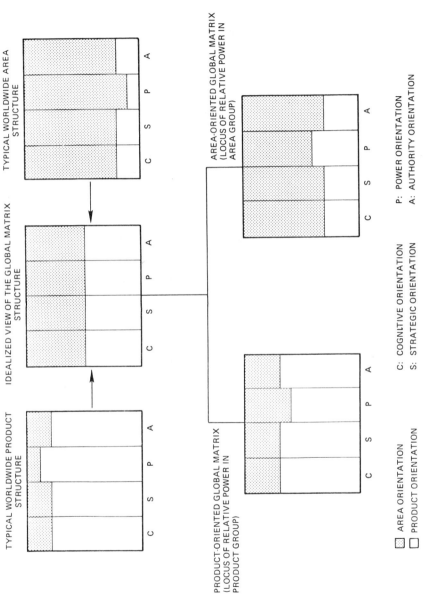

Fig. 5.1. Multinational organizational modes.

81

Organization of the Paper

The basic thrust of our findings will be presented in four parts. First, we will examine the process of gaining strategic clarity for a single business (in a multibusiness firm) in the context of a global matrix. This requires that management maintain the benefits of matrix structure while simultaneously gaining strategic focus by developing asymmetry in power. Second, we will outline the problems that arise when the business in question is a salient business in a given nation. A business is said to be salient if the host government perceives it to be important because of any of a variety of factors such as national defense (e.g., aerospace), national strategic autonomy (e.g., computers in France, telecommunications in several countries), employment (Philips in Belgium), or exports (MNCs in developing countries). As a result, these businesses attract the close scrutiny of the host governments and are often the target of governmental intervention. The managerial task in this setting is one of managing two sources of complexity - internal administration and external environment and still gaining strategic focus. We will next explore the problems of gaining strategic selectivity and focus in a DMNC operating in the matrix mode when the businesses are interdependent. Interdependence among businesses - based on technology, product flow, and common markets - imposes additional constraints on the strategist. An example of interdependence between businesses is the relationship between the radio, hi-fi, phono, and tape recorder product divisions at Philips. We will also examine the process of managing interdependent businesses in environments where some of the businesses may be salient. The schematic in figure 5.2 captures the development of the argument in the paper. Finally, we will speculate on the implications of the emerging patterns previously outlined.

RESEARCH METHODOLOGY

The research reported in this paper has evolved over a period of five years. Reports published at various stages of the research have discussed in detail both the methodology used and specific findings (Prahalad 1975, 1976; Doz 1976, 1978, 1979). This paper represents a synthesis of these efforts.

Two approaches were used in the research. First, an in-depth analysis was made of the management process for specific businesses and issues in several DMNCs. Typically, this sort of analysis required that the researchers spend from three to six months of effort studying an organization. Data collection was based primarily on in-depth interviews with executives at several levels in the organization at both cor-

Managerial complexity due to the choice of basic
strategic orientation in the DMNC

Managerial complexity due to the salience of the
business to (some) host governments

	Independent Businesses	Highly Interdependent Businesses
NOT SALIENT	PART I Providing strategic focus without sacrificing the benefits of matrix structure.	PART III Internal Interdependency due to technology flow, economies of scale, marketing, etc. Providing strategic focus to individual businesses and maintaining the interdependence of business in the portfolio.
SALIENT	PART II Providing strategic focus and incorporating the demands of host governments without sacrificing the benefits of matrix structure.	Interdependencies due to governmental intervention.

Fig. 5.2.   Schematic representation of the strategic issues
in managing DMNCs.

porate headquarters and subsidiaries in several countries. These interviews were coupled with an examination of documentary evidence, often of a proprietary nature, which was available within the corporation (this has caused some DMNCs to opt for disguise). Eight DMNCs were involved in in-depth studies and included in them were United States-based, European and Japanese MNCs.

The in-depth studies were conducted in the following DMNCs:

Table 5.1. Research Design for In-depth Studies

	Single Business	Interdependent Businesses
Business(es): Not Salient	Delta Corp* Various Automobile & EDP companies	Philips, Nippon Corp*
Business(es): Salient	LM Ericsson+	Brown Boveri & Cie G.T.E.

* Name disguised at company's request

+ Many one-industry companies operate a set of distinct product divisions corresponding to various product lines in a matrix mode. The diversity among product lines within the telecommunication equipment, and in automobile industries, for instance, justifies the development of several division.

The second research approach was to study extensively trends in industries and methods of governmental intervention from data available in the public domain (some of these analyses were also supported by data on similar issues collected by firms in our study). Typically, these studies included an analysis of worldwide competitive structure, economies of scale, growth and direction of technology, instruments of governmental intervention, and the patterns of DMNC response. The industries studied in depth were automobiles, electrical power systems, telecommunications, EDP, micro-electronics, and petrochemicals. Several interviews with selected senior officers in host governments added further insights. The findings reported here are the results of the twin approaches to data collection and interpretation.

STRATEGIC FOCUS FOR A SINGLE BUSINESS
IN THE MATRIX MODE

In a multinational matrix, area-oriented managers and product-oriented managers tend to compete for the identification, definition, and prioritization of the strategic and operating contingencies they face, and use them as sources of power (Crozier, 1964). Such competition leads to conflicts that can develop along a variety of dimensions.

For instance, major resource allocation decisions (a new large plant, for example) usually have to be approved by the head of the area where the plant is to be located, by the head of the worldwide product group it will serve, and by corporate managers under different pressures (such as better cash flow or earnings, or return on assets for the entire corporation). Furthermore, specialized technical workers to prepare and implement investment programs may be controlled by functional managers who deal with several product groups. For instance, in a petrochemical company studied in depth (Prahalad, 1975), the product groups, supported by functional groups like research and development demanded large-scale cost-efficient plants whose capacity would exceed the needs of individual national or regional markets and national subsidiaries. Area executives, on the other hand, advocated small plants and an area-specific product mix. Conflicts could also arise, for example, between area and product groups in making decisions about research and development, marketing strategy, and personnel policies.

In a matrix, the importance of multiple cognitive orientations to the plant decision in the example above need to be acknowledged and accepted. This enables the organization to factor in multiple cognitive orientation. Gaining multiple perspectives on problems and learning about them through an advocacy process (made possible through the acceptance of the need for a dual cognitive orientation), is different from making resource allocation decisions. The resource allocation decision is a reflection of the strategic orientation and the locus of relative power in the matrix. In other words, in a matrix, the process of gaining strategic focus in the deployment of resources rests on the ability of top management to choose an appropriate locus of relative power, keeping in mind the continuing need for a dual orientation. The locus of relative power has to be managed and cannot be allowed to be simply the result of an unpredictable set of pressures within the matrix. Stated differently, the trick for top management is to use the asymmetry in power as a strategic tool. At the same time, top management must ensure that the asymmetry is kept in check, so that the need for multiple cognitive orientation is not overlooked.

In our research we found that the locus of relative power affects the strategic and administrative orientation of a business. It has a major influence on the perception of strategic risk and opportunity, the orientation of control and information systems, the stability of joint ventures, the financial strategy, the career patterns and mobility of managers, and the acquisition and divestment decisions (Prahalad, 1976).

The essential question in strategic management in a matrix is therefore not how to equalize power but how to shift it to a desired locus and how to contain the asymmetry so that it does not lead to absolute power. If the asymmetry in power is left unchecked, it may lead to a situation where the cognitive orientations in the matrix may also degenerate into either a pure product or area orientation. Constant attention to both the locus of power and relative power is needed.

Top management can use a variety of organizational mechanisms to shift the locus of relative power in the matrix to correspond with the strategic orientation. In Delta, the locus of relative power shifted, during the period 1972-75, from the area to the product component of the matrix. This shift was managed by a blending of several key changes, most notably, change of the product manager. An aggressive, entrepreneurial manager with a proven track record was assigned to the product group. In addition, a Worldwide Product Planning Team (WPPT) was organized, with this new manager as chairperson. The members of the team were representatives of the various area organizations. The new product manager, using WPPT as a forum, attempted to standardize plant sizes and product specifications. Standardization of plants had an important effect on the balance of power. By denying area organizations the many options they enjoyed before like site selection, specification of size, and timing, the relative power shifted to the product group, with the tacit coalition with the functional component. The pattern of communication and control systems also changed in concert.

Containing relative power within reasonable bounds is often more difficult than shifting its locus. If the business group is the locus of power, for example, containing the power of that group, while at the same time motivating the area managers, is the key to managing in the matrix mode. We have noticed at least two basic approaches to this problem of containing relative power within reasonable bounds. One approach is the use of corporate staff or corporate functional groups. The other (often used to complement the first) is the involvement of direct top management in controversial decisions.

For instance, at LM Ericsson, corporate functional staff managers were used as arbitrators between the national subsidiaries and the product divisions headquartered in Sweden. Substantive knowledge, access to the president, and control

over key aspects of both the divisions' (export sales and overseas manufacturing) and the subsidiaries' (transfer of technology, supply of components) operations yielded considerable
influence to the corporate functional staffs. They could,
therefore, contain the relative power in either group (Doz,
1976).

In a similar vein, IBM had set up a planning and budget-
ing process that provided for the review and analysis of con-
tentions between area organizations and business groups by
corporate staffs, and the final decision by top management
(Katz, 1977). In both LM Ericsson and IBM the importance of
top management intervention, which would usually signal a
loser and a winner between the product and area-oriented
executive, was enough to lead to a resolution of most conflicts
in a balanced way which was at least marginally satisfactory to
both. Close substantive monitoring by corporate staffs en-
sured that conflicts would be genuinely settled rather than
smoothed over. Corporate staff monitoring and the possibility
of top management intervention worked as incentives to deter
both area and product managers from going too far toward the
seizure of absolute power. Furthermore, in both cases top
management was presented with the option of "taking the side
of the weaker group" as a matter of policy. This approach
was in evidence at several of the companies we examined.

In summary, in order to gain strategic focus for a business in global matrix, top management must choose a locus of
relative power - say the product or area dimension - and then
create mechanisms to contain the relative power of that dimension. In other words, they must manage the locus of relative
power.

What are the advantages of this approach? We believe
that it combines the ability to gain strategic focus with a dual
cognitive orientation.

Further, shifts in strategic orientation for a business can
be managed through shifts in the locus of power, rather than
elaborate reorganizations. For example, when Massey-Ferguson
(structured as a pure product organization) wanted to change
its orientation in response to a changing environment from a
worldwide product to an area orientation, a painful, almost
traumatic reorganization was required (Neufeld, 1969; Mathias
1978). Essentially, the matrix enables the DMNC to refocus its
business strategy without major structural or administrative
changes.

STRATEGIC FOCUS AND HOST GOVERNMENT CONTROLS

Managing a Salient Business in the Matrix Mode

A further source of complexity in managing a worldwide business derives from the intervention of host governments, particularly when host governments are also the primary customers, as in telecommunication equipment or electrical power systems. Safety and continuity of supply considerations (particularly for high technology goods of much strategic importance) as well as the constant state desire to generate national employment and minimize imports usually lead state-controlled customers to demand local production as a condition for selecting a foreign supplier. As a result, the world market is fragmented into a set of national oligopolies with very little trade between them (Surrey, 1972; Jequier 1976).

As deep, ongoing relationships built around a local manufacturing subsidiary develop between the company and its customers, a high degree of local responsiveness becomes necessary. Such responsiveness is best provided by an area-oriented management. It remains true, however, that in order to compete successfully for entry into new national markets the company must maintain some technological and economic superiority over local companies. Yet such superiority is best maintained through a worldwide product orientation. In mature markets, the MNC presence becomes threatened in the long run unless it can frequently transfer new technologies not yet easily available from other sources (Doz, 1979). This contradiction frames the dilemma facing managers of government-influenced businesses.

Further, governments often use their market power to try to gain a say in the making of key strategic decisions within the MNC, that is to compromise its strategic integrity. In some cases, economic efficiency, technological competence, or the weight of non-public customers make the bargaining posture of the company strong enough to retain its strategic integrity. For instance, Texas Instruments can have a 100 percent-owned subsidiary in Japan or resist successfully French government pressures to establish joint ventures. Most often, however, government control over market entry (such as that which exists in Brazil or Spain) or over the customers (such as telecommunication or power equipment) deprives the MNC of much of its bargaining power. Often the interests of the host government and those of the companies are sufficiently aligned to lead to a wholehearted agreement (Ford in Spain). In some others they differ and may lead to difficulties (Westinghouse's nuclear business in France or Germany). Specific outcomes depend upon the bargaining position of the company in its dealings with individual countries and upon the perceived costs and benefits of the particular trade-off. This makes the development of a clear overall worldwide strategy impossible. Strategy for a business becomes expressed as a preference for responsiveness in mature markets or for penetration of new ones, or as a desire to do both. Explicitly or implicitly, a matrix mode of management is needed for salient businesses. Within each business deviant subsidiaries will exist. For instance, after World War II, LM Ericsson kept two subsidiaries in very mature markets (France and Italy) that were run with very little involvement from headquarters in Sweden whereas others were guided and controlled more narrowly.

The dimensions along which to choose a strategic preference are simple: technological level (relative to competitors), and existing market positions. Companies such as Brown Boveri or ITT, with large market shares in major mature markets must show responsiveness in these markets and can afford the duplication of production facilities and still be competitive internationally. Rapid technological changes could also obsolete their large existing production capacities. Thus, they follow technical change when needed and when they can (in order not to lose their positions) but they do not lead. Conversely, technological leaders can both penetrate new markets and use their technology to try to provoke a redistribution of shares, to their advantage, in mature markets.

It remains, however, that most companies are both active in some mature markets and also actively pursue new markets - GTE for instance with mature operations in Belgium, Italy and several Latin American countries - and also a strong drive to gain strong positions in new markets, such as Korea or Iran. Most companies thus have to preserve a flexibility for specific decisions: some best made with national responsiveness as a major concern, others best made with global economic efficiency as a priority. Choosing which decisions to make with which priority is in itself difficult, and requires representation of various points of view in all decisions. This lies at the crux of the complexity of managing multinational government-controlled businesses: on the one hand managers have to recognize host governments' desires and give in to their demands, on the other hand these managers must develop and maintain technology and marketing strengths in their company to make it more than a conglomerate of national companies. Very high technology in new markets, or low technology in mature markets may permit a clear preference, but many markets and specific products are somewhere in between, where both the concern for political responsiveness imperatives (usually defended by area-oriented managers) and economic efficiency imperatives (usually defended by product-oriented managers) are about equally relevant, as shown in figure 5.3.

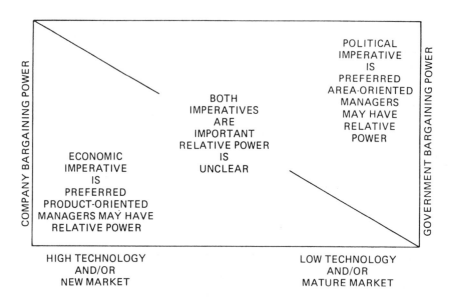

Fig. 5.3.   Bargaining power of MNC and host
government in salient businesses.

The various geographical markets and specific product
lines within a business are likely to cover the whole range of
situations described in figure 4, from high-technology products
(relative to competition) sold in new markets to low-technology
products (relative to competition) in mature markets.   In the
first situation, the MNC clearly has much bargaining power, in
the latter case almost none.   The major difficulty thus becomes
to preserve the ability to shift the preference between political
responsiveness and economic effectiveness from decision to decision according to the relative bargaining power of the MNC
and the host governments in the decision being considered.

In other words, the duality of political and economic imperatives in salient businesses calls for a flexible asymmetry in
power; the ability to allocate power to national subsidiary
managers for some decisions and to world wide product managers for some others.   For instance, the decision to prepare
and submit a bid to a particular utility, and the ensuing negotiation guidelines and limits, may need to be done differently
according to which national administration is involved.   For
some bids, worldwide product units may take responsibility,
for some others national subsidiary management.

Combining this indeterminacy of decision making with the
provision of a clear strategy embodied in consistent commitments of resources over time is a difficult task.   On the one

hand, one needs to preserve the duality of cognitive orientations and to make sure the relevant variety of data and points
of view are brought to bear on the analysis of strategic decisions (that is that competing strategic orientations are pro-
posed).

From a top management point of view, not only managers
with strong commitments, and thought patterns consistent with
their commitments, are needed, but also some neutral, uncommitted managers who can "oscillate between competing belief
patterns put forward by sponsors" (Steinbruner, 1976). The
complexity of managing so that both the economic and the
political imperatives receive adequate attention may thus be
thought to derive from the difficulty of managing power so
that a consistent, but heterogeneous, pattern of resource allocation can be set.

Basically, three different methods are used by managers
to simplify the management task and mediate between the
worldwide product-oriented managers and the nationally-
oriented managers within an organization that is, formally or
informally, run through a matrix management approach. In
our research, each of these elements was found to contribute
to making multinational government-controlled businesses manageable. First, given a strategic preference rooted in market
mix and technology level (that is, a preferred position on
figure 5.4), not all key decisions need to be made with a concern for both political responsiveness and economic efficiency.
Second, functional managers can provide the group of "uncommitted thinkers" who can be brought by top management to
participate in certain decision processes and influence specific
outcomes. Third, administrative procedures can be used by
top managers to provide for arbitration between competing
points of view from managers preferring national responsiveness or worldwide efficiency. These three approaches can
complement each other in a company. They are discussed
below.

Critical Decision Areas

Combining product and geographic cognitive and strategic
orientations is not equally important for all decisions. For
some decisions it is critical, largely because the way in which
these are made globally is likely to affect the subsidiaries'
situation in many countries. Foremost among these critical
decisions are those involving exports and R&D.

Judicious allocation of export business between various
national subsidiaries enhances both their local acceptability and
the overall company success by matching the demands of export customers in new markets to the specific competencies of
particular subsidiaries and to the policies of their host govern-

ments. Companies such as International Telephone and Telegraph and Brown Boveri & Cie reap large benefits from allocat-
ing orders to one of several full-fledged national subsidiaries,
and being sensitive in such allocation to both the needs of the
exporting country and of the importing one.

R&D is another area for reconciling the two orientations.
One unavoidable trade-off is balancing the demand for differ-
entiated products to meet the specifications of each particular
national customer with the need for a unified technological
effort. As a manager of a large electrical supplier put it:
"Remaining one step ahead of our national customers in technological competence is the best assurance of continued profitable business." Difficulties are further compounded by the
government's growing demands to have some "real" R&D
carried about locally instead of the minimal product adaptation
done by most MNCs. Thus, unless an extreme approach is
chosen (for instance LM Ericsson's development solely in Sweden of a very versatile electronic switching system adaptable
to almost any specifications through software changes) decisions on new product development and introduction often need
to involve close interfaces between subsidiary and product
managements.

For many other decisions, clear overall responsibility can
be assigned either to nationally-oriented subsidiary managers
or to product-oriented managers. At one extreme, marketing
in well-established national markets can be left entirely to the
local management; at the other, procedures for quality control
tests need to be developed centrally.

Which decisions to assign clearly and which to submit to a
more complex decision-making process involves a trade-off
between administrative complexity and adaptive capability.
The more decision responsibilities are clearly assigned, the
simpler the management process. The more decision responsibilities are left unclear, the more flexibly decisions can be
made, in an adaptive mode. The extent of decision responsibilities that can be left unclear depends largely on management's ability to use functional managers and administrative
procedures to guide decision-making processes.

Functional Managers

The substantive expertise of functional managers is needed by
subsidiary managers and worldwide product-oriented managers
alike. Product-oriented managers depend on the services provided by functional managers. Similarly, national subsidiary
managers depend on support provided by headquarters functional staffs even though they pursue national responsiveness.
As the power of functional managers is based on expertise

needed by both sides of the matrix, they may preserve a relatively uncommitted posture. Top management can relate closely with functional managers whose competencies are needed, and influence their alignment with either product managers or subsidiary managers on specific issues.

Yet functional managers, over time, may develop a functional logic that becomes aligned permanently with national responsiveness or worldwide coordination. For instance, manufacturing staffs can develop a logic that calls for integration and rationalization of production across borders or for flexible local plants serving separate national markets. Similarly, marketing staffs may develop their own logic on marketing differentiation or similarities among countries. Within each function, of course, further differentiation may develop, for instance rationalized efficient component plants and local-for-local, end-product plants may be favored, as in LM Ericsson.

By influencing corporate functional managers directly in the development of their preference for integration and responsiveness and by bringing them selectively to throw their weight to particular decisions and not to others, top management can develop a repertoire of intervention methods on the making of particular decisions.

Administrative Procedures

Various administrative procedures can be used to maintain a tension between economic and political imperatives without clearly assigning relative power. For instance, various committees and task forces may be used to manage along dimensions not formally favored in the matrix. Planning processes can be designed so that integration across borders and national responsiveness are given consideration, for instance, a contention process can exist between subsidiaries and product divisions under the coordination of corporate staffs as at LM Ericsson. Measure of performance for individual subunits and their managers can be set so their managers will see it as their duty to call top management's attention to "excessive" integration or responsiveness, such as at GTE (Doz, 1976). Finally, personal reward systems may be designed to reinforce tensions or ease them according to the measurement criteria or yardsticks used. Management of career paths can also be used to provide multiple views and facilitate coordination.

Similar to functional managers, administrative managers can be expected to develop their own operating logic over time. For instance, the controller's function may be expected to strive for uniformity of accounting practices and comparability of results, worldwide, thus opposing differentiation between subsidiaries in new or mature markets. Conversely personnel management may foster different career patterns between subsidiaries: expatriates to run subsidiaries in new markets, local nationals in mature markets. The way in which each administrative function develops its own logic can be managed so that its specific procedures support national responsiveness or integration across borders.

In summary, the allocation of responsibility for some decisions to product or subsidiary executives, and the use of functional managers and administrative procedures may permit top management to differentiate decision making within the matrix according to the relative importance of economic and political concerns for individual decisions and provide them with means to intervene in conflicts.

One of the top managers we interviewed commented:

> Conflicts do not develop over what a subsidiary does with its internal domestic market. That does not have much to do with product managers, and they only get into it on their tiptoes. Problems do come up between product vice-presidents who feel direct responsibility for all international marketing and the man who has the P & L of Europe, for instance. That's where conflicts sometimes come up and where they are irreconcilable.

> I have somewhat a tendency to side with product managers when they present overall technical arguments. If they tell me designing a part the way an area would like it would compromise our competitiveness for the next 20 years, I tend to lean on their side.

> Product managers have been around a lot so they know by themselves what to do and do not go too far. For instance we know that governments will not allow us to rationalize production, product managers have been here long enough to understand that.

> I decide for people, based on notions of integrity and honesty. I know who tends to exaggerate local pressures, who understands difficulties, what they have done in the past. Both sides call for clarity, but somehow this would destroy the spirit of what we do. So far each side has perceived that the other one is important. When product managers get assertive, and shift from advising to usurping (in the eyes of the area management), I may need to stop them. Sometimes they ignore the area managers in some correspondence and documents. I have to take care of who is attending which meetings, of who gets what documents, and all such detail. I need to

bring back the balance when they go too far (Doz, 1976).

One way to depict the use of corporate staff in managing salient businesses is shown in table 5.2 presented below:

Table 5.2. Top Management Intervention Spectrum

Strategic Issues	Cognitive Orientation	Power Orientation	Mechanism Used
Export Coordination	Dual	Product	Corporate Marketing
R&D	Dual	Product	Corporate R&D
Purchasing	Dual	Product	Corporate Purchasing
Marketing	Dual	Area	Area Marketing
Manufacturing	Dual	Area	Area Manufacturing

In sum, for salient businesses the appropriate locus of relative power is not set, nor can it be except on a decision-by-decision basis. When appropriate coalitions develop, decisions are made accordingly. When the emerging coalitions elicit strong discontent and concern from other managers, they bring the problems to the attention of top management. Functional and administrative managers can be used both to provide stability for certain classes of decisions without affecting others and also as levers by which top management can shift coalitions. In short, functional differentiation enables matrix management to provide operational flexibility and responsiveness to the conditions affecting each specific decision. The difference between the popular view of MNCs and the reality of managing salient businesses in developed countries can be shown schematically as in figure 5.4.

It is substantially more difficult to manage such a coalition-building process, which in some cases might be indirectly influenced by government desires and, in some cases, by individual decision, than it is to maintain a common stable locus of relative power for all decisions within a business. This difficulty may cause certain companies to stay carefully away from salient businesses. Another reason for DMNCs to stay away from salient businesses is that they are likely to weaken their bargaining positions in other businesses. For instance, Philips' desire to relocate some of its labor-intensive consumer

POPULAR VIEW OF MNC OPERATIONS
AND HOST GOVERNMENT RELATIONS

REALITY OF MNC
OPERATIONS AND HOST
GOVERNMENT RELATIONS

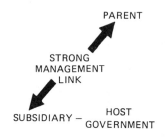

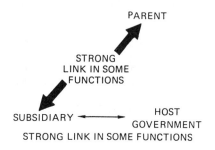

Fig. 5.4.   MNC operations and host government
relations: salient business.

electronics activities to the Far East were stifled for long by
possible threats from European governments to curtail their
orders for Philips' data processing equipment.

MANAGING EROSION OF STRATEGIC
FREEDOM - GOVERNMENTAL CONTROLS

Salience presents a problem because the significance of the
business to the host country induces her government to either
regulate or influence the strategy of the subsidiary.   In several developing countries, however, the mere fact that a firm
is a subsidiary of a multinational corporation is adequate reason for salience.   In other words, Philips' telecommunications
business is salient in France while its radio and television
businesses are less so.   In India, Philips is salient simply
because it is a multinational corporation.   Salience in a developed country tends to be based on issues (beyond products of
clear strategic importance, it is primarily issues of technology
and employment that lead to government interest); in a developing country, it is often a matter of ideology.   Governmental
influence and regulation - the response to salience - results in
an erosion of strategic freedom for the multinational corporation.
      India, for instance, has developed over the years a series
of regulations governing the operations of multinational corporation subsidiaries.   These relate to ownership, management
(expatriates), size and technology, repatriation of profits,
royalties, patents, and investments in either new business or

expansion. The overall intent of all these regulations is to ensure that multinational corporations contribute directly to the economic development of the country and that these regulations constitute the basis for control of corporate behavior. For example, the government has published a list of priority sectors and would like the MNC subsidiaries to contribute to the development of these sectors. Multinational corporations have responded to these regulations in one of two ways - either the multinational corporation is unwilling to compromise the strategic integrity of its worldwide operations (such as IBM, which pulled out of India) or it accepts the restrictions and works within the framework established by the regulations (such as ITC, formerly Imperial Tobacco Company). Unable to expand in their base businesses because of regulation, multinational corporations who have decided to stay have responded by diversifying - moving into priority sectors established by the government. The extent of diversification of multinational corporation subsidiaries operating in India, a measure of the influence of government policies, is given in table 5.3.

It is significant that the urge to diversify among MNCs in India occurred during the period 1970-75 - precisely at the time when the government was increasing its restrictions and tightening its implementation. It is also interesting to note that unrelated business strategy was adopted by 58 percent of MNC subsidiaries studied. Further, the diversification strategies of multinational corporation subsidiaries show marked differences. In their diversification, technology-intensive firms like Union Carbide and Philips have taken a route quite distinct from marketing-intensive firms like Brooke Bond and ITC. We can schematically present the differences as in figure 5.5.

The subsidiary managers of Union Carbide, with a base in batteries and chemicals, can identify capabilities of the parent in businesses and technologies like carbon products and agricultural chemicals - technologies sought after by India - as a basis for diversification. Union Carbide has moved beyond this basis for diversification, however. They are also involved in shrimp fishing for export (a priority sector), and are reportedly examining a ready-made clothing project, also for export. ITC, which has a secure base in tobacco, on the other hand, moved directly into shrimp, general exports, hotels, and paper and board. Unlike Union Carbide, ITC's parent, British American Tobacco could not provide access to advanced technology that is in the priority lists of the government of India. ITC had therefore to move into businesses totally unrelated to its core business. The expertise of its parent in the new businesses was also not significant. An ITC type of diversification - diversification into businesses where the parent may not contribute either technology, marketing skills, or management - represents a major break in the qual-

Table 5.3. Comparison of Diversification
MNC Subsidiaries vs. All Private Firms
(India, 1960-1975)

Strategy

Year	Single Business		Vertical Integration		Related Business		Unrelated Business		Average Number of distinct businesses per firm
2.1. Pattern of Diversification - MNCs (n=12)*									
	No.	%	No.	%	No.	%	No.	%	
1960	4	33.3	1	8.3	6	50.0	1	8.3	2.5
1965	2	16.6	1	8.3	6	50.0	3	25.0	3.5
1970	1	8.3	1	8.3	7	58.3	3	25.0	4.4
1975	1	8.3	-	0	4	33.3	7	58.3	6.1
2.2. Pattern of Diversification - All Private Sector Firms (n=50)									
1960	18	36.7	4	8.2	12	24.5	15	30.6	2.8
1965	13	26.0	2	4.0	12	24.0	23	46.0	4.0
1970	7	14.0	3	6.0	12	24.0	28	56.0	5.0
1975	6	12.0	2	4.0	9	18.0	33	66.0	6.0

*2 firms excluded (Glaxo and Siemens) for lack of data on their operations in 1960 and 1965.

1. Technology Intensive Multinational Corporations

Stage I	Stage II	Stage III
Original Business in India	Businesses sought by India and based on parent company strengths	Businesses Unrelated to parent company strengths

2. Marketing Intensive Multinational Corporations

Stage I	Stage II
Original Business in India	Businesses sought by India, but not related to parent company strengths.

Fig. 5.5.   Multinational diversification patterns in India.

ity of parent-subsidiary relationships. The only rationale for ongoing and continuing links between the two under such circumstances becomes purely financial. These links are further weakened when the government forces the subsidiary to reduce parent ownership to less than 50 percent. Government influence on subsidiary strategy in a country like India is significant, and it also affects the strategy of the parent.

Implicit in our analysis so far is the assumption that the business and functional groups at corporate head office and the national organization managers are the only actors involved in choosing a strategic orientation and that the host government, while attempting to reduce or contain multinational corporations' strategic freedom, ought to be seen as an outside part of the business environment. Increasingly, however, host governments like the Indian government are becoming active participants in the strategic decisions made by multinational corporations' subsidiaries. The differences between the popular concept of multinationals' operations in developing countries and reality can be shown schematically as in figure 5.6.

Faced with a dilemma like the one diagrammed above, the subsidiary managers go through several stages of frustration. (We have observed that subsidiary managers who ignored governmental regulations "as the handiwork of uninformed bureaucrats who do not know what is good for the country" become frustrated. They went through a phase when the dominant view was "how can you do business here." The persistence of

POPULAR VIEW OF MNC OPERATIONS
AND HOST GOVERNMENT RELATIONS

REALITY OF MNC OPERATIONS
AND HOST GOVERNMENT RELATIONS

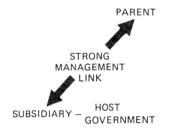

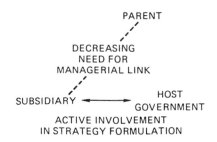

Fig. 5.6.   MNC operations and host government
relations: developing countries.

the government seems to have resulted in "If we can't beat
them, let's join them."   Other times, several subsidiary managers see regulations as an issue in their favor in dealing with
the parent.)   In other words the host government-subsidiary
link is reinforced if the subsidiary manager desires "strategic
independence" from the parent.   It is quite common in a regu-
lated environment to use "privileged information" in formulating
strategy.   "When I was with the minister the other day . . ."
is information that cannot be cross checked by corporate head
office.   At the same time, it may be crucial to the firm.   In
other words, subsidiary managers can gain independence from
the parent by forming a tacit coalition with the host government and involving the subsidiary in strategic moves which the
parent cannot monitor (a la ITC).   In order to avoid such
tacit coalitions with governments, some DMNCs are careful not
to appoint locals to all key management positions.   They usually appoint third-country nationals to key jobs or ensure that
one of the top two or three positions in the subsidiary is held
by an expatriate (e.g., Hindustan Lever in India).
     While governmental influence over multinational subsidiary
strategy may not be overwhelming (even in a country like
India), it is obvious that it is a growing phenomenon in several developing countries - Mexico, Brazil, Nigeria, Iran,
Indonesia - which resemble India in attempting to increase the
regulation of multinational corporations.   (In a private conver-
sation with one of the authors, a senior executive of a U.S.-
based steel company admitted that their excursions into totally
unrelated businesses in Brazil - (e.g., fast-growing lumber in
the savannahs - were due to restrictions on the expatriation of
profits.)

We do not yet have adequate data to identify the patterns of response of multinational corporations to this eventuality. We expect technology-intensive MNCs, like IBM, either to opt out of such markets or retain their freedom by constantly bringing in new technology (such as Philips and Union Carbide in India). Marketing-intensive firms may have to accept a greatly reduced role for the parent (such as ITC in India) in determining subsidiary strategy. Efficient scale-intensive firms often may offer packages which are so attractive in comparison to the alternatives of a local industry that they can develop a common interest with host governments and maintain their interdependence (such as Ford in Spain or Volkswagen in Brazil). In some cases, however, they may have to scatter inefficient small plants in a large number of small national markets (automobile assembly in Africa).

In our research we have seen three distinct approaches to managing strategic focus in a salient business. One is the constant use of market position and technological leadership to bargain with host governments and reduce intervention (as do TI and IBM). Another is the development of functional groups at the corporate office to arbitrate in area-product (and implicit host government) conflicts by gaining coherence in a class of decisions (such as R&D, manufacturing, marketing, and so on). Third, elaborate restrictions imposed by host governments have, in some cases, forced MNCs to alter the charter of their subsidiaries drastically (such as India and Brazil). The alternative seems to have been to opt out of that country (as did IBM in India or Brazil).

MANAGING INTERDEPENDENT BUSINESSES IN THE MATRIX MODE

Internal Interdependencies

As managing the locus of relative power in the matrix enables top management to influence the strategic orientation of a specific business, top management in the multibusiness firm can get overall focus for the portfolio of businesses by selecting the locus of power for each business. In other words, it is quite conceivable in a DMNC to find some businesses operating with a product orientation and others with an area orientation within the context of the companywide matrix. This approach to managing in the matrix mode, however, meets with limitations in MNCs in which the various businesses are interrelated. For example, in Philips, which operates in the matrix mode, the audio industry group (sales in 1977 about $150 million) consisted of four product divisions - radio, phono, hi-fi, and tape recorders. These divisions represented distinct businesses operating in worldwide competitive structure unique to those businesses. The economies of scale in manufacturing, the product characteristics, and Philips' market shares in various countries for each of these businesses all would suggest that the management of the audio industry group should develop different preferred strategic orientations for each of these businesses. However, the fact that these businesses were related to each other internally through product and technology flows created problems. The relationships between them involved marketing (shared distribution channels through the Philips national organizations - in each country where it carried out substantial business, Philips had set up a national management group, called the National Organization, regrouping its diverse activities under a single umbrella company), purchasing (components were bought from another Philips product group), product flows of subassemblies (for instance, recorders and phono products were used in hi-fi sets), and technology (divisions were drawing on common group level R&D laboratories). These relationships made strategic resource allocation somewhat difficult; for example, while the top management may want to give the hi-fi business an area focus, it may not coincide with the worldwide product focus for radios or phonos. At the same time, hi-fi may have to coordinate its plans closely with other divisions. Hi-fi, consistent with its area focus, might be concerned with customizing its products to meet the requirements of the national organizations, while the radio group, consistent with its product focus, might want to standardize its products and concentrate its operations in a few common international production centers. The strategic orientations of the two product divisions are not conducive to coordination. Cross-product flows, common distribution channels, overlaps in required technology and skill, common facility arrangements and sources of supplies among distinct businesses (as outlined above) represent one generic type of situation in which choosing a strategic orientation for a business is problematic (see figure 5.7).

External Interdependencies

In some cases, interdependencies were mostly external rather than internal. The difficulties at Brown, Boveri & Cie derived from such a problem. The overall organization of the firm is shown in figure 5.8. The distribution of total sales turnover of the company, both in terms of product groups and area organizations, is shown in table 5.4.

In addition to the above, a substantial percent of the Swiss, German and French subsidiaries' production was exported. In 1975, exports as a percentage of manufacturing for the three groups were about 80 percent, 40 percent and 30 percent, respectively.

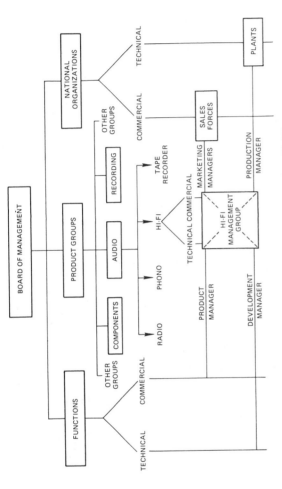

Fig. 5.7. Hi-Fi interdependencies in Philips.

Note: The Hi-Fi management group (product managers, development managers, marketing managers and/production manager) has to interface with other product divisions (recorders, radio and phono), with the National Organizations for production and sales and with the overall functional differentiation. It has to source components from two other product groups: components and recording equipment.

Source: Adapted from Joseph L. Bower and Yves Doz, Philips M.I.G. Audio A, B, and C 4-377-195 to 4-377-197 (Boston, Mass.: Intercollegiate Case Clearing House, 1976).

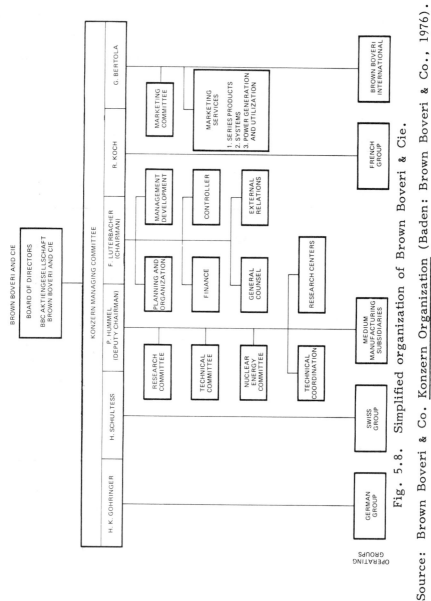

Fig. 5.8. Simplified organization of Brown Boveri & Cie.

Source: Brown Boveri & Co. Konzern Organization (Baden: Brown Boveri & Co., 1976).

Table 5.4. BBC Sales by Area and Product Group

Product Group	% of Sales (1975)	Area Organization	% of Manufacturing	% of Sales
Power generating equipment	20.7	Germany	43	40
Power conversion transmission and distribution	19.6	Switzerland	20	15
		France	15	13
Industrial & Transport Equipment	20.5	Medium sized Companies in Europe, Brazil India	17	16
Standard Products including Industrial Motors	17.7	Small Scale Operations in the Rest of the World		
Electronics	10.6		6	16
Others	10.9			

Source: Yves Doz, Brown Boveri & Cie, ICCH 9-378-115 (Boston, Mass.: Intercollegiate Case Clearing House, 1977).

The strategic conflicts at BBC can be characterized as follows: the national organizations wanted to retain control over all decisions within their territory, including decisions regarding mass-produced series products (such as motors); the national subsidiaries of BBC perceived such control as important in cultivating relationships with customers who were either owned or influenced by national governments, while on the other hand, a severe cost-price squeeze (East German prices were 30 percent lower) and the inroads of new competitors in standard products created strong pressures for rationalization and called for the development of a worldwide product orientation. The ambiguity was compounded by the fact that an offer to manufacture standard equipment locally could also entice developing countries to import power systems made by BBC in Germany, Switzerland, or France. The interdependencies among businesses in BBC were unlike those in the audio industry group in Philips, not primarily due to internal product or technology flows, but were due instead to the perceived political and business advantages of welding a relationship among businesses.

Managing Interdependencies

Essentially the dilemmas of both Philips and BBC can be conceptualized as follows: while some of their businesses were subject to worldwide product standardization and price competition (for instance, radios at Philips and motors at BBC), others were more affected by regional or national differences (power systems at BBC, hi-fi at Philips), leading to divergent strategic directions among businesses. The problem was further compounded by the fact that the interdependencies between these businesses led to a desire on the part of BBC national organizations to retain control over, say, motors, or on the part of the audio industry group management, to run all its divisions in the same administrative mold.

Under such circumstances, an approach to strategic coordination being tried by several companies is the use of corporate functional staff in conjunction with planning committees. At BBC the corporate marketing staff came closest to central product management. It coordinated exports; for example, it allocated total motor export business to the various country organizations. Marketing staff assisted the managing committee and the operating groups in the evaluation of systems, services, competition, and market potential. It also participated in the formation of corresponding product and marketing policies. In fact, because it monitored a wide range of information channels and because it played an important role in enhancing the export business, the corporate marketing staff was in a position to provide the nucleus of a more assertive product management function.

It was between various members of the corporate marketing staffs that trade-offs between businesses could be made at BBC and the interdependencies managed. Assisting the corporate marketing staff in the strategic coordination of each business were several levels of committees. Figure 5.9 shows the BBC coordination structure. Altogether there were sixteen BBC corporate business teams and over one hundred corporate product teams. These teams were basically a meeting ground for line managers from various manufacturing companies involved in the same business. Meetings took place every two months for business teams and twice a year for product teams. Their functions included the formulation of corporatewide objectives and business plans for their respective products. Formally, the product teams had to approve all capital expenditures for any significance; in practice, they seldom vetoed investments. Conflicts within a business were resolved within the business teams or by the management committee. Conflicts between businesses were dealt with by corporate staffs. As of 1977 the success of the dual coordination system was less than overwhelming.

The experience with corporate staffs attempting to coordinate related business operations worldwide in the context of strong national organizations is no different at Philips. Corporate planners were responsible for coordinating the capacity and investment decisions within the industry groups as well as across groups. Sudden shifts in the business climate in the hi-fi division, for example, were reflected in fluctuations in the work load of component factories managed by a separate industry group. The problem of sudden shifts in the work loads was further complicated by wide swings in inventory levels and an inability to offer new products to the market with short lead times. One of the side effects of corporate attempts to coordinate the businesses was wide swings in inventory and production levels for the component businesses.

The situation at both BBC and Philips indicated that managing interrelated businesses in the matrix mode and at the same time attempting to provide strategic direction to individual businesses (such as industrial motors at BBC or hi-fi at Philips) is very difficult. Typically, both organizations have attempted to use corporate functional groups and committees for strategic coordination within and across businesses. The results so far have not been strikingly encouraging, leading us to raise the question: In order to achieve strategic focus, should a multibusiness firm like Philips attempt to simplify its strategy first? This would require that Philips treat its various businesses as if they were independent. Alternatively, if the various businesses are closely related, and if top management wants to retain the benefits of that relatedness, can they then gain strategic focus for any one specific business?

TYPICAL ORGANIZATION
OF A MAJOR NATIONAL
COMPANY*

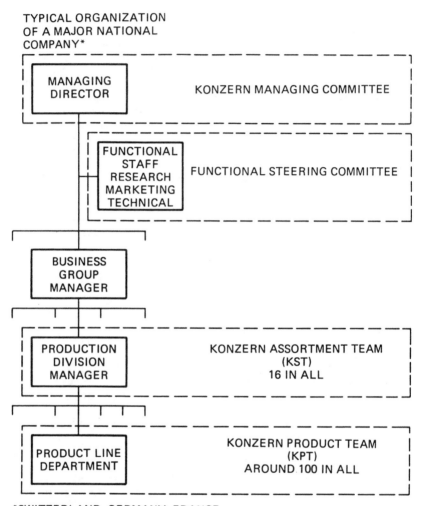

*SWITZERLAND, GERMANY, FRANCE
+3 BUSINESS GROUPS: HEAVY EQUIPMENT, SYSTEMS AND
ENGINEERING, SERIES PRODUCTS.

Fig. 5.9.   The Brown, Boveri and Cie intercompany
coordination structure.

Source: Yves Doz, Brown Boveri & Cie, ICCH9-378-115 (Boston, Mass.: Intercollegiate Case Clearing House,
1977).

It appears that top management must accept, as a trade-off, the complexity of a strategy (multiple interdependent businesses) with the complexity of developing an administrative system for providing a focus to businesses. This conclusion has several important implications. First, in order to provide strategic focus, some of the interdependencies among the businesses may have to be ignored consciously or the businesses operated as if they were independent. "Arms' length dealing" between business may be necessary. Second, top management must constantly evaluate the "worth" of these interdependencies in strategic terms. Third, the strategic worth of interdependencies depends on the judgments regarding the economic worth of these interdependencies as well as on an assessment of the administrative difficulties of providing a strategic focus.

A partial answer is to manage only the most critical interdependencies and ignore the others. For instance, International Telephone and Telegraph (ITT) recently reorganized some of its operations in Europe, spinning off the private telecommunication exchange business from its public exchange subsidiaries and moving it to its business-system group, with a worldwide product orientation. The move was made in answer to the aggressive intrusion of private exchange suppliers from the data processing industry. With this move, ITT was hoping to simplify the management of marketing interdependencies between private exchanges and office products and to deemphasize the interdependency of technology between various telecommunication products. Conversely, ITT has always ignored the management of the interdependency between end-products and electronic components divisions; this sort of interdependency has, on the other hand, always been of great concern to Philips and Siemens. So, between greater strategic clarity and extreme organizational complexity there are middle-of-the-road solutions where only the most significant interdependencies are recognized and managed. Over time, these interdependencies may change with technology or market conditions, as we have seen in the case of ITT, triggering structural or contextual changes. In some cases, divestitures are calibrated to the difficulty of fitting a particular business into the predominant strategic direction of the company.

Summary: Strategic Management In MNCs

The strategy of MNCs and the organizational forms that are used to manage them are a response to the changing business environment. The decade of the 60s was a period of significant economic growth and rapid development of MNCs. Many firms initiated their overseas operations during this time and established MNCs grew, using the opportunities created by the emergence of EEC, new technologies, and free trade (Vernon, 1971). As a result, earlier academic attention was focused on the organizational adaptations required to manage growth. The two stages of international operations - autonomous foreign subsidiary stage and the evolution of a worldwide product or an area structure - are well documented in the literature (Stopford and Wells, 1972; Brooke and Remmers, 1970; Franko, 1976). When the international operations of an MNC accounted for less than 15 percent of the total sales and assets, the subsidiaries were given significant autonomy and no attempt was made to integrate the domestic and international operations. When the significance of the overseas operations increased, attempts were made to integrate the domestic and international operations. Global structures were the result. However, the worldwide product and area structures, efficient along some dimensions, also blinded the organization to business opportunities and emerging problems. For example, while worldwide rationalization of production helped the MNC to realize competitive cost advantages, it made it difficult to respond to the unique needs and peculiarities of various country markets in which the MNC operated. On the other hand, while the area structure could be very responsive to local needs, it could not effectively utilize the benefits of large scale manufacturing, standardization of products and processes.

A further difficulty was brought about by the complexities of the technology, changes in the competitive structure, emergence of strong national champions and marked regional differences. These pressures led to the extensive use of a global matrix or grid structure. Managing the MNC matrix mode demands the use of very complex administrative systems and sophisticated managerial behavior. A matrix structure by design does not provide a strategic focus to businesses. It must be superimposed by the use of nonstructural mechanisms like relative power. The strategy of MNCs is further complicated by the action of host governments - by their desire to manage salient issues, businesses or the operations of the MNC in its entirety. The responses again are not necessarily structural. The method used by MNCs to cope with these issues are a combination of strategic choices (e.g., opt out of salient businesses) or bargain for a favorable (and manageable) situation and/or adapt. This progression in the complexity of MNC strategies, corresponding organizational responses, and the typical management problems associated with them are captured in a capsule form in table 5.5.

The strategy-organization relationship when the MNC strategy is complex, is an area where significant additional research needs to be done.

Table 5.5. Evolution of Multinational
Corporation Organizational Form

MNC Environment	MNCs Organizational Response	Typical Problems
I. Primarily domestic; Overseas business not significant.	Export department, International Division.	Inability to integrate overseas operations with domestic operations.
II. Overseas operations and opportunities significant - sales, investment, returns.	Global organization - worldwide product groups or area groups.	Missed opportunities due to a simple dominant orientation.
III. Business environment complex - simultaneous need for sensitivity to diversity in markets and ability to achieve economies.	Global matrix structure.	Inability to get strategic focus for businesses.
	Use of relative power for strategic focus.	Need for very sophisticated managerial behavior and systems.
	Use of corporate functional groups for strategic coordination. Use of corporate planning teams.	
IV. Host government's interest in containing strategic freedom of salient businesses.	Response contingent upon the relative bargaining strengths of host government and the firm.	Judging the relative bargaining strengths.
V. Host government's desire to contain the strategic freedom of all MNCs operating within its territory.	Opt out or adapt.	Businesses that the subsidiary is involved in do not reflect parents strengths. Tacit host government - subsidiary coalition.

STRATEGIC MANAGEMENT OF DMNCs - SOME
IMPLICATIONS

The emerging environment of the multinational corporation can
be best characterized as one which attempts to restrict and
contain the strategic freedom of the firm and will substantially
influence top management's attempts to balance strategic focus
and administrative adequacy. Host governments' attitudes and
regulations are clearly aimed at that goal.   As such, evaluating these influences is the key to understanding the
emerging difficulties in the strategic management of DMNCs.
It is possible to depict three scenarios on how MNCs may respond to the continuing erosion of their strategic freedom.

Scenario I - The Technology Response

As we have seen above, the relative bargaining power of the
nation-state with respect to a multinational corporation in a
specific business depends largely on: a) the sophistication of
the multinational corporation's technology, and b) the share of
the MNC's market that the country represents.   The bargaining power of the firm depends on its technology and that
of the country on its market share.   The result of India's
confrontation with IBM was as predictable as that of its confrontation with ITC.   IBM had the technology, and India, at
least for the foreseeable future, represented an insignificant
market for IBM.   Conversely, France or Brazil are large
enough markets for LM Ericsson to relinquish majority control
of its subsidiaries in these countries.   If we extend this argument further, we can speculate that the firms which can
continuously upgrade their technology and work on the state
of the art can continue to resist host country pressures to
contain their strategic freedom.   Texas Instruments, a technology leader, for example, can get away with 100 percent
subsidiaries even in Japan where most other American firms
had to accept joint venture partners.   The implication is that a
technology-intensive strategy is a viable response to increasing
pressure to contain strategic freedom.

Scenario II - The Two Tier Organization Response

While an MNC like Union Carbide may be able to take the reduction of its strategic freedom in India in its stride (Union
Carbide's business in India represented less than two percent
of the corporate turnover in 1976), if other developing countries follow the orientation of the Indian government, MNCs
may have to organize their global operations differently.   We

believe that once the number of countries that restrict strategic freedom goes beyond a threshold level for an MNC, it
would segment its global operations into two parts, operations
in those countries with little or no restrictions on their strategic freedom and operations in those with substantial restrictions.

Countries with little restriction on strategic freedom would
represent attractive opportunities for investment as well as
lending themselves to incorporation into a "global strategy" of
the multinational corporation. On the other hand, in order to
be able to operate in countries where restrictions are substantial, multinational corporations should be very responsive
and adaptive. Few such countries represent big markets for a
multinational corporation, but collectively they represent a
growing market. Organizationally, operations in countries with
little restriction can be managed with existing organizational
capabilities - some form of global organization. On the other
hand, as the needs of every country imposing extensive restriction are different and unique, a loose holding company
structure at corporate head office with little or no desire to
actively control specific operations in those countries may
emerge.

Scenario III: The Strategic Contingency Management

In some cases companies can respond by leaving much operating autonomy to their regional or national affiliates, while
maintaining central control of some key contingencies for their
overall evolution.

By varying the level of integration between decisions it is
possible to manage the activities most critical to the worldwide
success of the company in an integrated way, and to leave
considerable autonomy to the national subsidiaries for the
management of other activities or go to great length to satisfy
host countries. A company such as IBM, for instance,
pioneered this sort of approach by narrowly controlling technology but went to great lengths to provide employment, balanced trade, and local management in the various countries
where it does business. Central control over the substance of
decision was carefully maintained but decisions were made with
much concern for each country in which the company operated.

After attempting to maintain a product-area matrix structure (Davis, 1976), Dow Chemical then tried a different
approach by delegating all operational responsibilities to the
geographically-organized companies, but setting up a corporate
product department (CPD) to maintain a central perspective on
key contingencies. The CPD controlled long-term product
strategies and global functional support to specific product
lines. It was also in charge of setting overall product lines

targets and evaluating performance. All investment projects had to be supported by the CPD before approval. The Dow management structure provided much autonomy to the geographical units while maintaining central substantive control (and veto power) over key decisions affecting the worldwide results of a business. Contrary to IBM's approach, decisions were made locally, in the best interest of the local units, but with a close corporate check.

Conclusion

Multibusiness MNCs may well need to apply all of these scenarios for one business or another, according to technological, geographical, and strategic differences in their portfolio of businesses. How to manage and possibly combine these various scenarios and the organizational constraints they impose across the portfolio of businesses may well represent the challenge of the next decade for the diversified multinational company.

In order to influence MNCs successfully host governments must develop among the civil servants who deal with MNCs an understanding of the administrative differences between companies and a capability to identify, in the companies they interact with, the way in which various businesses are managed and the scenarios being followed by the company.

In the development of a more flexible organization that provides both responsiveness and capability in the MNCs as well as a better understanding among host country administrators of how these companies actually operate may well be the key to beneficial cooperation, or tolerance, between MNCs and host governments.

REFERENCES

Argyris, Chris. 1967. "Today's Problems with Tomorrow's Organizations." Journal of Management Studies.

Brooke, Michael Z. and Remmers, Lee H. 1970. The Strategy of Multinational Enterprise. London: Longman.

Corey, Raymond and Steven Star. 1971. Organizational Strategy. Boston: Harvard Business School Division of Research.

Crozier, Michel. 1964. The Bureaucratic Phenomenon. Chicago: Phoenix Books.

Davis, Stanley. 1975. "Unity of Command versus Balance of Power: Two Models of Management." Sloan Management Review.

---. 1976. "Trends in the Organization of Multinational Corporations." Columbia Journal of World Business.

--- and Paul R. Lawrence. 1977. Matrix. Reading, Mass.: Addison-Wesley.

Doz, Yves. 1976. "National Policies and Multinational Management." Boston: doctoral dissertation, Harvard Business School.

---. 1978. "Managing Manufacturing Rationalization within Multinational Companies." Columbia Journal of World Business.

---. 1979. Government Power and Multinational Strategic Management. New York: Praeger.

Franko, Lawrence, G. 1976. The European Multinationals. Stamford, Conn.: Greylock Inc.

Galbraith, Jay. 1971. "Matrix Organization Design." Business Horizons.

Jequier, Nicolas. 1976. Les Telecommunications et l'Europe. Geneva, Switzerland: Centre d'Etudes Industrielles.

Katz, Abraham. 1977. "Planning in the IBM Corporation." Paper presented at the TIMS-ORSA Strategic Planning Conference, New Orleans.

Mathias, Peter. 1978. "The Role of Logistics in the Process of Strategic Changes in Two Multinational Companies." Boston: doctoral dissertation, Harvard Business School.

Mee, John F. 1964. "Ideational Items: Matrix Organization." Business Horizons.

Neufeld, E.P. 1969. A Global Corporation: A History of the International Development of Massey Ferguson Limited. Toronto: University of Toronto Press.

Prahalad, C.K. 1975. "The Strategic Process in a Multinational Corporation." Boston: doctoral dissertation, Harvard Business School.

---. 1976. "Strategic Choices in Diversified MNCs." Harvard Business Review.

Steinbruner, John D. 1974. The Cybernetic Theory of Decision. Princeton, New Jersey: Princeton University Press.

Stopford, John M. and Louis T. Wells Jr. 1972. Managing the Multinational Enterprise. New York: Basic Books, Inc.

Surrey, A.J. 1972. World Market for Electric Power Equipment: Rationalization and Technical Change. Brighton, the U.K.: University of Sussex.

Vernon, Raymond. 1971. Sovereignty at Bay. New York: Basic Books.

6 Multinationals in Industrially Developed Countries: A Comparative Study of American, German, and Japanese Multinationals

Anant R. Negandhi
B.R. Baliga

The research project upon which this paper is based began in 1976. The project is a collaborative effort by six academicians of three different national origins, – German, Indian, and Swedish – and different academic training and orientations.* The research is being supported by the International Institute of Management (I.I.M.), Science Centre, West Berlin and the International Business Institute of the Stockholm School of Economics, Sweden. The project grew out of earlier research (Negandhi and Baliga, 1979) on a comparative study of multinational corporations in the developing countries.

In recent years, a number of studies have been undertaken at both intranational and international levels which elaborate on the premise advanced by Chandler (1962) concerning the linkage between strategy and structure (Stopford and Wells, 1972; Franko, 1974; Yoshino, 1978; Lawrence and Davis, 1978; Channon, 1973; Allen, 1976; Rumelt, 1974; and Thanheiser, 1972).

Chandler's main premise that structure follows strategy, and strategy and structure should be in congruence with each other to generate high performance and organizational effectiveness, seems to have some surface validity. However, it assumes "supremacy" on the part of the firm to establish and implement its strategies, while the role and influence of the external environment/client groups on the firm's strategy are considered less important.

*The research team consists of Professor A. R. Negandhi, University of Illinois, Urbana-Champaign; Lars Otterbeck, Anders Edstrom and Gunnar Hedlund, Stockholm School of Economics; B. R. Baliga, University of Wisconsin, Eau Claire; and Martin Welge, University of Koln.

Secondly, the "rightness" of congruence between the firm's strategy and structure is inferred through the economic performance criteria, though the linkage between the strategy, structure, and performance has not yet been empirically verified (Galbraith and Nathanson, 1978). It is conceivable, however, that economic and financial performance of the firm may be a function of market and economic conditions rather than the firm's strategy and structure (Bain, 1958).

A previous study in six developing countries (Negandhi and Baliga, 1979), which dealt with MNC's conflicts with the host governments and other publics in host countries, clearly indicated that the assumption concerning the "supremacy" of the firm (MNC) in setting its own strategy is highly unrealistic, especially when the other client groups in the environments are active agents. (See our recent book <u>Quest for Survival and Growth: A Comparative Study of American, European, and Japanese Multinationals</u>, 1979. A summary of the results of this study is presented in another chapter in this volume entitled "Adaptability of American, European, and Japanese Multinational Corporations in Developing Countries." In other words, the remark of Vernon that "sovereign states are feeling naked . . . sovereignty and national economic strength appears curiously drained of meaning" (Vernon, 1971, p. 3) appears increasingly invalid. The reality has been well expressed by Bergsten: "Sovereignty is no longer at bay in host countries . . . the degree of this shift in power . . . is virtually complete in most industrial host countries and some developing countries" (Bergsten, 1974, p. 138-39). This change in the bargaining powers of various nations, MNCs, and other parties constitutes reality as we see it. We believe that multinational corporations can no longer unilaterally control their own fate but will have to deal with the demands of various interest groups in the environment. Those who are able to cope with these changes in their bargaining position will be the ones to survive and grow. Briefly, then, we were guided by the following premises:

> The MNCs' strategies are influenced by demands made by constituents in both the host and home countries. Such demands are being made, not in the context of free economy market forces, but in terms of controls and regulatory measures imposed by governments on MNCs. On the basis of this premise, we hypothesized that the MNCs' strategies should be in congruence with the home and host countries' policies and demands.

> In order to be effective in the varied environments of home and host countries (varied demands and policies of home and host countries) the MNCs may have

to devise different strategies for their home offices and their subsidiary operations. In other words, a master plan (e.g., the IBM and Coca Cola policy on 100% equity in all foreign operations) may become dysfunctional and nonoperational if the demands made by host countries are different.

Structures and processes of HQs and Subs must be consistent with the different strategies utilized by HQs and Subs to cope with the home and host countries' demands (environments).

The lack of congruence between the demands of the home and host countries and HQs' and Subs' strategies, Headquarters and Subsidiary strategies and respective structures and processes will be reflected in tensions and conflicts between HQs and Subs, between HQs, home, and host countries, and between Subs and host countries. These conflicts and tensions were very visible in the developing countries (Negandhi and Baliga, 1979).

Specifically we sought to examine:

Strategies adopted with respect to transfer of technology; investment policies; manpower and personnel policies; product and marketing policies.

Structuring of MNCs both at headquarters (HQ) and subsidiary (sub) levels.

Organizational processes such as mechanisms for controls and coordination, long-range planning and environmental scanning, personnel training, performance reviews and feedback mechanisms utilized at headquarter and subsidiary levels.

Decision making and relative influences of HQs and Subs in major and minor decisions.

The nature and intensity of conflicts in decision making between HQs and Subs.

HQ-Sub relationships and the nature and intensity of conflicts and conflicting issues between them, including the modes of resolutions and consequences of conflicts.

The nature and intensity of conflicts and conflicting issues between MNCs and governments and other publics in both the home and host countries (Negandhi and Baliga, 1979).

The paper reports the findings of the study related to interaction between MNCs (American, German, and Japanese) and
their constituents.   Certain focal issues between HQ and subsidiaries are also discussed in terms of their impact on external interactions.

THE RESEARCH DESIGN

The project was conceived in a comparative vein; we endeav-
ored to study American, German, French, British, and Japanese multinationals and their subsidiaries. (A study in France
was dropped at a later stage due to our inability to find a
suitable collaborator).   Our aim was to collect detailed information on many aspects on multinational operations at both
headquarter and subsidiary levels.   Subsidiaries of German,
Japanese, and American multinationals operating in Europe
(West Germany, France, United Kingdom, Spain, Portugal,
Belgium, and the Netherlands) and their respective headquarters constituted the universe for the research reported in
this paper.   The universe was determined from investment
directories and listings provided by chambers of commerce and
manufacturing associations.   Considerable efforts were made to
ensure that the listings were as current as possible.   The
universe was restricted to firms that were engaged in some
form of manufacturing activity.   Hence, firms in travel,
banking and other service sectors were omitted from consideration.   Given the problems associated with field research on
multinational corporations, it was thought prudent to contact
the chief executives of all firms in the universe in order to
ensure a fairly reasonable final sample.   Letters detailing the
nature of the research project and requesting a personal interview with the chief operating officers and/or representatives of
the top management team were then mailed out.   Surprisingly,
despite the rather credible sources of information on investment cited above, a number of letters were returned as
"undeliverable," i.e., the addresses provided were either
incorrect or the companies had relocated without a current for-
warding address on file.   This paper reports the data obtained
from 23 American, 15 German, and 19 Japanese subsidiaries
operating in European countries.   (The total data base consisted of 44 HQs and 120 Subs.   Countries in which the subsidiaries' operations were studied included: West Germany,
United Kingdom, the United States, Brazil, India, Iran, Spain,
Portugal, Belgium, the Netherlands, France, and a number of
developing countries.)
     At this juncture, it appears appropriate to make some re-
marks on the nature of the ultimate sample that was utilized in
the analysis.   Ideally, in order to have the utmost confidence

(statistically) in the results, the organizations would have either to be perfectly matched or a large enough random sample drawn from the universe. Matching was impossible as historical patterns of Japanese, German and American investments in Europe have been quite different, with Japanese multinationals being a more recent phenomenon. As there were considerable uncertainties about the cooperation that could be obtained from multinational corporations' executives, a conscious random sampling procedure was not adopted. It can, however, be asserted that the final sample that did result was random in that every firm in the universe had the same chance of participating or not participating in the study. However, in order to increase the generalizability and external validity of the study, considerable supplemental information was obtained both on companies that had participated in the study and otherwise. Despite these efforts, the reader is cautioned to bear the limitations of the sample in mind when reading through the analysis and discussions.

Indepth interviews were then conducted with chief executive officers and/or top management representatives from all firms that had agreed to participate in the study. The interviews lasted about four to eight hours on the average and in most cases included luncheon and dinner sessions. These luncheon and dinner sessions proved to be extremely valuable as the executives tended to relax, and, in narrating episodes related to organizational functioning, revealed significant, though subtle, aspects of their operations – an excellent example of empirical opportunism (Bixenstine, 1966). In those instances where organizational members other than the chief executive were present, consensus or majority responses were the ones utilized for analysis.

SOME COMPARISON WITH DEVELOPING COUNTRIES

It is generally recognized that the nature and intensity of issues (conflicts) between MNCs and developing countries are more pronounced than those between multinationals and the industrially developed countries. To provide a comparative perspective on MNCs' relationships with the industrialized countries, we will examine some of the issues that have generated conflict in the developing countries, the nature of conflict, and the manner in which American, European, and Japanese multinationals have dealt with this conflict. Mikesell (1971, p. 30) has identified the following factors as having the potential of causing conflict between MNCs and host governments, particularly with respect to the mineral and petroleum industries:

Division of total net revenues from operations between the foreign country and the host government.

The control of export prices, output, and the other conditions affecting the level of total revenues.

The domestic impact of foreign company operation.

The percentage of foreign ownership.

Bergsten (1974, p. 152) suggests that the differences between the domestic socio-economic objectives of the host government, and the objectives of the foreign investor, give rise to conflicts between these two parties. In more specific terms, he identifies the following issues over which conflicts and tensions are bound to arise:

Job quota requirements by the host government; quantitative and qualitative aspects.

Requirement for use of local inputs and parts in manufacturing.

Research and development activities.

Export requirements.

Market power of foreign investors; a demand for reduction in order to promote local enterprises.

External financing requirement.

Building up a high-technology enterprise.

Reduction of imports.

Ownership requirement: a reduction of foreign share, and an increase in local participation.

A U.S. State Department study analyzing the nature of conflict between American firms and host countries (predominantly "developing") indicated that of the 198 cases of conflict, approximately 68% were related to equity issues (see table 6.1). A previous study in developing countries (Negandhi and Baliga, 1979) surfaced three conflict-ridden issues: equity, localization of managerial control, and transfer pricing (see table 6.2). The study further indicated that American and European multinationals had problems in effectively managing their interactions with host government representatives and their agencies, whereas Japanese multinationals had prob-

Table 6.1.   Issues Causing Conflict Between U.S. Investors
and the Host Countries

	60	61	62	63	64	65	66	67	68	69	70	71	Total
Equity	-	1	1	-	2	2	1	3	-	5	39	74	128
Participation	-	-	-	1	-	-	-	-	-	-	-	6	7
Pricing Policy	-	-	-	-	-	-	-	-	-	-	-	3	3
Controls by Government	-	1	1	2	12	-	-	-	1	2	6	25	50
Expansion of Exports	-	-	-	-	-	-	-	-	-	-	-	-	-
Interference with Host Economy	-	1	-	-	-	-	-	-	-	-	1	4	6
Interference with Socio-Cultural Norms	-	-	-	-	-	-	-	-	-	-	-	2	2
Interference by MNCs' Home Governments with Host Governments' Policies	-	-	-	-	-	-	-	-	-	-	-	1	1
Conflict with National Sovereignty	-	-	-	-	-	-	-	-	-	-	1	-	1
	-	3	2	3	14	2	1	3	1	7	47	115	198

Source: U.S. State Department: Disputes Involving U.S. Foreign Investment: July 1, 1971 through July 1, 1973, Bureau of Intelligence &
Research RECS-6, Washington, D.C., February 8, 1974.

Table 6.2.　Issues Causing Conflict
Between MNCs and Host Countries

Causes of Conflict	Far East			Latin America			Both Areas			Total
	U.S. MNCs	European MNCs	Japanese MNCs	U.S. MNCs	European MNCs	Japanese MNCs	U.S. MNCs	European MNCs	Japanese MNCs	
Equity Participation by Locals	13	14	0	0	0	1	13	14	1	28
Management of Control in the Hands of Local Nationals	15	17	13	2	3	2	17	20	15	52
Control on Exchange	2	3	0	0	1	0	2	4	0	6
Control on Imports	3	0	1	0	1	0	3	1	1	5
Expansion of Exports	3	2	2	1	1	0	4	3	2	9
Transfer Pricing (Pricing Policies)	6	6	2	5	2	0	11	8	2	21
Use of Local Inputs	0	2	0	0	0	0	0	2	0	2
Interference by Host Governments in Corporate Affairs	2	2	0	0	1	0	2	3	0	5
Contribution to Economic Plans of Host Nations	2	0	0	2	0	0	4	0	0	4
Interference with Socio-Cultural Norms	1	0	1	1	1	0	2	1	1	4
Interference by MNCs' Home Governments with Host Governments' Policies	1	0	0	1	0	0	2	0	0	2
Total	48	46 Total 113	19	12	10 Total 25	3	60	56 Total 138	22	138

Source: Negandhi, A. and B. R. Baliga. Quest for Survival and Growth: A Comparative Study of American, European, and Japanese Multinationals. West Germany: Athenaeum Verlag, 1979, pp. 15.

lems dealing with labor, distributors, and local managers. In specific terms, the type of problems experienced by American and European multinationals centered around equity dilution, reduction in royalties, and technology and management know-how transfer, while Japanese MNCs were concerned about their relatively higher turnover rates, absenteeism, and low productivity of their employees.

NATURE OF ISSUES BETWEEN MNCs AND EUROPEAN COUNTRIES

Although many of the West European countries are operating as "free and open markets" and are generally very congenial to foreign investors, particularly Americans, lately, they too have begun to question the utility of unchecked foreign investments. In other words, the governmental decision-makers as well as other public groups (labor unions, consumer advocates, environmentalists, and so on) are discovering that national needs, ambitions and objectives can be at variance with the MNCs' objectives, goals, and strategies. This invariably creates a climate of tension and eventually conflicts among MNCs, host governments, and other constituents in host countries.

The range, nature and intensity of these issues, of course, differ considerably from country to country, depending upon the prevailing political climate and economic conditions (unemployment, inflation, balance of payment position) and the level of industrial and economic development. For example, some two years ago, in a study of MNCs in developed countries, Fry (1977) reported that the issue of worker participation ("Mitbestimmung") was the most prominent in West Germany, and the traditional issues such as providing new technology, employment, upgrading wages and the developing local resources were considered secondary by the governmental officials.

In contrast, in Belgium the major issues pertaining to multinational corporation functioning were related to employment capabilities, potential effect on balance of payments position, research and development activities (lack of), development and utilization of local resources and worker participation in management. Simultaneously, however, MNCs emphasized their importance in terms of increasing entrepreneurial spirit, providing new technology and making available consumer goods at lower prices. These differences in expectations between government and multinational corporations' priorities are clearly highlighted in table 6.3.

Table 6.4 illustrates the issues of contention between MNCs and host government/publics that emerged in the current study.

Table 6.3.   Largest Impact Profile Differences*

	Germany	
Impact	Government Wants More	Firms Give More
Worker Participation	GGGGGGGGG	
Increase Competition		FFFFFFFFF
Capital Inflows		FFFFFFF
Increase Skilled Employment		FFFFFFF
Create Entrepreneurial Spirit		FFFFFF

	Belgium	
Impact	Government Wants More	Firms Give More
Increase General Employment	BBBBBBBBBBBB	
Increase Skilled Employment	BBBBBBB	
Balance of Payment Effects	BBBBBBB	
Increase R & D Efforts	BBBBBB	
Develop Local Resources	BBBBB	
Worker Participation	BBBBB	
Worker Awareness	BBBBB	
Increase Quality of Consumer Services	BBBBB	
Social & Cultural Values		FFFFFFFFFFFFFF
Increase Entrepreneurial Spirit		FFFFFFFF
Provide New Technology		FFFFFF
Create Lower Prices		FFFFF

*The numbers of characters for each impact have no absolute meaning.   They are of indicative value in a relative sense only.   They indicate magnitude of differences and direction.

Source: David E. Fry.   Multinational Corporations - Host Government Relationships: A Empirical Study of Behavioral Expectations.   Unpublished D.B.A. dissertation, Kent State University, 1977.

Table 6.4. Host-Country Expectations*

	Germany N/%	U.K. N/%	Spain N/%	Portugal N/%	France N/%	Total
Technology	0/0.0	3/21.4	0/0.0	0/0.0	0/0.0	3/5.3
Exports	0/0.0	1/7.1	0/0.0	0/0.0	1/12.5	2/3.5
Employment	0/0.0	2/14.3	0/0.0	0/0.0	0/0.0	2/3.5
Economic Development	3/23.1	5/35.7	10/90.9	9/81.8	7/87.5	34/59.6
Ambivalent	1/7.7	0/0.0	0/0.0	0/0.0	0/0.0	1/1.8
No specific	9/69.2	3/21.4	1/9.1	2.18/2	0/0.0	15/26.3
	13/22.8	14/24.6	11/19.3	11/19.3	8/14.0	57/100

*Raw Chi Square = 43.19530 with 20 degrees of freedom. Significance = 0.0019.

Source: Interview data collected by the authors.

As can be seen from table 6.4, economic stagnation, triggered by the oil crisis, has generated traditional economic demands even in the more industrialized nations of the world. However, except in the case of Spain and Portugal, the European countries in which field research was undertaken have not yet legislated these demands as has been done in the developing countries. Also it appears that these countries do not discriminate unduly in favor of domestic corporations over multinational corporations. This could partly be a result of the pervasiveness of EEC ideals.

It should be obvious that the greater the incongruence between host government expectations and MNC priorities, the greater the probability of fairly intensive conflicts. This has been demonstrated by Fry (1977), and Negandhi and Baliga (1979).

One thing appears clear: the less economically developed a country, the more demands does it place on multinational corporations and the more willing it is to legislate these expectations. This is clearly evident from table 6.4, where Spain and Portugal are both greatly concerned with overall economic development. Also, the more developed countries - Germany and France - had hardly any expectations of the multinational. The United Kingdom, which was going through a phase of economic stagnation during the period of study, was keen to overcome this stagnation through encouraging high technology and high employment potential investment. Furthermore, as Fry (1977) has indicated, the expectations are heavily influenced by current political issues.

RESULTS AND DISCUSSION

At first glance, it appears from table 6.5, that problems for American, German and Japanese MNCs arise from different sources. This is not accurate as the significance of the association has been heightened by the fact that labor is the source of almost half the problems faced by the multinationals. However, U.S. and German subsidiaries have, proportionately, more labor problems than Japanese companies. The underlying theme of labor-management problems is, however, quite different in the various countries. In Germany, for instance, industry representatives were involved in challenging the constitutional validity of the "codetermination" laws and influencing the election of representatives who were against the codetermination laws. The U.S. multinational subsidiaries, owing to workforce size stipulations in the law, were most susceptible to the laws. Given the confrontationary nature of management-labor relations in the United States, American multinationals initially had a difficult time accepting the col-

Table 6.5. MNC Ownership by Sources of Problem in Host Countries*

	Host Government N/%	Labor N/%	Political Groupings N/%	Local Competitors N/%	Multiple Sources N/%	No Problems N/%	Regional Economic Grouping N/%	Total
U.S. MNCs	1/25.0	11/40.7	1/100.0	1/100.0	1/100.0	8/38.1	0/0.0	23/100
	1/4.3	11/47.8	1/4.3	1/4.3	1/4.3	8/34.8	0/0.0	
German MNCs	0/0.0	12/44.4	0/0.0	0/0.0	0/0.0	3/14.3	0/0.0	15/100
	0/0.0	12/80.0	0/0.0	0/0.0	0/0.0	3/20.0		
Japanese MNCs	3/75.0	4/14.8	0/0.0	0/0.0	0/0.0	10/47.6	2/100.0	19/100
	3/15.7	4/21.0	0/0.0	0/0.0	0/0.0	10/52.6	2/10.5	
Total	4/100	27/100	1/100	1/100	1/100	21/100	2/100	57/100
	4/7.0	27/47.4	1/1.8	1/1.8	1/1.8	21/36.8	2/3.5	

*Raw Chi Square = 20.42215 with 12 degrees of freedom. Significance = 0.0595.

laborative philosophy. More recently reported cases of serious problems have become fewer and fewer, fostering the impression that American MNCs are now able to deal with these demands.

Outside Germany all multinationals, especially the larger U.S. and German multinationals, have been the targets of leftist ideology oriented labor unions. This has been particularly true of Spain and Portugal where rising nationalistic expectations have made the issue even more difficult to handle. Japanese multinationals appear to have avoided serious problems with labor, to some extent, by their small size and willingness to go into joint ventures with either government organizations or private entrepreneurs. This finding is interesting in the light of the fact that, despite being involved in joint ventures or minority holdings in the developing countries, Japanese organizations had considerable problems with labor (Negandhi and Baliga, 1979). These problems stemmed mainly from historical factors and efforts made by Japanese to impose their management style. It appears that the Japanese multinationals have learned from their experience in the developing countries of Asia and South America, and have restricted the use of Japanese management style (such as life-time employment, and demanding loyalty to the company) in industrialized countries.

Japanese subsidiaries were involved, however, in conflicts with the EEC commission. Problems were centered around charges of "dumping" by Japanese organizations, despite the fact that the Japanese companies accused had manufacturing subsidiaries in EEC countries. The Japanese organizations responded by adopting a legalistic stance while simultaneously emphasizing their local manufacturing activities in efforts to make the "dumping" charge untenable.

The Environment and its Impact on Organizational Functioning

One of the fundamental problems that multinational corporations have had to contend with in the developing countries has been a set of explicit demands and implicit expectations of the host governments. This has resulted in considerable constraints to multinational activity and has also been the source of numerous conflicts between multinationals and organizational members in host environments. This, coupled with numerous uncertainties that arose out of the developmental process, meant that a very organic mode of organizational functioning had to be adopted. Organizations that were successful in doing so were effective, and organizations that could not adapt found that more and more of their energies had to be devoted to coping with escalating levels of conflict. The organic mode required utilizing a size (small) that permitted flexibility, a personalized approach to external relations and meeting environmental demands without undue loss of organizational control. The Japanese multinationals were invariably successful in doing so, whereas the insistence of U.S. multinationals on large-size units, retaining 100% equity control and a formalistic approach to external relations, meant relatively ineffective functioning as far as external relations were concerned (Negandhi and Baliga, 1979).

A major advantage that all multinationals saw with reference to operating in Western Europe was that the host environment was more similar than dissimilar to the home environment. As a result, organizational strategies that had proved successful at home were transferred with little fear of failure. Also as can be seen from table 6.6, Japanese, German, and American subsidiary executives interviewed perceived only moderate uncertainty along with a number of critical environmental dimensions. As a result, points of tension were few and almost similar for Japanese, German, and American multinationals. In contrast to the developing countries, the political dimension of strategy was less significant in Western Europe.

Table 6.6.   Perceived Uncertainty of Environmental Factors

Environmental Conditions	Mean	Standard Deviation
Overall Environmental Uncertainty	2.737	1.996
Predictability of Market Conditions	1.947	0.833
Predictability of Political Conditions	2.053	0.895
Predictability of Supply	1.526	0.081
Predictability of Capital	1.246	0.576
Predictability of Labor Market	1.860	0.972

Scale:

1	5
very easy	very difficult

Approach to External Relations

A key finding of our comparative study of multinationals in developing countries was that Japanese multinationals utilized personal contact by top-level executives and trade associations to maintain external relations with significant members of the host environment. American multinationals, on the other hand, maintained external relations through press releases, public relations departments, and the use of lawyers. Our study has concluded that the "personal mode" employed by the Japanese multinationals was very effective. This pattern was, however, not discernible in Western Europe. No significant differences between the Japanese, German and U.S. multinationals existed in the industrialized countries. This could be possible due to the fact that, in the industrialized countries, the multinational phenomenon is fairly commonplace and the conventional approach adopted by domestic corporations to external relations can safely be employed by the multinationals too.

HQ-Subsidiary Issues

Just as no significant differences among multinational corporations arose with regard to their interactions with the host governments and other publics, no significant statistical differences in terms of HQ-subsidiary relationships arose, as can be seen from table 6.7. However, it is illuminating to note that for U.S. MNCs, approximately 42% of the issues that were reported to us in the course of the field investigation were concerned with decision-making authority. U.S. subsidiary managers complained over and over again that they felt very impotent in their role. In contrast, approximately 67% of issues reported by Japanese executives related to operational issues. Reflecting the relatively laissez-faire system, few issues resulted from external requirements of host governments as they did in developing countries. Significantly, however, headquarter influence prevailed over subsidiary influence almost three times as often. It is not surprising, therefore, that a fair proportion of the issues between HQ and subs were centered around decision-making authority. American subsidiary executives were very vocal in voicing the complaint that the tremendous degree of centralization left them almost impotent. That this degree of centralization has not reduced their effectiveness to the extent it has in the developing countries is more a reflection of environmental characteristics (less demanding) than any inherent U.S. superiority in the organizational structure and process.

CONCLUSIONS

In direct contrast to our findings in the developing countries, U.S., German and Japanese multinationals appear to have similar patterns of interactions with members of their environment. Any differences are one of degree and not of substance. These findings appear to support the contention that organizations are becoming more similar than dissimilar; that

Table 6.7. Issues between Headquarters and Subsidiaries*

	No Response N/%	Capital Investment N/%	Operational Issues N/%	Personnel Issues N/%	External Requirement Issues N/%	Decision-Making Authority N/%	No Significant Issues N/%	Total
U.S. MNCs	1/100.0 1/4.3	3/60.0 3/13.0	2/25.0 2/8.7	1/33.3 1/4.3	1/100.0 1/4.3	5/62.5 5/21.7	10/32.3 10/43.5	23/100
Germany MNCs	0/0.0 0/0.0	2/40.0 2/13.3	2/25.0 2/13.3	0/0.0 0/0.0	0/0.0 0/0.0	3/37.5 3/20.0	8/25.8 8/53.3	15/100
Japan MNCs	0/0.0 0/0.0	0/0.0 0/0.0	4/50.0 4/21.0	2/66.7 2/10.5	0/0.0 0/0.0	0/0.0 0/0.0	13/41.9 13/68.4	19/100
Total	1/100	5/100	8/100	3/100	1/100	8/00		

*Raw Chi Square = 13.63656 with 12 degrees of freedom. Significance = 0.3245.

Note: Top row refers to column percentages, bottom row refers to raw percentages.

133

is, effects of culture are being suppressed by technological and environmental forces. This appears to be increasingly true of multinational corporations which, through their international activities, appear to be developing an organizational form geared more to the problems of coordinating global operations than emphasizing a geocentric form of management. Given the changing political, economic and social conditions in Europe and other industrialized countries, it may not be too long before the developed countries themselves begin to legislate some of their needs, expectations, and concerns in specific policies governing foreign private investment (such as generation of employment). On the other hand, the emergence of multinational corporations from the developing countries may soften present policy-restrictions on multinational corporations in the developing countries.

REFERENCES

Allen, Stephen A. 1976. "A Taxonomy of Organizational Choices in Divisionalized Companies." Working paper IMEDE, Lausanne, Switzerland, October 19, 1976.

Bain, Joe. 1958. Industrial Organization. New York: John Wiley.

Bergsten, Fred C. 1974. "Coming Investment Wars?" Foreign Affairs 53, no. 135.

Bixenstine, E. 1966. "Empiricism in Latter Day Behavioral Science." In Some Theories of Organization. ed. Rubenstein and Haberstroh, Homewood, Ill.: Doresey Press.

Chandler, Alfred D. 1962. Strategy and Structure. Cambridge, Mass.: M.I.T. Press.

Channon, Derek. 1973. The Strategy and Structure of British Enterprise. London: MacMillan.

Franko, Lawrence. 1974. "The Move Toward a Multi-Divisional Structure in European Organizations." Administrative Science Quarterly 19:493-506.

Fry, David. E. 1977. Multinational Corporations - Host Government Relationships: An Empirical Study of Behavioral Expectations. DBA dissertation, Kent State University.

Galbraith, Jay and Nathanson D. A. 1978. Strategy Implementation: The Role of Structure and Process. St. Paul: West.

Lawrence Paul, and Stanley Davis. 1978. Matrix. Reading Mass.: Addison-Wesley.

Mikesell, Ray F. et al. 1971. Foreign Investment in the Petroleum and Mineral Industries. Baltimore, Maryland: John Hopkins Press.

Negandhi, Anant R. and Baliga, B.R. 1979. Quest for Survival and Growth: A Comparative Study of American, European and Japanese Multinationals, Konigstein, West Germany: Athenaeum. New York: Praeger.

Rumelt, Richard. 1974. Strategy, Structure and Economic Performance. Boston: Division of Research, Harvard Business School.

Stopford, John and Wells, Louis. 1972. Managing the Multinational Enterprise. London: Longmans.

Thanheiser, Heinz. 1972. Strategy and Structure of German Firms. Ph.D. dissertation, Harvard Business School.

Vernon, R. 1971. Sovereignty at Bay. New York: Basic Books.

Yoshino, M.Y. 1978. Japan's Multinational Corporations. Cambridge, Mass: Harvard University Press.

7 Adaptability of American, European, and Japanese Multinational Corporations in Developing Countries
Anant R. Negandhi

INTRODUCTION

The purpose of this paper is to examine the management strategies, philosophies, and orientations of American, European, and Japanese multinational corporations (MNCs) in coping with the increasing demands of the host, particularly in the developing countries.

In recent years, MNCs have come under considerable scrutiny by both the home and host countries, as well as by the international bodies, such as the United Nations and the International Labor Organization.

In their home countries, MNCs have been criticized for exporting jobs, creating balance-of-payment problems, and making it difficult for the national government to implement foreign policies.

In the host countries, MNCs have been attacked for exploiting labor, using monopolistic power to crush the local firms, being involved in "unethical" transfer pricing practices, and using leverage to gain favorable rates for large financial credits from local capital markets.

At the same time, they have been questioned by the host nations about their specific contributions to the socio-economic plans of the host countries. In more specific terms, many of the developing countries, in order to maximize their returns from foreign private investment, have enacted legislation that requires a majority local equity in foreign enterprises, higher proportion of local nationals in top positions, and increased exports and foreign exchange earnings and reduction of imports of raw material and spare parts.

Such demands from the host countries have to some extent constrained the MNCs to rationalize the world-wide productive capacity they seem to possess. For this purpose, MNCs, for their part, have made demands on the host countries to provide them with efficient infrastructural facilities, reduce bureaucratic controls and interference in corporate affairs, and provide conducive labor legislations and more flexible expansion policies.

COMPARATIVE FOCUS

Generally speaking, the host countries have attempted to apply uniform and non-discriminatory regulations on the multinational corporations originating from the different countries. That is, American, European, and Japanese multinationals, for example, are not being treated differently in terms of policy, by the host nations. However, in spite of apparent similarities of regulations and controls, MNCs from different countries have interpreted and responded to such regulations in different modes.

It was the purpose of this study, therefore, to examine the similarities and differences among American, European, and Japanese MNCs' strategies, philosophies, and orientations in coping with the controls and regulatory measures imposed on them by the host country. To examine such similarities and differences, we began by asking questions concerning the nature of the conflicting issues and causes and consequences of the conflicts between the MNCs and the host governments and other publics in the host countries. (For the sake of brevity, we will henceforth refer to conflicts among the MNCs and the host governments and the other publics in the host countries as MNCs-environmental-unit conflict in the host country.)

CONCEPTUAL SCHEME, RESEARCH SETTINGS, SAMPLE, AND METHOD

Initially, as shown in figure 7.1, the research model postulated that the nature and intensity of the conflict between the MNCs and the environment units in the host country may be a function of certain internal attributes of the MNCs (such as ownership, size, type of industry, years of operation in the host nation, level of capital investment, level of technology used, and pattern of equity holding in the subsidiary by the parent organization), and certain attributes of the host nations themselves (such as level of industrial and economic development, and socio-economic and political stability and diversity).

The research was conducted in six developing countries: Brazil, India, Malaysia, Peru, Singapore, and Thailand. Senior

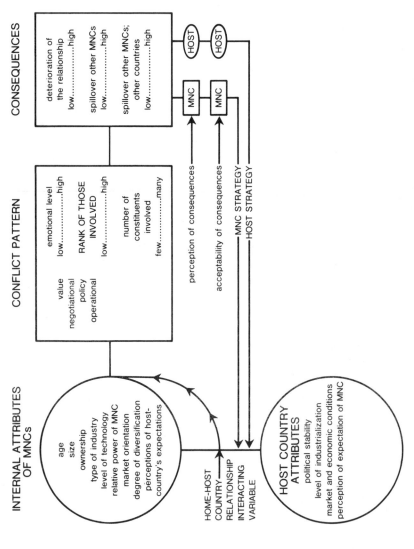

Fig. 7.1. The conceptual scheme.

executives of 124 MNCs operating in those countries were interviewed with the aid of a semi-structured interview guide.
We also interviewed senior government officials, executives of the trade and professional associations, banking and
investment companies concerned with foreign investment, and
other knowledgeable persons in those countries to collect background information and to obtain the perspectives and viewpoints of those persons on the multinational activities in those
countries.

Thus far, our attempts have been concentrated on examining the impact of certain internal attributes of MNCs and
MNC-host country relationships. An analysis of results of this
aspect is reported elsewhere (see Negandhi and Baliga, 1979).
These results are briefly summarized below.

BRIEF SUMMARY OF RESULTS

1. American and European MNCs tend to have a larger number of interface conflicts in the host countries than the
   Japanese MNCs.
2. Japanese MNCs tend to have more operational problems
   than the European and American MNCs.
3. Wholly-owned and majority-owned subsidiaries tend to
   have more interface conflicts than the minority-owned
   subsidiaries.
4. Firms operating in a seller's market and a moderately
   competitive market, tend to have a larger number of interface conflicts than those operating in competitive
   markets.
5. MNCs with larger expectation differences between themselves and the host governments face more interface conflicts than those with smaller expectation differences.
6. The type of industry, number of years in operation, size
   of employee force, level of capital investment, level of
   technology used, and extent of product diversification did
   not make significant impact on the MNC's host-country
   relationships.

As indicated earlier, the purpose of this paper is to
analyze the impact of managerial strategies, philosophies, and
orientations on the MNCs' host-country relationships. The
following discussion on this aspect is based on the in-depth
interviews with the senior executives of 124 MNCs (subsidiaries) and the governmental officials and other knowledgeable
persons in those six countries studied.

MNC-MANAGEMENT ORIENTATIONS

As researchers, our bias was clearly in favor of quantifiable factors, but we were not blind to Oscar Wilde's observation that, "A cynic is a man who knows the price of everything, and the value of nothing." (Nowotny, 1964) Or to put it differently, as the thoughtful businessman Nowotny reminds us:

> We tend to put everything in life in quantifiable "fact" and/or non-quantifiable 'value' terms. We have done so since the beginning of human history, and it is improbable that this dual way of looking at things will ever be replaced by a purely factual approach which eliminates all value judgments. (1964, p. 101)

Nowotny goes on to say:

> Top executives, like all other people, will continue to base their decisions on so-called objective facts, on the one hand, and subjective values, commonly referred to as management or business philosophy, on the other hand . . . .Value judgments will usually have priority over factual considerations in making vital business decisions. (1964, p. 101)

During the last two decades or so, much has been written about differences in management orientations of managers from different countries. The U.S. managerial orientation, for example, has been characterized as aggressive, egalitarian, and conscious of human relations. In contrast, the European managerial orientation has been characterized as authoritarian, passive, and paternalistic (Nowotny, 1964). Finally, Japanese management, has been described as paternalistic, culture-bound, and secretive (Yoshino, 1969).

Nowotny, among others, has argued that in terms of managerial philosophy, the American management is future-oriented, aggressive, mobile, informal, quantity-conscious, and organization-minded, while European management is past- and present-oriented, values wisdom over vitality, stability over mobility, convention over informality, quality rather than quantity, and diversity over organization (1964).

Although much cross-fertilization has taken place, not only between Americans and Europeans, but also between managers in developed and developing countries, our observations indicate that subtle but noticeable differences still exist between the three groups of multinationals under consideration - American, European, and Japanese. We found that these differences were quite evident in their management philosophy and approaches to dealing with host governments and other environmental units. They not only utilized different investment strategies, but also had different objectives in investing abroad. The host governments, on their part, also recognized differences in the actions and behavior of these multinationals. Some of these differences are elaborated below.

COMPANY EFFICIENCY VERSUS SYSTEM EFFECTIVENESS

In general, the U.S. multinationals studied seem to be operating with a notion of efficiency that differs from that held by their European and Japanese counterparts. To American managers, the cardinal principle of efficiency was the profitable production of quality goods and services at a price the consumer could afford or was willing to pay. This notion was continually reinforced by the home office, which rewarded the subsidiary on the basis of its annual bottom-line performance. Thus, plant productivity, cost of goods purchased, and similar financial indices became the main concerns of the overseas manager. The very legitimacy of overseas operations and their subsequent worth was seen in terms of the operational efficiency.

In contrast, the Japanese and Europeans measured success or failure not so much in terms of the operational efficiency criteria used by American multinationals, but in terms of system effectiveness, i.e., the degree to which their organization was able to adapt to and cope with the stimuli (e.g., new control or regulatory mechanisms) emanating from the environment. In order to do so, they were often willing to sacrifice some short-term operational efficiency. Furthermore, the home office often reinforced the policy of long-term effectiveness by stationing an expatriate manager in one country for substantial periods of time. The manager's role was evaluated, not so much in terms of bottom-line profits as in terms of the ability to cultivate and maintain a harmonious interaction with host-government officials and others in the environment. In contrast, most U.S. executives perceived such activities as a "waste of resources," contributing only to a decrease in efficiency and profitability. In fact, U.S. subsidiary managers were rarely asked by the parent organization to cultivate interface and boundary relationships.

With respect to the short-term profit orientation of American multinationals, the managing director of an American subsidiary, a local national, said:

> Americans are interested in taking out their investments in five years and are then willing to let the company decline and die. . . . (They) develop a habit of walking out from a given market at the

slightest provocation. They are too temperamental and don't give a damn about understanding host countries' problems and aspirations. What they want is their fair return . . . their ability to get back their investments in five years, and then remit profits to the maximum extent possible.

A European executive in Southeast Asia expressed a similar viewpoint:

Americans come here on a temporary basis and set up fly-by-night type of operations, and they disappear as fast as they come. We do not come with such intentions. Because of this American attitude, they (U.S. executives) get very annoyed when the government changes policies. We, too, do not like sudden changes in policies, but this is the name of the game and one should adapt to it. (See also Franko, 1976, p. 225, for similar observations.)

We also observed that European and Japanese executives were given enough leeway and freedom to set their own targets in a given country, while U.S. subsidiary executives were programmed by their headquarters to produce, sell, and make profits at certain levels.

As the managing director of a large American petroleum company lamented:

Those computer kids in New York tell us what to do, when to eat, and when to travel. We have no freedom like the Japanese and Europeans . . . .They must be paid half as much, but carry a lot of decision-making power.

Another characteristic displayed by U.S. executives was their misguided notion that they were doing the host nations a big favor by their very presence. If the host nations did not appreciate this fact, they said they would be only too glad to leave, and gleefully watch the nation's downfall. The following quotations from our interviews provide further insights into the workings of the U.S. overseas executive's mind.

The managing director of a large American MNC in Malaysia, pounding his hand on the desk, said:

We came here because they needed us. We can help them. This little country and her little people need help, but they must be reasonable, otherwise we will get out of here.

Commenting on the status of his own company, he said:

> We are number one in the world in the manu-
> facturing of _____ , and I want you to know, and
> the world to know about this fact, and I want you to
> tell this to everybody else.

In contrast, a European MNC's executive reflected:

> We came here to stay for a long time. We have
> been here a long time, and intend to stay unless or-
> dered out by the host country. Of course, then we
> must go . . . .We are, after all, their guests.

Franko, in his study of European multinational companies,
underscored this highly-adaptable attitude of European MNCs
in these words:

> The continental presence was more discreet
> . . . the flags of the home countries of continental
> enterprises did not connote ambitious or superpower
> capabilities of recipient countries. (1976, p. 222)

The Japanese multinationals' overall attitude toward host
nations was even more conciliatory than that of the Americans
and Europeans. The overall Japanese view was:

> We came here as guests, and our nation is small
> and needs natural resources, as well as foreign
> trade and investment to survive.

Japanese multinationals generally emphasized their role in
contributing to the overall welfare of their host and home
countries. They seem to believe that each and every one of
them has a national responsibility to secure resources for Japan, to provide opportunities for small manufacturers from
Japan to invest overseas, to sell their advanced technology,
and to help host nations achieve their own socio-economic objectives. Of course, such a "collective" orientation, in contrast to the "individualistic" orientation of the U.S. executive,
strongly reflects Japan's national heritage and religious beliefs
(Kitagawa, 1976, p. 21).
Whether such differences between Americans, Europeans,
and Japanese are substantial or not, government officials and
opinion leaders (press, academicians) in the countries studied,
perceived the existence of such differences. A high-ranking
government official in Singapore, a country very cordial to the
United States, said:

Americans are more jumpy, impulsive, and reactive, while Europeans are very conservative and go with a step-by-step approach in decision making . . . Europeans come here to stay, and Americans come on a short-term basis.

Not surprisingly, this attitude was apparent in the MNC's investment strategy, reaction to changes in host-government policies, and the selection and training of overseas managers. This is examined in greater detail in the following section.

ADAPTIVE VERSUS REACTIVE BEHAVIOR

Generally speaking, American multinational executives perceived policy changes in host countries as a substantial threat to their operations. Their usual reaction to change was belligerent. Instead of negotiating discreetly, they preferred to overreact and ignore diplomacy. In the majority of cases, they failed to distinguish between an actual governmental policy change, and merely apparent shifts in the host government's attitude adopted only in order to placate political factions within a nation. In certain cases, U.S. MNCs precipitated policy changes through reacting prematurely to inconsequential statements made by the host government's representatives.

In contrast, the Japanese generally saw the source of their problems with host governments in actions taken by third parties . . . students, organized labor, consumer groups, and even American multinationals. During times of conflict, they assumed a very low profile and waited for the tension to dissipate.

European executives generally assumed a "philosophical" position on any issue that arose. They blamed neither the government (as Americans did), nor other publics (as the Japanese did). They were generally charitable to American MNCs facing specific problems with the host country. In brief, they preferred to stay on the sidelines, and were very willing to compromise. As a Swiss executive in Brazil explained:

MNCs should operate within the framework of Eastern philosophies: no public debate, no press releases, no big announcements, no big fanfare, just do the job. . . . (They should) follow the example of the Hindu Atma and get lost; lose identity into nothingness.

He went on to recommend,

a philosophy of harmony and cooperation instead of raising issues, . . . keeping a low profile, asking no questions, and working within host-government policies, and solving problems at a personal level, rather than at the public level.

Similarly, a European executive in Malaysia, referring to a sudden change in that country's investment policies (requiring that a fixed proportion of employees be "Bhumiputras") said:

The government goals and objectives do change, and we must adapt to these changes. This is what international business is all about; we must constantly adapt to new circumstances, and nobody can say that the government has to keep its goals and policies the same for all time.

With reference to the same policy change, an American executive reacted by saying,

The recent two acts are unconstitutional and amount to illegal takeover of foreign companies. (The government) is tyrannical, and no different from that in other developing countries . . . I will not advise my company to invest any more in Malaysia.

Such differences in MNC-behavior patterns and reactions were further revealed through examining the perceived intensity of conflicts, the consequences of conflicts, and the extent of the involvement of senior executives in these episodes.

Table 7.1 shows that of all the conflicts faced by American MNCs, 45 percent were described by their executives as very intense. On the other hand, only 14 percent of conflicts were rated as less intensive by the U.S. executives. The European MNCs were not far behind: 40 percent of their conflicts were described as highly intensive. However, the Japanese MNCs noticeably played down the intensity of their conflicts in the host countries. Only 21 percent of their conflicts were evaluated as highly intensive.

The low-profile strategy adopted by the Europeans and Japanese had favorable payoffs in terms of the ultimate consequences of the conflicts. American MNCs had twice as many breakdowns in relationships than the Europeans, and three times more than the Japanese. Apparently, Europeans and Japanese prevented their conflicts from ending in dire consequences (Franko, 1976; Boddewyn and Kapoor, 1972; Heller and Willatt, 1975).

The Japanese MNCs' desire to maintain a low profile is further shown by the relative lack of direct involvement in any

Table 7.1. Intensity of Conflict by Origin of Controlling
Ownership of MNC

OWNERSHIP	INTENSITY OF CONFLICT		
	HIGH	MEDIUM	LOW
	N %	N %	N %
U.S.	10/45	17/41	7/14
EUROPEAN	13/40	12/34	9/26
JAPANESE	6/21	6/21	11/48

Source: Authors' interviews as reported in Negandhi and Baliga, Quest for Survival and Growth, West Germany:
Athenaeum Verlag, 1979, p. 47.

conflicts of their senior personnel. Approximately half of the
U.S. and European MNCs' conflicts involved senior personnel,
whereas in Japanese MNCs, junior- and middle-level executives
took the heat. This strategy could be followed largely because
of the fact (as shown in a latter section) that Japanese firms
filled even lower-level managerial positions with Japanese expatriates.

MANAGERIAL ATTRIBUTES AND CONFLICT RESOLUTION

In their responses to our question, "What talents do you consider are most needed by the executive-personnel dealing with
host governments?" all MNC-executives interviewed seemed
pretty much in agreement. They all ranked interpersonal competence and influential contacts as most desirable qualities. In
addition, the Japanese MNCs placed major emphasis on the
"political" and diplomatic skills of their executives.
     The American, European, and Japanese executives, how-
ever, differed considerably in applying their resources to conflict resolution. The American approach, in most cases, was
to place all their cards on the table, and to attempt to resolve
their problems in public. They appeared to be under the impression that their interests would be best served through a
general and open discussion of the issues involved. They
tried to generate such a dialogue through press releases, and
by pressuring government officials independently, through in-

dustry associations, or even through U.S. embassies and consulates.

A European executive in Brazil commented on this approach, and contrasted it with his own (European) approach thus:

> The American way of bringing things out into the open . . . is stupid. What do they achieve? We do not understand the American way . . . The company should be careful not to raise any dialogue or do anything via debate . . . I would suggest complete secrecy and solving problems discreetly at the personal level.

Another European executive in Malaysia expressed similar thoughts:

> Americans get into conflict with government . . . this is the American way of life. They do not like governments to tell them what to do, and they get on right away (in debate) with the government officials and fight if the officials attempt to control them. This may be the life style in America, and they are used to this life style . . . and think it applies equally here (in host nations).

The host-government officials also perceived Americans as aggressive and far too vocal. A Brazilian government official, for example, stated,

> Americans bring out everything in public. . . . We do not understand it. It is okay philosophically, but washing dirty linen in public does not solve anything . . . . We do not understand the American way.

In contrast, both European and Japanese executives were adept at keeping a low profile, and did their best not to raise questions in public. They preferred to work discreetly and make very subtle efforts to influence decision makers. In times of stress, they (especially the Japanese) did not hesitate to push their "big brothers" (U.S. MNCs) into the limelight, taking shelter in their shadows.

RESPONSES TO POLICY CHANGES

Substantial differences between the three groups of MNCs were clearly reflected in their responses to specific issues and policy changes that were being debated at the time our study was carried out. We examined three policy changes that were announced recently in three countries - Malaysia, India, and Peru - in order to illustrate these differences.

Malaysian Case

The Malaysian government now requires all foreign corporations to increase equity holdings by nationals and also specifies proportions in which various ethnic groups are to be employed in an organization. The required percentages are: 30 percent Chinese, Indian, and those of other national origins who are Malaysian citizens; 40 percent Bhumiputras, who are considered to be the "true" Malaysians; and 30 percent foreigners (expatriates).

To implement this policy, the government has formed a ministerial-level committee, which has begun to issue letters of invitation to various foreign companies to appear before the committee and discuss their plans for compliance with the stated policy.

In response to the question, "What would you do if you got a letter of invitation from the committee?" the typical answer of Japanese MNCs was:

> We have already done so and implemented this policy of the government in terms of equity requirements, and will attempt to do the same with respect to the employment of the different national groups. Of course, this is somewhat difficult, and time-consuming, but the government understands our problems and is sympathetic.

The European response was:

> Fine! We have already made plans and look forward to discussing intelligently with the government officials; we are not scared or afraid; we will make every effort to implement this policy.

In commenting on the fairness of this Malaysian policy, a European expatriate manager echoed this reaction, saying:

> The government policy of Malayization is correct. And as a matter of fact, they are trying to tell us: "look, MNCs, we like you and would very much like your operation here, but we have this problem of inequity which may create troubles and a potential revolution. This is not good for you or us," . . . we do not need revolutions, but to avoid

this, we must get down to work and remove this in-
equity; otherwise, neither you nor we will be here
. . . (To us) this is a realistic situation, and we
are prepared to work with the government.

In contrast, an American executive's reaction to the same
policy was:

These policies are political in nature and will
and should not be implemented; but if they are, it
will hurt the country and the inflow of foreign investment.

The American executive's response was to make a long-
distance call to the vice-president of the international division
of the company, and then fly home for detailed instructions.
The majority of the American expatriate managers interviewed
felt that the policy was unconstitutional, and that they would
rather pull out than implement it.

In reality, however, neither the Japanese nor the European MNCs in Malaysia had made any serious efforts to increase the employment of "Bhumiputras" in the proportions
desired by the government. American MNCs, on the other
hand, had a higher proportion of locals on their employee ros-
ters. As we will see in a later section, Europeans and Japanese have been relatively slow in placing local nationals in
top-level positions, not only in Malaysia, but also in other developing countries.

Further, American MNCs have shown the greatest reluc-
tance in complying with equity-dilution requirements, while the
Europeans and Japanese have demonstrated a greater flexibility
in doing so (Franko, 1976). The American refusal to do so
appears to have placed them in an awkward position, which the
host-government officials have variously attributed to "American stubbornness, inflexibility, imperialism, and indecisive-
ness."

The Indian Case

Analogous to the Malaysian case, the Government of India's
Foreign Exchange Regulation Act (FERA) of 1973, requires
that all foreign equity holdings be diluted to 40 percent, unless the firm is operating in the "priority sector" designated
from time to time by the government, and/or the firm is exporting at least 65 percent of its production.

Here again, the typical response of European MNCs was
to either increase their exports to the required amount, dilute
their equity, and/or to increase investments in the "priority
sectors." It was interesting to note, for example, that a well-

established European tobacco company (a non-priority industry), sought the advice of an Indian consulting firm in order
to find ways and means of investing its large accumulated capital in cement manufacturing. When we asked some American
executives about this move by the European company, the majority of them felt that the company was "out of its mind."
The Americans also felt that if they were to recommend to
their home office investment in some unrelated but priority industry, they would be immediately fired or called home and
demoted. They, accordingly, spoke more in terms of pulling
out of India, or exerting pressure on the Indian government
through the U.S. State Department and other American, and
international agencies. (Two recent cases of IBM and Coca
Cola's withdrawals from India exemplify this point.)

The Peruvian Case

Similar reactions were observed in Peru with respect to the
Andean Pact Regulations, particularly "Decision 24," which requires all foreign companies to become "mixed companies" with
51% local ownership within 15 years (Council of the Americas,
1973). The typical European and Japanese response to this
regulation was, "We will do it when the time comes," or "We
have already done so." The Americans frequently talked about
leaving or putting pressure on the Peruvian and other Andean
Pact countries to change the Andean pact regulations.

Differences in Interpretation

Our extensive interviews further confirmed the fact that the
examples described above were not unique. A detailed analysis of the conflict-response patterns led us to believe that in
interpreting government policies, the Japanese managers were
inclined to follow what they called "political instructions" which
were communicated orally by government officials or reported
in the press, regardless of whether such instructions were
spelled out in the policy framework or not. In contrast, the
American tendency was to refer to the documentations of policies, and act accordingly. The usual reasoning of American
MNCs seemed simple and straightforward. "If the governmental policies are favorable to our company's overall interests, we
will come (forward to invest) and continue our operations; if
they are not, we will not (come forward to invest) and pull
out our existing investments." The actions of American
petroleum companies in India and Malaysia amply illustrate this
attitude. In India, one company decided to withdraw its investment in petroleum refining and marketing operations when the
government of India began to implement its petroleum policy of

increasing the market share of the public-sector companies. In Malaysia, when the Government announced its interim royalty rate (7-1/2 percent of the total revenue) for oil exploration undertaken by foreign MNCs, an American MNC, which did not agree with the rate, decided to stop its drilling operation. This particular situation in Malaysia generated heated arguments between company and government officials, which also affected other multinationals. In response to a company's reaction to the Malaysian petroleum policy, Mr. Razaleigh, then the Chairman of the government-owned petroleum company, said, "We are prepared to listen to reason, not threats. . . . Petronas will (government-owned company) not submit to threats of pulling out "huge investments" from Malaysia . . . they must realize that the oil belongs to this country and our people, and we will not allow them to take all our wealth away."   (New Strait Times, 1975).

Preference for Clarity in the Governments' Policies

Our interviews also revealed that the American MNCs found it difficult to operate with vague and diffuse policies. As the top executive of an American petroleum company in Singapore explained:

> What is important to us is not what the rules of the game are, but their consistency. We can operate under strict controls, or no controls at all . . . but what is terribly difficult is when you gear your approach to certain markets and, all of a sudden, more controls are slapped on overnight, or when you had a tightly controlled situation, and the controls are taken off.

Such preferences for clarity and consistency in policies are natural, and they do make life easier for the multinationals. However, uncertainties and changes are a fact of life, particularly in international business and by and large, American MNCs have reacted poorly to changes in their environment.

The Japanese, on the other hand, viewed unregulated situations as advantageous to them; lack of specific policies meant that no specific constraints had to be contended with. Whenever clarification was needed, they felt, it could be gained by talking to influential persons, government officials, bankers, and their own embassy's personnel.

To the Europeans, the existence of confused situations meant that the world is dynamic. They also felt that if certain policies were too restrictive currently, they would change in due course of time, and that one should be prepared to wait out such eventual changes.

Apparently, such insistence on clarity by the U.S. multinationals conveyed an impression of stubbornness and inflexibility to host-government officials, whose own socio-cultural
background made them tolerant of vagueness.

PERSONNEL POLICIES

American MNCs' Practices

The personnel policies as well as the overall management system of American MNCs have been acclaimed as most advanced
and sophisticated. This was acknowledged not only by host-
government officials, educators, and union leaders, but also
by executives of the European and Japanese multinationals
themselves.

American MNCs have been regarded as fair and equitable
in dealing with their employees in terms of providing attractive
wages and salaries, fringe benefits, training, and promotion
opportunities. Because of such enlightened personnel policies,
other industrial and commercial enterprises, including European
and Japanese MNCs, have experienced difficulties in attracting
and retaining a high-level workforce in the developing
countries.

American MNCs were also the first to deal with the widespread demand of the developing countries to localize management of foreign companies. In our earlier study of 56 U.S.
subsidiaries in six developing countries (Negandhi, 1975), we
found no more than two dozen expatriate American managers
in these companies. In the present study, we noted the continuation of this trend in the declining use of expatriate managers by U.S. multinationals.

As shown in Table 7.2, the majority of the top-level
executive positions in the U.S. subsidiaries were filled with
local nationals. In fact, in our study we found only one company that did not have any national in a top-level position.
In contrast, fifteen Japanese multinationals (78.9 percent) did
not employ even one single national in the top-level management ranks. The table indicates that European MNCs had localized their operations considerably more than the Japanese,
though to a lesser extent than the American MNCs.

Our study also indicates that Japanese mulitnationals are
particularly likely to employ Japanese personnel, even low
down the organizational ladder, despite the availability of
skilled and competent personnel in the host country. It was
not uncommon in Japanese multinationals to find that their
first-line supervisors were Japanese nationals. Such practices
contributed quite significantly to the operational-level problems
with which the Japanese multinationals were plagued.

Table 7.2. Extent of Localization of Top-Level
Management by MNCs

LOCALIZATION OF TOP-LEVEL MANAGEMENT	MNC OWNERSHIP		
	U.S. (n = 44)	EUROPEAN (n = 33)	JAPANESE (n = 19)
	n/%	n/%	n/%
100	12/27.3	3/9.1	0/0
75-99	14/31.8	13/39.4	0/0
51-74	7/15.9	4/12.1	2/10.5
1-50	10/22.7	8/24.2	2/10.5
0	1/2.3	5/15.2	15/78.9

Note: Chi square = 53.03
           D.F. = 8
           Level of significance = 0.01

Source: Authors' interviews.

European MNCs' Practices

In recent years, European MNCs have made considerable
strides in catching up with the Americans with respect to their
management systems and personnel policies. Although there
are still subtle differences between the basic orientations,
management philosophy and practices of American and European
companies, the gap between the two with regard to their
personnel policies for local employees, is fast narrowing.
Especially, at the levels of unskilled and skilled workers, and
supervisory and middle management, there are no great
differences in wages, or in type of training and promotion
opportunities available. However, as we will discuss later, at
the higher technical and managerial levels, the American and
European countries are still somewhat different.

Japanese MNCs' Practices

Among the multinationals we studied, the Japanese seem to
have the most severe problem with their employees. They
experienced the greatest difficulty in attracting, retaining,
and motivating employees at all levels. Generally, the Japanese MNCs followed two distinctive modes in their personnel
policies. The one was to practice the Japanese style of management. Here, they would attempt to introduce the Japanese

practice of life-time employment and promotion on the basis of seniority, and demand complete employee loyalty to the company. The other mode was to treat the local employees in the same manner they were treated by domestically-owned companies. This resulted in maintenance of the status quo, and holding employees in low esteem as was the custom in many local enterprises and government agencies. However, because of rising expectations and a better understanding of the status of workers in other countries, these policies have resulted in low employee morale, productivity, and higher absenteeism and turnover rates (Negandhi, 1973). Although the expatriate Japanese managers failed to see the causes of their problems, they did admit that they had serious manpower and personnel problems in their operations.

Background and Career Patterns

The American overseas manager is always on the move. Both occupational and intercompany mobility is a built-in feature of the manager's working life. The usual tenure of a U.S. subsidiary manager in a given position was between three to five years. In our interviews, we found only a handful of American expatriates who had lived in a given country more than five years. Many of them were newcomers and were hoping that their assignments overseas would not be a manifestation of their having been demoted. Even those who had taken up their assignment less than a year ago expressed the desire that they soon be transferred home again.

In contrast, the European and Japanese managers thought of their overseas career as long-term. They felt that, basically, they were international executives, and had assumed their present positions to strive for long-term objectives, both for their companies and for themselves. A typical response of a Japanese expatriate manager to the question, "Where do you go next, and when?", was:

> I came here only five years ago, and it will depend upon that man (pointing to the picture of the president of his company), but I came here to stay.

The response of the European executive was the same as that of the Japanese, except that there was no picture to be pointed to. As one German manager in Malaysia explained:

> This is not quite heaven, but it is a good place to live and raise a family . . .

Speaking on behalf of all other Europeans, he said:

We are international executives, and we have, by choice, decided to pursue overseas careers and, unlike Americans, for us the question does not arise where to go next.

The United States is a very mobile nation, so an attitude toward an overseas assignment by the typical U.S. overseas manager like that described above is both realistic and understandable. But, the contrast between American, European, and Japanese attitudes toward and expectations in their career goals creates an unfavorable image of the American MNCs. Partly because of the short term of their assignments, American overseas managers are thought of by host officials as "second-rate" executives, not given much decision-making power by their headquarters. European and Japanese expatriates, on the other hand, are regarded as influential and important persons, possessing high status within their companies. Whether such a situation was true or not, this was considered to be a fact in the eyes of host-government officials and leading local businessmen. Frequently, government officials in developing countries have demanded that U.S. subsidiaries call in their vice-presidents or presidents for even minor discussions, thus implying that expatriate managers are not considered important enough in the management hierarchy, or lack sufficient influence or authority to make important decisions.

Significant differences were also observed in the background and training of American, European, and Japanese executives. As one would expect, a large majority of the expatriates interviewed were college graduates. However, the nature of their studies differed considerably. Approximately two-thirds of the American expatriates were either business and/or engineering majors. A large majority of Japanese expatriates specialized in international economics and social science. A larger number of the European managers, on the other hand, took their degree in the humanities and liberal arts.

With respect to the American overseas manager, more than a decade ago, we found, in another large-scale study, that over 50 percent of the graduates were business or engineering majors, with approximately 44 percent from the humanities and liberal arts (Gonzalez and Negandhi, 1967). More recently, however, greater emphasis is being placed on business administration education. This is quite evident from the survey of Fortune's 500 chief executives. The study reports that "more than half of today's top officers majored either in business or economics, and more than a quarter studied in graduate school" (Burck, 1967, p. 176).

In contrast, in earlier studies by Newcomer (1950) and Warner and Abegglen (1955), it was found that less than one-third were business graduates. The Fortune survey also reports an increasing trend toward legal and financial training among top executives. The survey states:

> The expanding size and complexity of corporate
> organizations, coupled with their continued expansion
> overseas, have increased the importance of financial
> planning and controls. And the growth of govern-
> ment regulation and obligations companies face under
> law has heightened the need for legal advice. The
> engineer and the production man have become . . .
> less important in management than the finance man
> and the lawyer. (Burck, 1967, p. 177)

Our interview, however, indicated that such a trend,
while true for high-level corporate officials, has not yet pen-
etrated to the level of managers of subsidiaries in the developing countries. The emphasis, here, is on the "nuts and
bolts" part of the business bottom-line profits, internal
efficiency and productivity. As mentioned earlier, these executives do not devote sufficient time to interface relationships
(Boddewyn and Kapoor, 1972).

In contrast to such training received by American expatriate managers, European and Japanese managers, both in
their formal education and in in-company training, are indoc-
trinated to be sensitive to the demands of the external
environment. They are very much concerned with the
"positioning" of their organizations in such a way that they do
not "stick out like a sore thumb" (Franko, 1976, pp. 220-225).
As we discussed earlier, their primary concern was to adapt to
the socio-cultural environment while the American executives
perceived themselves as "change agents." The Americans
usually found the socio-economic and political environments in
the developing countries hostile and not conducive to the
private enterprise system.

The American Dilemma

In spite of the proven superiority of American management
practices, and despite the efforts to localize U.S. overseas
operations, the personnel policies of the American MNCs are
being increasingly criticized by their own employees and by
government officials. The apparent slowness of European and
Japanese MNCs in placing local nationals in responsible positions has, however, been overlooked by the host governments.
Why so?

Host-government officials, as well as top-level local employees interviewed, felt that while American companies have
responded to the desire of host governments for more local
managers, they have merely followed the letter of the law and
not the spirit. In localizing overseas operations, the critics
contend, they have not only withheld decision-making powers
from local nationals, but also from the remaining expatriate

managers. It was also frequently pointed out to us by government officials that the quality of American expatriate managers was "inferior" to their European and Japanese counterparts. Common expressions of host government officials we talked to were: "Americans cannot make decisions."; "They are too inflexible."; "They do not have enough power." A most illustrative and striking example of such an evaluation on the part of host-government officials of American expatriates, was reflected in the public demand of a senior Malaysian governmental official that the president or vice-president of a company come from the United States to discuss some problems. Until that time, the official had declined to grant even a courtesy appointment to the subsidiary manager.

Simultaneously, the presence of a sizeable number of expatriates in the European and Japanese MNCs appears to have been conceived by the host countries in generally positive terms. They have been credited by the host government as possessing substantial decision-making power, and being more flexible in their attitudes than the Americans. They are also regarded as having closer ties with their headquarters, and even the ability to influence major decisions affecting subsidiary operations.

Thus, it seems to us that the localization of management by American MNCs has turned out to be a disadvantage for the U.S. companies. Some of the American expatriate managers interviewed felt that it was a mistake on the part of their companies to do so. As one American in Thailand said:

> We should not have done it in the first place, but now we do not know how to go back and bring more expatriate managers . . . European and Japanese are smart . . . they have not gone too far in this respect.

HEADQUARTER-SUBSIDIARY RELATIONSHIPS

In order to obtain a better understanding of the problems facing the executives of American subsidiaries, we attempted to explore various facets of headquarter-subsidiary relationships and their impact on MNC (subsidiary) host-country relationships.

Interviews with American executives indicated that they felt strongly about their inability to participate in decision making. Many of them admitted that they were little more than "peons" in terms of their head-office hierarchy, and that communication between them and the head offices' bosses were strictly formal and minimal in nature. At the same time, many of these executives complained a great deal about the excessive

demands made by their head offices for reports and data on
subsidiary operations. They felt that these reports and data
were for the entertainment of the "computer men" and, as one
American executive in Thailand put it:

> For these whiz kids who are playing around
> with the figures but really don't know what to do
> with the data. . . . [The] more you supply, [the]
> more they want . . . and my two (expatriate) assis-
> tants and I spend sixty percent of our time in gen-
> erating reports and data, and I surely hope some-
> body is using them at least as toilet paper.

In a similar vein, another American expatriate, who had
been posted to India after twenty-five years of service at the
home office, said:

> Headquarters demand a lot of documentation
> from here . . . (but) as far as top brass is con-
> cerned, they seem to know very little about what is
> happening in these countries.

Explaining his relationship with the home office, he
pointed out:

> We leave home . . . take a week off to go to
> our headquarters . . . socialize with the people we
> know, but communicate with nobody on substantial
> matters . . . I sometimes wonder whether the pres-
> ident or even the vice-president of our international
> division will recognize me . . . . They simply do
> not care.

Yet another American executive in Thailand echoed his frustration, saying:

> I really question whether the top brass at the
> home office listen to what we say and report . . . I
> think they are not mature enough to know the con-
> ditions prevailing here. . . . We are just beating
> the drums, nobody cares to listen back home.

And lastly, a returning American executive who had served for
eight years in Malaysia summed up the problems of the U.S.
subsidiary home office relationship. When asked about what
report he would have to file on his return regarding his experience abroad, he responded:

> I am on my way to San Francisco on my next
> assignment. . . . They did not call me to report

> at the head-office. . . . If they want to know
> something about the operation which I started here,
> they would call me long-distance. . . . Hell, they
> do not need me . . . they know it all!

In contrast to such apparent tension and misgivings between the U.S. subsidiaries' managers and their head offices,
the European and Japanese managers felt very comfortable in
their relationship with their head offices. Although there was
relatively much less formal reporting to be found in the European and Japanese MNCs, the overseas managers felt that they
were involved in and informed about the major strategic decisions undertaken back home, and their own voices and viewpoints were seriously considered during the formulation of
major policies affecting their operations. They also felt they
had considerable latitude in running their operations. In this
respect, most of the American expatriate managers we interviewed felt that their role and duties were very narrowly defined; they were simply just another cog in the corporate
machine.

The foregoing rather rosy picture of European and Japanese overseas managers does not necessarily mean that they
did not experience any tension and conflict in dealing with
their home-office personnel. Yoshino's study (1975), for example, shows the existence of tension and certain levels of
conflict between the Japanese subsidiary and the home office.
He ascribes this tension to the unique decision-making system
that the Japanese employ. This "bottom-up" decision-making
system is known in Japan as the "Ringi" system. In under-
scoring the practical limitations of this system, Yoshino states:

> Japanese have extended the Ringi system of de-
> cision making to international operations with virtual-
> ly no alterations. . . . (However) the extension of
> the Ringi system . . . has several immediate as well
> as long-range implications. . . . First . . . it has
> created some practical difficulties for the management
> of foreign subsidiaries, because it is they who must,
> somehow, bridge the gap that is created by their
> physical operation and isolation from the parent com-
> pany. This diverts their attention from the pressing
> needs of management of the local enterprise and is
> often a great source of frustration for them. Fur-
> thermore, the decision process can be extremely
> time-consuming when circumstances require rapid re-
> sponses. . . . [The] long-term implications of ex-
> tending the Ringi system . . . are that it makes the
> participation of non-Japanese nationals in the deci-
> sion-making process extremely difficult. (Yoshino,
> 1975, p. 163).

In criticizing this type of decision-making system used in Japanese multinationals' overseas operations, Yoshino further states:

> Japanese management is a closed, local, exclusive, and highly culture-bound system, and the Ringi system epitomizes it. . . . Compared with the Japanese, the American system is less culture-bound, has greater flexibility, and has a considerable degree of tolerance for heterogeneous elements. (1975, pp. 164-165)

Yoshino's description of the Japanese decision-making system is illuminating. However, in our opinion, he has failed to differentiate between the problems created at operation levels, and those at interface levels.

The Japanese do face a great number of operational problems; this may be due to their particular management orientation, including the Ringi system in decision making. However, such an orientation has not created problems for them in dealing with the governmental officials in host countries. As indicated earlier, the officials interviewed by us felt that the Japanese managers were much more flexible and had more decision-making power than the Americans.

The American system of management was much more advanced, and also preferred by employees. But the lack of self-esteem of the managers, coupled with their restricted decision-making power and a lack of adequate communication between the subsidiary and its home office has caused a large number of interface problems for American MNCs.

The European multinationals overseas appear to be in the best position. Unlike the Japanese, they were not found to be experiencing major operational problems. Although their management system may not be as sophisticated as the American MNCs', they are not far behind. Our studies in a number of developing countries indicate that local people would generally rather work for American than European MNCs, owing to their higher wages, better training, and promotion opportunities (Negandhi and Prasad, 1971, Chs. 7, 8). However, once the qualified employees reach higher management positions in U.S. subsidiaries, they seem to be frustrated with their lack of decision-making power and the excessive reporting requirements of their home offices. At this stage, the most able and qualified local employees in the American subsidiaries seek alternative opportunities, either in large local enterprises or in governmental agencies. However, there has not been a massive exodus.

In contrast, the European MNCs do not initially create such high expectations among their local employees, but they do promise better job security and a more stable career path.

Local nationals do not appear to have as good a chance of reaching top positions in European operations, but at the lower positions they are made to feel important and wanted. Such a feeling of being "wanted" is lacking in the American subsidiaries.

There is little substantial difference between American and European MNCs with regard to their interface conflicts. However, our interviews clearly showed that Europeans have learned to adapt better to changing circumstances. In fact, it would not be foolhardy to predict that European multinationals in the years to come, will experience less conflict than those from the U.S. (provided that present trends continue), since their flirtation with U.S. management practices seems to be on the wane (Heller and Willat, 1975).

INVESTMENT POLICY AND STRATEGIES

The American, European, and Japanese multinationals all desire to have one hundred percent equity holding in their subsidiaries. However, Europeans and Japanese appear to have reconciled themselves (Franko, 1976, pp. 121-130) to the leverage possessed by host governments, and have more readily accepted majority or even minority (especially the Japanese) positions. American MNCs, however, have often made threats of divestiture in order to retain one hundred percent equity. Such an attitude has begun to hurt American MNCs. Because of their insistence on one hundred percent equity, some host governments are bypassing them whenever large-scale projects have to be developed in the public sector.

Furthermore, U.S. MNCs appear to be reluctant to enter into fields in which they do not possess the necessary know-how. Acquisition of know-how through partnership with some other American firm is generally not pursued. There is a great concern with the notion of internal efficiency, expressed, for example, in a strong desire to build plants that achieve economies of scale. In contrast to these American policies, the Japanese have an investment policy that is very flexible. If they had to, they would even settle for minority equity holding, or go into partnership with others, including Japanese trading companies, other Japanese investors, local investors, as well as governmental enterprises. Usually, Japanese overseas investment was undertaken by a large trading company, which coordinated its efforts with other firms (generally Japanese) possessing the requisite know-how. In a sense, Japanese trading companies serve as catalysts for Japanese manufacturing investment in Southeast Asia, as well as in Latin America.

Despite the frequency of minority equity holding, a significant proportion of Japanese firms nevertheless manage to retain management control through use of various subagreements with respect to raw materials, spare parts, disposal of the end-products, etcetera. The Japanese were also willing to spread their investment over diverse operations. In other words, their limited amount of capital investment was channeled into a number of activities, both to minimize risk, and to demonstrate the flexibility to the host country. When questioned by host governments about their contribution toward socio-economic development, they would point out the extensiveness of their involvement and investment, their impact on employment generation, and the variety of products they were manufacturing. In this way, they would stress their intense concern for the socio-economic development of the host country. However, when the multinationals came under fire, they would disappear from public view and take an extremely low profile, saying, "we are not big . . . we are not multinationals . . . we have only small equity holdings, as required by host governments."

In our interviews, large trading companies like Mitsui, Marubeni, Mitsubishi, and others, doing business in the range of 250 to 400 million dollars per year in a given country, claimed that they were not multinationals, while much smaller American manufacturing companies with investments of less than $50,000 would widely advertise their international stature (Franko, 1976, pp. 218-219; Heller and Willat, 1975, p. 219). To cite a typical example, a Japanese company operating in Thailand, with an investment of no more than one million dollars, managed to control four textile companies, three steel mills, one food company, one large trading company, and ten other companies with products ranging from tissue paper to metal fabrications. The sales volume of this firm was about 450 million (U.S.) dollars per year; and it claimed to provide employment for 10,000 locals. In the same country, a typical American investor would invest about one and a half million dollars in a single plant providing employment for approximately 300 to 400 employees. Nevertheless, the American company would maintain a high profile while the Japanese firm would be barely noticeable.

As indicated earlier, we found that the Japanese investor was willing to enter into areas in which his company currently lacked the know-how. In other words, the possession of a particular technique or product was not the criterion for overseas investment. In fact, it was the other way around. Japanese multinationals were generally very receptive to whatever the host government wanted to be done. When the negotiating firm did not possess a technique, it would invite other Japanese or foreign investors to join. The Japanese also showed a willingness to enter into innovative terms of agreement. Such agreements might include provision of technology and know-how in return for long-term raw material supplies, or end-products for Japanese, European, and American markets. The European mode of investment fits in between that of the U.S. and the Japanese. The European strategy was one of diversification. However, the Europeans generally preferred to retain a larger proportion of equity than did the Japanese, though their insistence on a one hundred percent equity position was not as great as the Americans. Also, the Europeans were not necessarily against entering into joint ventures with host governments (Franko, 1976, pp. 121-130).

REFERENCES

Boddewyn, J., and Kapoor, Ashok. 1972. "The External Relations of American Multinational Enterprises." International Studies Quarterly 3, no. 2: 433-453.

Burck, C. G. 1976. "A Group Profile of the Fortune 500 Executives." Fortune XCIII: 176-177.

Council of the Americas. 1973. Andean Pact: Definition, Design and Analysis: 38-54. New York: Council of the Americas.

Franko, L. G. 1976. The European Multinationals. Stanford, Conn.: Greylock Publishers.

Gonzalez, R. F., and Negandhi, Anant R. 1967. The United States Overseas Executive: His Orientations and Career Patterns. East Lansing, Mich.: Michigan State University.

Heller, R., and Willatt, Noris. 1975. The European Revenge. New York: Scribner's.

Kitagawa, K. 1976. "A View of Modern Management in Japan." Management Japan 3.

Negandhi, A.R. 1973. Management and Economic Development: The Case of Taiwan. The Hague: Martinus Nijhoff.

———. 1975. Organization Theory in an Open System. New York: Dunellen.

———, and Baliga, B. R. 1979. Quest for Survival and Growth: A Comparative Study of American, European, and Japanese Multinationals. Konigstein, W. Germany: Athenaeum Verlag. New York: Praeger.

---, and Prasad, S. B. 1971. Comparative Management. New York: Appleton-Century-Crofts.

Newcomer, Mabel. 1950. The Big Business Executive: The Factors that Made Him, 1900-1950. New York: Columbia University Press.

New Strait Times (Malaysia). 1975. June 27.

Nowotny, Otto. 1964. "American Versus European Management Philosophy." Harvard Business Review 42, no. 2.

Tindall, R. E. 1975. "Mitsubishi Group: World's Largest Multinational Enterprise." MSU Business Topics 22.

Vernon, Raymond. 1971. Sovereignty at Bay: The Multinational Spread of U.S. Enterprises. New York: Basic Books.

Vernon, Raymond. 1977. Storm Over the Multinationals. Cambridge, Mass.: Harvard University Press.

Warner, Lloyd W., and Abegglen, James C. 1955. Occupational Mobility in American Business and Industry. Minneapolis, Minn.: University of Minnesota Press, pp. 95-114.

Yoshino, Michel. 1976. Japan's Multinational Enterprises. Cambridge, Mass.: Harvard University Press.

Yoshino, Michael Y. 1969. Japan's Managerial System: Tradition and Innovation. Cambridge, Mass.: M.I.T. Press.

Yoshino, M.Y. 1975. "Emerging Japanese Multinational Enterprises." In Ezra F. Vogel, Modern Japanese Organization and Decision-Making , Berkeley, Calif.: University of California Press.

8 Multinationals and the Communist World: A Comparative Study of American, European, and Japanese Multinationals in Eastern Europe and the U.S.S.R.
Joseph C. Miller

INTRODUCTION

One of the many controversial issues about multinational corporations (MNCs) is the process through which they adapt to the ever-changing regulations and other policy requirements of the home and host countries in which they operate. Several critics of the MNC (for example, Barnet and Mueller, 1975) have argued recently that these firms command sufficient political influence virtually to dictate the terms of the tax, investment, and other regulatory policies. Far from constraining MNC functions to serve the needs of broader public purposes, the adaptive process, according to this view, primarily consists of lobbying and other forms of political manipulation. The opposite position is taken by some defenders of MNC, who contend that the MNC is a passive victim of a bewildering and continually tightening web of bureaucratic demands. Caught in this net of governmental controls, the MNC is able to adapt only by good luck, evasion of the rules, or escape to some other country as a haven of freedom.

Arguments and evidence have been marshalled by both critics and defenders to prove that their view of adaptation by the MNC is correct. It seems fair to say, however, that neither side is persuasive simply because the evidence presented is incomplete, selected carefully to support the argued position. More objective, unbiased research is needed on MNCs' processes of adaptation.

Such research would also help fill an important gap in our understanding of government-business relationships. As Lindblom (1977) has recently observed, the interface between public policymaking and corporate adaptation has been largely ignored by research scholars. On the one hand, political scientists are interested mainly in political policies and administrative processes within governmental bodies; and, on the other, economists and business researchers concentrate on decision making in the corporation and the effects of regulation on the market. Neither group of researchers has spent much effort examining the interplay of negotiation, reaction and conflict between corporations and government bodies. This paper examines the processes of adaptation of Western MNCs to the strict and comprehensive policy requirements of the USSR and its six East European partners in the Council for Mutual Economic Assistance (CMEA).

NATURE AND PURPOSE OF THE STUDY

The empirical findings below are the result of comparative research on the adaptive processes of American, West European, and Japanese MNCs. Thus, the basic objective of the study is to compare the functioning of MNCs from these different countries as they adapt their organizational structures and corporate strategies to the regulations and policies of the Soviet Union and the six Eastern European countries (Bulgaria, Czechoslovakia, East Germany, Hungary, Poland, and Romania). Differences are hypothesized between the MNCs of the several Western countries and Japan based on the following:

1. Functional modes of operation and management styles may differ among three types of modes, as suggested by Barrett and Bass (1970).
2. Some of the home countries' (such as Japan and France) governments assist their MNCs in dealing with the host country to a much larger degree than other home countries (such as the United States).
3. A much larger percentage of the West European MNCs than U.S. or Japanese MNCs have long-established (that is, pre-World War II) relationships with the Soviet Union and the East European countries (as documented in studies by the ECE, 1973).
4. Closer geographic proximity may favor the West European MNCs over the U.S. and Japanese MNCs as they compete for joint venture and other cooperation contracts with the Soviet and East European state enterprises.
5. In so far as U.S. MNCs are perceived by the East Europeans or Soviets as being technologically more advanced than the other MNCs, the U.S. MNCs may have this advantage.

These underlying reasons will help explain some of the differences between the MNCs in their processes of adapting to the Soviet and East European policies, but they are given only as preliminary grounds for the comparative hypotheses.

Other, more complete explanations emerge from the executive interview data reported below.

The specific processes of adaptation that are analyzed for differences between MNCs are as follows:

1. Basic contractual framework. Typically, the form of the industrial cooperation agreement (or joint venture in Hungary or Romania) is negotiated between the MNC and the Eastern governmental agency and becomes the institutional framework within which the partners operate. Thus, the process of adaptation here occurs during the contract negotiation, and the result is to a large extent fixed for the life of cooperation venture. However, in some cases the contract is negotiated or extended into more complex mutual undertakings.

2. Transfer of MNC technology. In the simplest forms of cooperation agreements (such as a licence), the host country policies are satisfied by a once-for-all transfer of the technology. In the more complex, ongoing cooperation arrangements, however, the process of adaptation may entail required updating of the transferred technology, exchanges of information, and joint research and development.

3. Financing and payment. Confronted with hard currency shortages and growing balance of payments deficits, the East European countries are more anxious to obtain Western credits and to find means of repaying these loans through the sale of goods (jointly produced by the MNC and its Eastern partner) in the West. For the MNC, the process of adaptation requires an imaginative use of barter, buy-back financing, and (sometimes) use of soft currencies.

4. Operating authority or control. Of the seven host countries, only Hungary and Romania (and in a limited number of cases, Poland) permit any equity ownership by an outside firm, and this ownership is strictly confined to a minority interest. Thus, the MNC must find other grounds on which to base its need for operating authority or control, and the adaptive process of working together has resulted in an interesting variety of management contracts, operations checkpoints, and other forms of informal controls.

5. Product quality control. An especially important subcategory of operating authority is the adaptive process concerned with product quality controls. Western MNCs have generally had difficulties trying to achieve a level of product quality comparable to that in the West, and the process of adaptation has not been made easier on the MNC by the Eastern partner's insistence on obtaining advanced technologies and marketing the jointly-produced product in the West.

6. Marketing distribution. While some of the East European or Soviet state enterprises are able to match Western MNCs in product quality, virtually none of them has the experience or organization to distribute and market their products effectively. The result is that heavy demands are placed

on the partner MNC, particularly when the product is to be sold in Western markets as an increasing number of cooperation arrangements are attempting to do. MNCs must also face the prospect of increased competition in the latter case.

Other adaptive-process issues could be added to the above list, but the six issues outlined here are sufficiently well-defined and important to serve our needs in the analysis of the processes.

DATA SOURCES AND METHODS

The research findings in this study are based on samples of 110 U.S. MNCs from an estimated total of 250 U.S. firms operating in the host countries, 98 West European MNCs from an estimated total of 400 firms, and 14 Japanese MNCs from an estimated 60 firms. Preliminary work on the U.S. sample began late in 1974 with a letter questionnaire to 1068 companies, the names of which were suggested by the business press, chambers of commerce, and other private and public agencies. Direct responses from over 70 percent of these companies, aided by follow-up inquiries, suggested that an estimated 250 U.S. corporations had signed cooperation contracts or were actively engaged in Soviet or East European operations as of January 1, 1976. The remaining 818 companies were in most cases either simply engaged in trade with the USSR or East European countries or had expressed only some interest in setting up operations in these countries. Further examination of the active 250 firms led to the selection of 110 MNCs, which are in nearly all instances large corporations with extensive global operations, and in-depth interviews of executives were taken in each of these MNCs.

Identification of the sample of West European MNCs began in 1970 with the compilation by the ECE of data on individual MNCs and their cooperation contracts. Preliminary results were published in 1973 based on 202 projects and the experience of 50 West European MNCs whose executives were interviewed. Further data were collected in 1974 and 1975, nearly doubling the sample of companies (98 as of January 1, 1976), and the sample number of cooperation contracts analyzed was enlarged to 298. The ECE also has added more of a comparative dimension to this data base by including 25 and 27 Japanese and U.S. contracts, respectively.

Interview data from Japanese MNCs are more limited than information in our U.S. and West European samples, but the ECE sample and two recently-published surveys of Japanese MNCs in the USSR and Eastern Europe provide an adequate basis of comparison. The first of these two supplemental surveys (Stankowsky, 1974) focused on the experience of Japanese MNCs in the Soviet Union, Poland, Czechoslovakia, Romania, Bulgaria and Hungary during 1972-73. The second survey (Chung Sung-Beh, 1975) was limited to the Soviet Union, and it described the role of Japanese MNCs in ten cooperation projects.

ANALYSIS AND INTERPRETATION OF RESEARCH FINDINGS

The analysis that follows is subdivided into six sections, each referring to one of the processes of adaptation briefly identified above. Each adaptive process is a dependent variable, and the independent or explanatory variables hypothesized are classified as host-country policies, MNC strategies, and external or home-country policies. The underlying rationale of this framework (shown in table 8.1) is that the process of adaptation may be explained by pressures of host-country policies, the operational needs of the MNC, and policy demands of the home country.

Each of the independent variables in table 8.1 is defined below, and its hypothesized relationship to the dependent variable is discussed. Where it appears that the relationship is significant, comparisons are made between the American, West European, and Japanese MNCs. Thus, our objectives in this analysis are to identify variables that help to explain the processes of adaptation, suggest hypotheses for these relationships, and to compare the functional performance of the three groups of MNCs in the adaptive processes.

Basic Contractual Framework

Most researchers in the area of East-West industrial cooperation regard the form of the initial or basic contract as the most fundamental dependent variable describing the processes of adaptation by the Western MNC to the policies of the Soviet or East European host institutions. A list of various contract categories, ranging from a simple technical assistance contract to an equity joint venture, that are in common use between Western MNCs and Eastern bloc countries is given in this chapter's appendix. It should be emphasized that the form or specific contents of a contract are almost infinitely variable, and that elaborate combinations of licenses, know-how and subcontracting clauses, for example, are not uncommon in a single contract.

In its simple or complex form, the contract is a fundamental dependent variable describing the adaptive process for two major reasons. First, it embodies most (if not all) of the

Table 8.1. Hypothesized Relationships

Dependent Variables	Independent Variables		
	Host-Country Policies	MNC Strategies	External or Home-Country Policies
1. Contract	Planning Preference	Time-Horizon	Technological Status
2. Technology Transfer	Development Needs	Competitive Life-Cycle Position	Export Controls
3. Financing/Payment	Import-Export Policies	Debt/Equity Ratio	Loans & Guarantees
4. Operating Authority	Joint Venture Laws	Technological/Financial Leverage	Home-Host Country Agreements
5. Product Quality	Industrial Development	Trademark/Patent on Product	Product Complexity
6. Marketing Distribution	Export Policies	Global Marketing Organization	Service Needs of Product

important agreements that emerge from the months-long negotiations between the MNC and host country. The precontract
negotiations are in many cases the most comprehensive and
concentrated process of adaptation that the MNC will have to
undergo; since the Soviet and East European style is to include every conceivable detail in the contract, the parties must
work out compromises on a large agenda of issues requiring
months or even years of discussions. With few exceptions,
neither the MNC nor the host-country negotiating team ever
divulges much information about the adaptations as they occur
in the process of negotiations, but the final contract itself is
the result of the negotiations and from it we can infer a good
deal about this adaptive process.

The contract is rarely fixed or static after it has been
signed, however, as our more recent research indicates, and
the dynamics of its further development point to the second
reason for viewing it as a fundamental adaptive-process variable. Just as the original contract is a summary statement of
the adaptations and compromises that are negotiated, the second or third contracts (or protocols, which are extentions of
the basic contract) contain the results of adaptations that the
partners find useful in the course of their joint operations.
Not all of the operational conflicts are resolved in a protocol or
new contract - some lead to a dissolution of the cooperative
arrangement, some are arbitrated, and most are settled informally - but the important changes in the parties' relationships
are almost invariably reduced to writing in a contract. Such
important changes include new policies promulgated by the
host-government partner, increases in the prices of basic inputs, and provisions for new-product or marketing developments.

The first explanatory variable is the host-country policy
of preference for a particular type of cooperation. As shown
in tables 8.2a, 2b, and 2c, the Soviet Union appears to have a
strong preference for turnkey contracts, i.e. contracts for the
delivery of entire plants. The percentage of all Soviet contracts accounted for by turnkeys is 67.6 percent in the predominantly West European MNC sample (table 8.2a) and 66.1
percent in the U.S. MNC sample (table 8.2b) the corresponding percentages for Bulgaria are 42.9 percent and 27.3
percent, and for East Germany, 59.9 percent and 38.5 percent, respectively. No other type of contract has such an
apparently strong host-country preference, except perhaps
co-production/specialization with 47.3 percent of Hungary's
projects with West European MNCs.

Why do the USSR and, to a lesser extent, Bulgaria and
East Germany prefer turnkey contracts? No definite statement
of policy has been made by any of these countries, but business executives suggest that this preference is related to more
general policies that limit the interaction of Western managers,

Table 8.2. Types of Industrial Cooperation Contracts with Host Countries (%)

	Licenses and Know-How	Turnkeys	Co-Production	Subcontracting	Joint Ventures
a. West European MNCs (n = 98, no. of contracts = 298)					
U.S.S.R.	8.1%	67.6%	21.6%	2.7%	--
Bulgaria	35.8	42.9	14.2	7.1	--
Czechoslovakia	50.0	--	40.1	9.9	--
East Germany	--	59.9	40.1	--	--
Hungary	33.2	13.1	47.3	5.7	--
Poland	31.4	28.3	37.4	3.0	--
Romania	20.8	39.6	15.1	11.3	13.2
b. U.S. MNCs (n = 110, no. of contracts = 371)					
U.S.S.R.	25.0%	66.1%	5.4%	3.5%	--
Bulgaria	63.6	27.3	9.1	--	--
Czechoslovakia	63.6	30.3	6.1	--	--
East Germany	53.8	38.5	--	7.7	--
Hungary	57.1	14.3	14.3	5.7	8.6
Poland	56.8	29.7	8.1	5.4	--
Romania	49.0	43.4	3.8	--	3.8
c. Japanese MNCs (N = 14, no. of contracts = 22)					
U.S.S.R.	25.0	62.5	12.5	--	--
Bulgaria	50.0	50.0	--	--	--
Czechoslovakia	--	100.0	--	--	--
East Germany	--	--	--	--	--
Hungary	50.0	50.0	--	--	--
Poland	25.0	50.0	25.0	--	--
Romania	--	100.0	--	--	--

Sources: ECE (1973 and 1976); Holt, Marer and Miller (1976), Chung Sung-Beh (1975); and Stankowsky (1974).

engineers and other MNC personnel with their host country counterparts. Under a turnkey contract, the MNC constructs the plant, arranges for the delivery of machinery and equipment and provides the necessary know-how to see the plant operating on stream. Thereafter, the MNC is largely disengaged from the project, in contrast to the typically longer-term cooperation involved in co-production, subcontracting, or joint ventures. Soviet and East German policies are well known for their efforts to minimize Western participation or MNC interaction within the country, and the turnkey form of contract seems to fit well with such policies.

Comparing U.S. and West European MNCs with respect to contract form, we see no significant difference between the percentage of U.S. and West European turnkey contracts with the USSR (66.1 percent and 67.6 percent, respectively), but some differences with respect to East German and Bulgarian turnkey projects (38.5 percent vs. 59.9 percent and 27.3 percent vs. 42.9 percent) with U.S. MNCs because of the more recent arrival of the latter.

The Japanese MNCs display an interesting difference from the U.S. and West European MNCs (see table 8.2c). Contracts between Japanese MNCs and Soviet state enterprises follow virtually the same pattern as the U.S. and West European contracts, with 62.5 percent concentrated on turnkey agreements, but unlike the other MNCs the Japanese firms negotiated high percentages of turnkeys with more of the other host countries (50 percent in Poland, Bulgaria and Hungary, and 100 percent in Czechoslovakia and Romania). This strong propensity by the Japanese MNCs for turnkey contracts may be explained by greater language barriers, less experience in dealing with the East Europeans or Soviets, and global policies that have generally proceeded cautiously on long term foreign investments.

The second explanatory variable refers to the planning time horizon of the MNCs. In one sense, this variable reflects the MNC side of the first independent variable since both partners to a cooperation agreement have time-frame preferences based on planning objectives. The main distinction relates to the method of research: because nearly all interview information came from MNC executives (host-country officials were almost impossible to interview), many of the MNCs underlying reasons for longer-or shorter-term contracts were made explicit. We are therefore able to examine these underlying explanations in the context of technology transfer, financing, product quality and marketing (below), and time horizon becomes a less composite variable for the MNCs than the host countries.

Among the three groups of MNCs, the longest time horizon with respect to cooperation contracts was held by the West European MNCs and the shortest by the Japanese MNCs, with the U.S. MNCs in between and somewhat closer to the West

Europeans. The West European perspective in part reflects the generally earlier entry and long association of these companies in Eastern Europe and the USSR's. However, this variable looks to the future, and the U.S. MNCs indicated sophisticated planning processes and long-term objectives. The Japanese MNCs have similarly detailed long term planning procedures, but their stronger preference for turnkeys and other short-term contracts places them in a significantly distinctive category in this context.

The third explanatory variable describes the environmental state of the state of the technology being transferred through the contract. The hypothesis was that simpler technologies would explain licenses or other forms of short-term, simple contracts and that the more complex co-production or joint venture contracts would be based on more complex technologies. Some examples of cooperation contracts can certainly be found that support this hypothesis, but taking the sample as a whole no significant relationship was indicated. Some of the licensing and turnkey contracts involve complex technologies, as a result perhaps of the MNCs' unwillingness to make such technologies the subject of closer or longer-term cooperation, and some co-production contracts are based on simpler technologies, pointing to other, marketing or managerial reasons for the agreement. Technology is analyzed further in the next section, where it is treated as a dependent variable.

Transfer of MNC Technology

One of the adaptive processes of MNCs in Eastern Europe and the USSR that has received considerable attention by home country policy makers is the transfer of technology from the MNC to the host enterprise. Some members of the U.S. Congress and others are concerned that U.S. MNCs are selling the Soviets technology of national security or military importance. Indeed, there are legal constraints on the transfer of technology in most of the home countries, as discussed further below. Our first concern here is to identify technology transfer as an adaptive process, one that begins with the exchange of technical information in the negotiations stage and continues after the contract is signed with the application of Western know-how and equipment. The process may continue even after the partners have concluded their cooperative work together, with further learning and application; and our research indicates that it may also become a two-way transfer in some instances, to the technological gain of the MNC.

The host-country variable that explains part of the technology adaptation process is the set of industrialization objectives in the five-year development plan. These objectives are controlled to some degree by international specialization plans of the CMEA, but the national development plans have shown considerable independence in practice. For example, the CMEA plan was to have the Soviets specialize in computers, but Czechoslovakian and Hungarian scientists made several important developments in this field, and now all seven of the countries are engaged in some aspect of computer manufacture. Where a country has natural resources that the others lack, some technological specialization may follow, as e.g., the existence of petroleum in the USSR and Romania have led to the adaptation of Western extraction and pipeline technologies. In most cases, however, the type of technology and hence the adaptation process are related more, directly to the development plan objectives for setting up various types of plants.

Tables 8.3a, b and c present summaries of the types of technologies being transferred by U.S., West European and Japanese MNCs, respectively, through cooperation projects in each of the seven host countries. Among the host countries, the USSR receives the largest share of petroleum-extraction technology, with 86.7 percent of U.S. MNCs contracts in this sector. The Soviet Union also receives a large share (53.3 percent) of the construction technology by U.S. MNCs, a consequence of the high concentration of turnkey projects in that country. The only other type of technology concentrated in the USSR is food and agricultural technology (41.8 percent of West European and 42.8 percent of U.S. MNCs projects), reflecting the emphasis in recent Soviet five-year plans on raising agricultural productivity and food-producing capacity.

The second largest industrial country of the seven, Poland, is the recipient of substantial shares of MNC technologies in the chemical (19.6 percent of U.S. MNCs and 25.0 percent of West Europe MNCs), machinery (15.7 percent and 31.3 percent), and electronics (14.7 percent and 50.0 percent) sectors. Specialization is also seen in Romania, the third largest country, with its large shares in transport equipment (none by U.S. MNCs but 27.9 percent of the West European MNC total) and machinery (12.3 percent in the U.S. MNC sample and 25.3 percent West European MNC).

As suggested by the percentage figures given, there are differences between the U.S., West European and Japanese MNCs. The most basic difference is that only 13.4 percent of the West European MNCs technology-transfer contracts are with the USSR in contrast with 51.0 percent of U.S. MNCs contracts. When we adjust the percentage distributions of the other six countries for this major difference (which be explained in part by the Soviet preference for the larger-scale U.S. technology), the apparent discrepancies largely disappear. For example, machinery technology transferred from U.S. MNCs to Polish enterprises is 34.1 percent of all such transfers to the six East European countries, and 29.4 percent in the case of West European MNCs. Some small differences

Table 8.3.   Technology Transfer, By Project,
As a Percentage Distribution in Host Countries

a. U.S. MNCs (N = 110, no. of projects = 371)

	USSR	Bulgaria	Czech.	East Germany	Hungary	Poland	Romania	7-Country Total
Agriculture & Food	44.4%	11.1%	7.4%	3.7%	14.8%	14.8%	3.7%	100%
Textiles, Paper	30.4	4.3	21.7	8.7	8.7	8.7	17.4	100
Chemicals	48.5	8.2	7.2	3.1	5.2	19.6	8.2	100
Metals	59.1	--	4.5	--	4.5	22.7	9.1	100
Machinery	53.9	1.1	7.9	--	9.0	15.7	12.4	100
Electrical Equipment	50.8	6.2	3.1	--	10.8	15.4	13.8	100
Transport Equipment	33.3	4.2	4.2	8.3	12.5	16.7	20.8	100
Mining	86.7	--	--	--	--	--	13.3	100
Construction	53.3	6.7	6.7	8.9	6.6	8.9	8.8	100
Services	62.5	6.3	9.4	--	3.1	6.3	12.5	100

b.   West European MNCs (N = 98, no. of projects = 298)

	USSR	Bulgaria	Czech.	East Germany	Hungary	Poland	Romania	7-Country Total
Food & Agriculture	41.8%	16.7%	--	8.3%	8.3%	8.3%	16.6%	100%
Light Industry	15.0	--	--	--	55.0	20.0	10.0	100
Chemicals	25.0	3.8	3.8	1.9	25.0	25.0	15.5	100
Metals	31.8	--	--	--	4.5	45.5	18.2	100
Machinery	6.8	6.8	6.8	3.9	29.1	25.2	21.4	100
Electrical Equipment	6.1	3.0	3.0	--	39.4	36.4	12.1	100
Transport Equipment	4.7	2.3	9.3	2.3	37.2	16.3	27.9	100
Services	7.7	7.7	--	--	23.0	30.8	30.8	100

c.   Japanese MNCs (n = 14, no. of projects = 22)

	USSR	Bulgaria	Czech.	East Germany	Hungary	Poland	Romania	7-Country Total
Light Industry	33.3%	--	--	--	33.3%	33.3%	--	100
Chemicals	50.0	--	30.0	--	--	--	20.0	100
Metals	25.0	25.0	--	--	--	50.0	--	100
Electrical Equipment	--	--	--	--	50.0	50.0	--	100
Transport Equipment	50.0	--	50.0	--	--	--	--	100
Services	--	100.0	--	--	--	--	--	100

Sources: See table 8.2.

are seen, but they are not very significant. Comparisons with the sample of Japanese MNCs reveal one large difference: there are no technology transfers in the agricultural and food equipment industries. This difference is probably more apparent than real, however, unless the smaller scale of Japanese agriculture is an important factor.

The second explanatory variable is the MNC executives' perception of the lifecycle and competitive position of the technologies being transferred. The hypothesis was that the adaptive process of technology transfer would be more readily agreed to and more quickly accomplished in the cooperative project, the more mature the technology was in its life cycle and the larger the number of (Western) competitors it had. In the opposite extreme, a new technology that enjoys a highly advantageous competitive position is not likely to be transferred because its owner will want to exploit its advantages in Western markets before sharing it with an Eastern enterprise. Obviously none of the technologies examined are in the latter category since they are all being transferred through the cooperation project. However, the degree to which the technology is fully transferred can be estimated by the duration and complexity of the contract and by the described use of the technology. For example, a low-level transfer is indicated by a simple and short term licensing agreement under which the use of the technology is limited to a small number of applications. The technology hypothesized to be the subject of this type of agreement is at an early life-cycle stage, virtually unmatched by competitors. A more complete transfer is seen in a co-production or joint venture agreement in which the technology uses are extensive. Our hypothesis suggests that the latter will be a mature technology with numerous Western competitors.

The sample data provide some support for the hypothesized relationship, but the results are rather inconclusive. One source of difficulty may be the fact that many of the cooperation projects are developing rapidly from initial uncomplicated arrangements to ones of greater complexity and wider uses of technology. A more meaningful test of the hypothesis may be possible only after more of the projects ripen into full development.

The third variable that helps explain the technology transfer process is the environmental variable describing home-country laws that limit the export of certain types of technologies. The U.S. federal regulations requiring technology licenses (that is, government permits) are the best known of these laws, although the West European countries and Japan also have a variety of formal or informal controls. Recognizing that most technologies are available from several sources in the industrialized world, policy makers in the NATO countries have established a coordinating agency to oversee matters of military concern.

While technology-export controls probably are effective, their effect is almost always an absolute prohibition which cannot be observed in a sample of operating (and, therefore, governmentally-sanctioned) projects. Aside from a few cases in which permission to export the technology was first denied and later approved, there is little that can be said about the process of technology adaptation where a flat prohibition remains as it does on direct military applications, advanced computer hardware, etc. Our conclusion on this environmental variable is therefore similar to that on the MNC-related variable: a longer-term, more comprehensive appraisal is needed in testing its significance.

Financing and Payment

Although the combination of financing and payment creates a complicated dependent variable, the linkage between the two in many Soviet/East European projects requires that we consider them together. Our analysis of these cooperative arrangements indicates that: a) a high proportion of them are financed through counter-purchase agreements, under which the MNC buys products (not necessarily those of the joint project) from the host country; b) the Eastern partner often undertakes such arrangements to enlarge its hard-currency export capability; and c) a significant share of the MNCs contribution consists of intangible assets (such as patents, know-how and trademarks) and services (such as engineering, managerial and marketing know-how). Thus, the financing/payment variable suggested should indicate the number of counter-purchase agreements each weighted by the dollar value of such purchases relative to the total value of the contract.

The host-country variable is the balance of payments (current plus capital accounts) position of each country contemporaneous with (and expected in the immediate future of) the life of the project. Tables 8.4 and 8.5 present the available estimates of this independent variable, the trade balances (exports minus imports) and hard-currency debt of the host countries with West Europe, the United States, Japan and other Western developed countries. Our hypothesis is that the host countries with the larger hard-currency debts and trade balances are also the countries with the most counter-purchase processes of adaptation in their cooperation contracts. The underlying rationale is that the host country becomes less able to secure financing as its trade deficit and debt increase, hence policy demand shift more to counter-purchase financing as a substitute.

The results provide some support for this hypothesis, but a strong relationship is not indicated. A rank order of the host countries, from highest trade deficit and debt to the

Table 8.4. Soviet and Eastern European Balances of Trade
With the Developed West, 1970-75
(Millions of U.S. Dollars)

	1970	1971	1972	1973	1974	1975
USSR	-514	-303	-1356	-1748	-912	-6281
Bulgaria	-64	-53	-39	-77	-525	-841
Czechoslovakia	-134	-146	-135	-247	-392	-578
East Germany	-292	-281	-523	-820	-894	-1044
Hungary	-65	-241	-112	-50	-641	-747
Poland	61	24	-375	-1368	-2368	-3050
Romania	-206	-146	-217	-248	-534	-511

Sources: Farrell and Ericson (1976); Zoeter (1977).

Table 8.5. Eastern European Countries:
Hard Currency Debt at Year End
(Billions of U.S. Dollars)

	1970	1973	1974	1975	1976
Bulgaria	0.7	0.8	1.2	1.8	2.3
Czechoslovakia	0.3	0.8	1.1	1.5	2.1
East Germany	1.0	2.1	2.8	3.8	4.9
Hungary	0.6	0.9	1.5	2.1	2.8
Poland	0.8	1.9	3.9	6.9	10.2
Romania	1.2	2.0	2.6	3.0	3.3
Total Debt	4.6	8.5	13.1	19.1	25.6

Source: Zoeter (1977).

lowest, suggests that Poland, followed by East Germany, the
USSR, Bulgaria, Czechoslovakia, Romania and Hungary engage
in the highest to the lowest counter-purchase financing. East
Germany and the Soviet Union are exceptions, as a result of
the special relationship of the former with West Germany and
the large reserves (including gold) of the latter. Also, the
high debt positions of Poland and Romania (third, after East
Germany) are explained in part by the fact that these two
countries are the only ones among the East European six that
have received U.S.-government guaranteed credits (further
discussed, below).
     On the MNC side, the explanatory variable is the cor-
porate debt/equity ratio. The rationale for this variable is

similar to the host-country variable: the higher the long-term debt position of the MNC, the more pressure it feels to accede to a counter-purchase arrangement. Conversely, MNCs with lower debt/equity ratios are better able to obtain conventional financing, either internally or through banks, and thus enter into fewer of the counter-purchase agreements. However, our tentative results show this variable to be less significant than the host-country variable, suggesting that: a) host-country demands and policies are more important in determining the adaptive process of financing and payment; and b) considerations affecting the MNC adaptation are more complex than indicated by the debt/equity ratio.

The third independent variable is the policy of the home government with respect to the guaranteeing of credits for co-operative projects. As shown in table 8.6, the West European governments have extended a much larger share (79.9 percent) of the publicly-guaranteed credits to the Eastern European countries than either Japan (7.4 percent) or the United States (1.7 percent). Such credit has undoubtedly had an important effect in encouraging the growth of contracts between MNCs and the host-country enterprises, but it fails to explain the large influx of U.S. MNCs since 1972 with or without counter-purchase financing. U.S. MNCs have obviously had at their command a host of other financial resources, including internally-generally capital, private bank credits and a willingness to use barter and counter-purchase financing.

Operating Control or Authority

In one sense a comprehensive set of processes, the dependent variable describing the degree of operating authority or control exercised by the MNC, is a process of adaptation central to the administrative function. We measure this variable as the percentage of equity ownership held by the Western partner in a joint venture or, in other types of cooperation contracts, the degree of MNC participation in the fundamental decisions of the agreement. The latter method of measurement is in part the subjective perception of the Western executives, but it corresponds rather closely to the complexity of the contract (table 8.2), from a simple licence in which the MNC has minimal control or authority to a co-production agreement in which MNC control can be very extensive.

As the host-country explanatory variable, the statutory (or constitutional) authorization for equity joint ventures is a variable of limited usefulness. Only three of the host countries, Hungary, Poland and Romania, permit joint ventures, and all four of the other countries in effect prohibit such forms of cooperative contracts. Thus, except for a ranking of the three (from the most open to joint ventures, Hungary, to

Table 8.6.   Government-Guaranteed Credits to the East European
Countries (end of 1975)
(Millions of U.S. Dollars)

	Total	Bulgaria	Czech.	East Germany	Hungary	Poland	Romania
West Germany	1380	110	240	(n.a)	50	600	380
France	2365	300	155	390	40	1250	230
U.K.	2201	51	70	75	70	1700	235
Italy	670	70	59	36	40	310	155
Austria	1246	20	190	290	7	700	39
Sweden	418	35	19	84	1	250	29
Japan	768	75	55	57	1	400	180
U.S.	181	0	0	0	0	122	59
Other	1139	61	110	130	32	700	106
Total	10368	717	898	1062	241	6032	1413

Source: East-West Markets (September 20, 1976 and October 4, 1976).

181

the least, Poland), the explanatory variable is dichotomous. Further analysis of the host-country legal environment might reveal movements in the four countries toward the establishment of joint venture laws, but in the absence of such information we conclude that this variable is not significant.

A more finely discriminating explanatory variable is the perceptions of MNC executives as to their firms' technological and financial leverage in achieving operating authority. As expected, this variable is significant in "explaining" not only the equity-based authority in joint ventures but also the degree of MNC participation in basic decisions of the cooperative project. When we compare U.S., West European and Japanese MNCs, however, differences are not indicated. Rather, it appears that in all these groups of MNCs, the willingness to use technological or financial leverage as a means of securing control varies rather widely among corporations.

The third, external variable refers to intergovernmental agreements between the home and host countries for the promotion of enterprise cooperation. Examples include the West German and French agreements with a number of the Eastern countries, under which financial and scientific support is pledged. The U.S. "detente agreements" with the USSR are also agreements of this type, but we do not include the several scientific and technical agreements that have followed since they are between U.S. corporations and Soviet state agencies. The rationale of the hypothesis linking this variable with the dependent variable is that home host-country support and encouragement will strengthen the position of the MNC. Our results provide some support for the hypothesis and point to inter-MNC differences: the West European MNCs capitalize on their home-government support to realize a somewhat higher degree of operating authority, especially in co-production and joint venture contracts.

PRODUCT QUALITY CONTROL

The adaptive process of developing adequate product quality control is a variable based on the MNC executives' perception of the success or failure of the cooperative project in achieving such quality control. In general, the more problems the executives saw in the area of product quality, the less successful was the project rated. One research problem that emerged, therefore, was the intervening effect of the length of time during which the partners had been working together. In most cases, problems of product quality were solved within the first two or three years of the contract. Thus, some of the more recent projects with U.S. or Japanese MNCs may appear less successful than the longer-established projects with West European MNCs.

The level of industrial development of each of the seven host countries is hypothesized to explain a significant part of the variation in product-quality control. In general, one expects projects in the less-industrialized countries (Bulgaria and Romania) to have more problems of product quality than projects in the more-industrialized countries (Poland and East Germany). However, the results show no significant relationship, for the following reasons: 1) the level of industrial development does not distinguish sharply between most of the countries; and 2) this independent variable is too aggregative to be useful in explaining project variations. A better (but, unfortunately unavailable) host-country variable would measure intercountry differences at the disaggregated industry or product level.

The MNC-related variable, the MNC patent or trademark policy, is considerably more useful. Where the ouput of a project is sold under the MNC-partner's trademark or patent, we hypothesize that the success of the project in achieving adequate product quality is high. Conversely, the MNC executive is less concerned with product quality and willing to accept a less than adequate quality control in those projects in which the MNC trademark or patent is not involved. This relationship appears to exist across the three groups of MNCs, with little difference between U.S., West European, and Japanese MNCs. A more likely distinguishing factor is the product type or competition in world markets', which points to the greater or lesser use of trademarks or patents in some industries.

Some of the interproduct differences are captured in the external explanatory variable, the degree of technical complexity of the product type. The more complex the product, the more likely it is, we hypothesize, that problems of product quality control will arise. The research results provide some examples of projects that support this hypothesis, but overall this variable is not significant. One explanation for the lack of significant association is the high concentration of technically-complex products makes it difficult to distinguish among degrees of complexity. Also, the very complexity of the product seems to be related to greater efforts by both partners to solve quality-control problems.

Marketing Distribution

Since our main concern is with the ability of the cooperative project to market its products in markets outside the host countries, we measure this adaptive-process variable by the percentage share of the project's sales or output that are exported to Western and Third-World markets. At best, this measure is an approximation, since data on project sales are not available and the MNC executives could only estimate it. National data on exports of particular product-classes are of some value, but are usually too aggregative.

The host country explanatory variable describes the relative importance that policy makers attach to the encouragement of exports. Ideally, this variable would be based on a rank-ordering of specific industries, from the most emphasized to the least in export promotion policies. However, such industry- (or product-) specific policies are difficult to infer from the development plans or actual export performance data. The results of this variable are therefore not significant.

On the MNC side, the explanatory variable measures the global marketing organization of the corporation as the ratio of foreign to home sales of the MNC. We hypothesized that the cooperation project would have a higher share of Western and Third-World sales, the more extensive the global marketing capabilities are of the MNC. This relationship proved to be significant, and, not surprisingly, the Japanese MNCs (followed by the U.S. MNCs, and lastly the West European MNCs) are seen to have more extensive global marketing organizations. The implications of this finding are that the East Europeans may favor the Japanese MNCs, when all other factors are equal, to help them develop much needed export capabilities.

Finally, the external variable refers to the after-sales service needs of each product, and it is not significantly related to the project's export sales. Some products conformed to the hypothesis that the cooperation project would not be able to export products that require large investments in after-sales service, but in other cases the marketing help of the MNC provided the needed after-sales support and the project was a strong exporter.

CONCLUSIONS

Several interesting conclusions emerge from the above analysis of adaptive processes. First and most basic, the MNCs are neither passive victims nor powerful manipulators of the host-country policies. Rather, they accept to a very high degree a comprehensive set of conditions prerequisite to their entry, and pursue strategies of adaptation to these conditions through joint-management decisions on operational matters of technology, financing and marketing. The processes of adaptation are therefore more realistically seen as the mutual accommodation of the MNC and its partner state-enterprise to the changing needs of their cooperative venture.

Second, the two specific processes of adaptation that provide the MNC and its Eastern partner with apparently the most opportunities for adaptation are the contract negotiation and the decisions that define operational authority. As shown above, the process of contract negotiation in the USSR or the East European countries is typically very detailed and comprehensive. Knowing that most of the terms of the agreement will be included in the contract and few, if any deviations from the contract will be permitted, executives of MNCs justifiably view the negotiations as a critical stage at which to achieve desired modifications or adaptations. Once the contract is signed and the partners are working, some problems unforeseen during negotiations arise. To solve these problems and often to use the opportunity as a means of winning additional authority in the on-going venture, either partner will apply a point of advantage – control of inputs, technology, financing, or management know-how.

The third conclusion is actually a set of conclusions, each referring to the hypotheses set forth to explain the adaptive processes by host-country, MNC and home-country (or external) variables. Our tentative findings here indicate the following: a) the contractual framework appears most closely associated to both host-country preferences and MNC planning objectives; b) the type of MNC technology being transferred seems to be explained largely by host-country plans for industrialization; c) the degree of operating authority on the part of the MNC in a cooperative venture depends on the MNC executives' perception of their company's financial or technological leverage, and on the number and scope of umbrella agreements between the governments of their home country and the host country; d) product-quality problems are much more likely to occur in those cooperation projects in which the MNC trademark is being used; e) and finally, the ability of a cooperative venture to export its products to Western or Third World markets depends importantly on the strength of the MNC's global marketing organization.

The remaining hypotheses are not adequately supported by the information developed in this research. However, further refinement and testing seems well warranted, especially with respect to the hypotheses on financing and payment and marketing distribution. One promising approach to these questions would seem to be the use of industry-level data, as opposed to either national aggregates or micro-firm data, to measure, for example, the host-country ranking of export products.

Finally, the comparisons between Japanese, West European and U.S. MNCs yield interesting results. The greatest differences are seen in the preference for types of contract (table 8.2), with the Japanese MNCs favoring turnkey contracts with the East European enterprises. Some differences are also observed in the types of technology being transferred (table 8.3), although the contrasts are not as great. The global marketing networks of the MNCs reveal some differences, with the Japanese leading the U.S. and West European MNCs in the impact of this variable on export sales outside the CMEA countries.

APPENDIX: CATEGORIES OF COOPERATION CONTRACTS

1. Know-how or technical assistance contracts.
2. Licenses, with payment in cash, royalties, or resultant products.
3. Subcontracting, by the MNC in the host country, refers to contracts under which the MNC provides technical (construction) know-how and machinery, equipment and parts, but does not have significant on-site installation/ supervision responsibilities.
4. Turnkey contracts includes all agreements under which the MNC as supplies has significant on-site installation or supervision responsibilities.
5. In a co-production contract each partner specializes either in the production of parts of a product that is assembled by one or both partners, or in the production of a limited number of finished products that are exchanged to complete each partner's range of products.
6. Joint venture provides for the co-ownership of capital, co-management, and the sharing of risk and profit.

Sources: ECE (1973), Holt, Marer and Miller (1976); McMillan and St. Charles (1974).

REFERENCES

Economic Commission for Europe. 1973. Analytical Report on Industrial Cooperation Among ECE Countries. Geneva: ECE.

Barnet, Richard J., and Mueller, Robert E. 1975. Global Reach: The Power of the Multinational Corporations. New York: Simon and Schuster.

Barrett, Gerald V., and Bass, Bernard M. 1970. "Comparative Surveys of Managerial Attitudes and Behavior." In Comparative Management. ed. J. Boddewyn. New York University.

Bolz, Klaus, and Poletz, Peter. 1974. Erfahrungen aus der Ost-West Kooperation. Hamburg: Verlag Weltarchiv.

Chung Shung-Beh. 1975. "Japanese-Soviet Economic Relations." Le Courier des Pays de l'Est, no. 183 (March): 3-29.

Farrell, John T., and Ericson, Paul. 1976. "Soviet Trade and Payments with the West." In Soviet Economy in a New Perspective, A Compendium of Papers submitted to the Joint Economic Committee. Washington: U.S. Government Printing Office.

Holt, John B., Marer, Paul, and Miller, Joseph C. 1976. East-West Industrial Cooperation: The U.S. Perspective. Mimeographed. Washington: U.S. Dept. of Commerce, Bureau of East-West Trade.

Lindblom, Charles. 1977. Politics and Markets. New York: Basic Books.

McMillan, Carl H., and St. Charles, D. P. 1974. Joint Ventures in Eastern Europe: A Three-Country Comparison. Montreal: C. D. Howe Research Institute.

Marer, Paul, and Miller, Joseph C. 1977. "U.S. Participation in East-West Industrial Cooperation Agreements," Journal of International Business Studies 8 (Fall-Winter): 17-29.

Stankowsky, Jan. 1974. "Japanese Economic Relations with the U.S.S.R. and Eastern Europe." In Japan in der Weltwirtschaft, ed. A. Lampe. Vienna: Wiener Institut fuer Internationale Wirtschaftsvergleiche.

U.S. Congress, Subcommittee on International Security and Scientific Affairs of the Committee on International Relations, House of Representatives. 1977. Technology Transfer and Scientific Cooperation Between the United States and the Soviet Union. Washington: U.S. Government Printing Office.

Economic Commission for Europe. 1976. A Statistical Outline of Recent Trends in Industrial Cooperation. Mimeographed, restricted. Geneva: ECE.

Wilczynski, Jozef. 1974. Technology in COMECON. London: MacMillan.

Wolf, Thomas, A. 1973. U.S. East-West Trade Policy. Boston: Lexington.

Zoeter, Joan C. 1977. "Eastern Europe: The Growing Hard Currency Debt." In East European Economics Post Helsinki: A Compendium of Studies Submitted to the Joint Economic Committee, U.S. Congress. Washington: U.S. Government Printing Office.

9 A Model of Market Opportunity Expropriation in State-Controlled Economies: A Case of the Shipping Industry
Robert G. Vambery

INTRODUCTION

During the 1960s, analysts of multinational corporate behavior viewed the MNCs as positive and constructive agents of international economic development. The MNCs were lauded for being instrumental in the transfers of much needed capital, high technology, and advanced management methods. They were credited with providing employment, paying local taxes, and generating economic, social, and cultural advancements for host countries. Many analysts also claimed that most of these benefits were achieved with little or no harm to the MNCs' parent countries. Through their multinational involvement the MNCs' parent companies derived sales growth, market-share protection, and increased income. Furthermore, the activities of the MNCs outside the parent country's national borders resulted in a return stream of earnings through the repatriation of profits.

The international business literature of the 1970s altered this favorable interpretation of MNC impact. Instead, it focused on the inadequacy of the multinational corporations' contributions to host countries, their disruptive effects on host-country societies and government procedures, and on their manipulative and malintentioned activities.

The earlier calls for attracting more and more direct investment from abroad and encouraging additional incentives to attract further participation by MNCs, as means of accelerating the economic development of host countries, were replaced in part by an emphasis of the urgency of establishing codes of conduct for multinational corporations and the desirability of economically squeezing multinational corporations in order to create a new economic world order more rapidly. In discussions of the new economic world order, the reasonable expectations of profit-oriented multinational corporations were pushed out of the forefront of thinking. The special, and sometimes unreasonable, economic demands of host countries came to occupy the center of attention.

During what remains of the 1970s and in the early years of the 1980s, more in-depth analysis needs to be made of the impact of multinational corporations on the industrialized nation-states, especially the countries from which specific multinational firms emerged. The examination should not focus on issues just from corporate viewpoints but also from the viewpoints of the public interests of industrialized countries, especially the parent country. The need arises from what appear to be some counterproductive effects of MNCs on their countries of origin.

First, multinational corporations often favor foreign production over exportation. This foreign production orientation can shift most of the international economic activities outside the country of the parent company. Though multinational corporation sales figures resulting from manufacturing and sales abroad are impressive, the foreign activities may provide only very limited income for the home nation. The primary benefits may be in the form of repatriated earnings and the contributions these earnings make toward the improvement of the parent country's balance of payments position. However, the advantages for the nation would be substantially greater if the foreign sales were the results of domestic production and exportation rather than foreign production and foreign sales.

A second example of counterproductive impacts of MNCs is offered by nonequity methods of participation in multinational business. Nonequity methods include licenses, royalty arrangements, and management contracts, all of which can generate revenues that are preferable to no income but do appear to give away substantial portions of the capital gains and growth opportunities that can be realized through leveraged direct investments in foreign countries.

Specifically, the Communist Bloc has frequently managed to capture the best of all worlds in its business relationships with Western multinational corporations. Generally, the Communist countries either buy or license equipment, technology, and know-how and tend to enter into short-term rather than long-term relationships. These relationships result in major productive synergistic effects for the Communist countries, whereas they simply provide short-term income benefits for industrialized country corporations. The transactions usually do not involve equity investments or equity rights. Moreover, often few or no follow-up contracts result from the important initial concessions made by the Western corporations to their Communist trading partners. Although the annual reports of individual multinational corporations are improved by these

East-West business associations, they provide minor benefits for Western nations in comparison with the economic value provided to the Communist Bloc countries. Indeed, developing countries also try to follow this model by not allowing or severely restricting equity ownership by MNCs and simply milking the industrialized country corporations of the most productive contributions they have to make. These contributions consist of technology and know-how transferred in exchange for relatively small fees, such as three to six percent royalties on gross sales. The tremendous equity value growth opportunities of direct ownership are thus denied to the industrialized corporations and indirectly to the Western nations.

Prices charged for technology sales present a third problem area. Multinational corporations and industrialized country corporations frequently observe that their income from product sales to foreigners are marginal even when high technology goods are involved. Therefore, if opportunities arise to sell technological capabilities and designs, they may feel that whatever additional profits can be generated through the sale of these technologies are better than the present low level of profits. The outcome of this thinking is that the resulting incremental income derived is much smaller than the macroeconomic value of the technology being sold. The pricing of industrialized country technology is not strictly a corporate question. Technology development costs are largely borne by the public at large not only by the company that holds patents to specific inventions. The tax deductibility of research and development costs, the government financing of specific R and D efforts, and, beyond, the vast cost of educating and training highly skilled people who conduct research are all borne by the nation rather than the corporation. Therefore, the nation, not only the corporation, should derive substantial benefits from the eventual sale of technologies to foreigners. The MNCs are expected to be and should be instruments in this process.

COMPETING AGAINST STATE POWER

The increased influence of state owned corporations in transnational shipping presents major threats to established shipping companies whose survival depends upon their ability to earn profits in the competitive international shipping markets. Similar threats are presented to these companies by the presence of government agencies and ministries which negotiate with one aggressive voice in the interest of all the shipping lines of their nations.

The first important illustration of these threats arises from the destructive price cutting practices of COMECON fleets

as well as the stringent import/export cargo reservation practices from which COMECON fleets benefit.

The second illustration comes from the threat the release
of the UNCTAD Code of Conduct for Liner Conferences may
present to established operators who derive large shares of
their revenues from third-country trades.

Because the political and national economic implications of
these two issues are as great as their commercial implications,
associations of ship owners vigorously urge shippers' groups
to joint them in mobilizing the support of their respective governments in fighting the new threats.

The actual threats are difficult to quantify but the causes
of the arising fears can be readily identified.

The COMECON Case

On the COMECON issue two factors cause fears: a) Soviet
merchant marine fleets are being expanded much more rapidly
than may be justified by the Soviet's cargo carrying needs.
Their general cargo liner capacity is already about four times
over the capacity needed and continues to grow; and b) much
of the excess capacity is placed at the disposal of third-country traders at low rates which are termed "noncommercial" by
many liner conference members (CEJSA, 1977).

Mere arguments emphasizing that the low rates are possible because the Soviet Government extends heavy subsidies
to its merchant marine sector are not very effective, since
many other governments also provide far-reaching capital and
operating subsidies to their maritime industries.   However,
rates that are 35 percent to 45 percent below prevailing liner
conference tariffs are probably marginal, rather than fully
distributed, cost based. Waging effective "commercial" competition against such "dumping rates" may be nearly impossible.

Furthermore, the Soviets follow usual unfair competition
practices.   While they can offer services to shippers of many
countries, foreign flag lines commonly are not permitted to
compete for contracts to carry Soviet cargos.   On the supply
side, the Soviets benefit from a rather free, international competition environment, while on the demand side they practice
exclusion and monopolism.

The Soviets show willingness to discontinue their predatory pricing only in exchange for large, guaranteed shares of
the traffic normally carried by the established steamship
lines.   Even in bilateral trades where the liners of each country ought to be able to compete for a fair share of the traffic,
the Soviets move to capture the overwhelming portion of the
cargoes.   Of the traffic moving between the Netherlands and
the USSR, for example, in 1976 Soviet vessels carried 88 percent of the import and 78 percent of the export cargos while

the Dutch were able to capture only 1.5 percent and .5 percent respectively (United Nations, 1977).

The discussions concerning COMECON fleets can at times be unfair to certain shipping lines. Currently the criticism of the behavior of Soviet lines is almost automatically extended to the lines of all communist countries. However, top officials of the Polish Ocean Lines, for example, vigorously reject the charges of "non-commercial" behavior and point to POL's friendly participation in or cooperation with some seventeen conferences. Moreover, POL claims that even on routes where conference membership is not likely in the near future, POL avoids freight rate wars and attempts to behave in the manner of the tolerated outsider (Bejgar, 1976).

Shippers' groups are cognizant of these facts but are not likely to join an anti-COMECON fleet movement quickly. Actual and latent threats of low COMECON fleet rates can be effective against the cartel power of conferences. Therefore, it is to some degree in the interest of shippers to help maintain the downward pressure on freight rates exerted by COMECON government-controlled liner companies.

The UNCTAD Code Case

The UNCTAD Code of Behavior for Liner Conferences is far from a perfect document, yet many liner conference members feel that they could live with the Code, at least on a trial basis.

One economic provision of the Code, however, goes radically against the principles of open competition in international maritime transportation. Though the Code is subject to several interpretations, it appears to give statutory right for the carriage of up to 40 percent of the trade between two countries to the conference liners of each of the two countries. Only the remaining 20 percent of cargos would be left for third-country shippers.

The 40-40-20 formula of course is not compulsory. But it does give strong credibility to cargo reservation arrangements in which national flag carriers are favored in the assignment of cargos to conference lines. In effect the market is expropriated binationally, irrespective of competitive economics or the capital investment or operating cost efficiencies of specific national flag conference line companies.

TRANSNATIONAL SHIPPING INDUSTRY STRUCTURE

Corporations active in the shipping industry can be classified into two categories: 1) those that perform shipping tasks within the borders of their country; and 2) those that perform shipping tasks that cross national borders. The first type of corporation may be called "domestic shipping corporation" while the second may be called "transnational shipping corporation."

The preceding classification offers an "activity-" rather than "ownership-" oriented definition. It is a very broad definition which can be useful, because it specifies that any shipping corporation involved in moving goods and commodities across one or more national border is automatically a member of the group of the "transnationals."

The difficulty of the defining process, however, immediately becomes evident because the bisectional definition does not yield a clear, mutually exclusive division of companies into two groups. Some domestic shippers are also transnationals while some transnational corporations are involved in domestic shipping. It is appropriate to identify "overlapping" or "conflicting" conditions: a) foreign-based transnationals providing domestic point to domestic point services; and b) domestic-based shipping corporations providing domestic point to foreign destination point services.

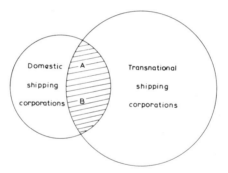

Fig. 9.1.   The plurality of activity structure
in the shipping sector

Conflict No. 1.   Companies involved in moving cargos from domestic sources to domestic destinations may also be involved in the transport of imports and exports. The import/export services can be separately or jointly operated with domestic services. No necessary relationship exists between domestic tonnages and import/export tonnages, nor do revenues from sales of domestic transport services need to exceed revenues from the sale of import/export transport services.

Conflict Resolution: Under the same corporate name or under several names this company functions both as a domestic and as a transnational corporation. Though examinations of the company's operations and finances are complicated by joint control and management arrangements, it is possible to separate the transnational "activities" from the domestic and to include the transnational portion of the firm in studies of transnational corporation behavior.

Conflict No. 2. A shipping company may be strictly domestic under the "activities" definition (it moves cargos only within one country's borders) but be owned or controlled by a foreign corporation.
Conflict Resolution: This company could be considered a domestic firm from an operational viewpoint but would qualify as a transnational, because its owners or managers are exercising control over its activities and are deriving benefits from it across national borders, that is, transnationally.

Conflict No. 3. The "activities-" based definition presents a dilemma in differentiating between companies involved in international shipping but having local versus foreign nationalities: A company owned and operated by nationals of a country qualifies for the "transnational shipping corporation" designation, because it moves cargos for the country's importers and exporters and also provides trade services for third countries. A second company may be servicing the same shipping needs but be under the ownership and management of citizens of another country.
Conflict Resolution: While both of these corporations are "transnationals," the first may be called a "national transnational shipping corporation" or alternately a "domestic transnational shipping corporation," while the second would be referred to as a "foreign transnational shipping corporation." The treatment afforded to these two types of transnationals by a country's government may be nondiscriminatory or it may be very different depending on whether the firm is a "domestic" or "foreign" transnational corporation.

There are three more types of corporations which should be included in formulating policies for the control of transnational shipping companies.

First, certain shipping operations are conducted through joint-venture arrangements among corporations and/or governments of two or more nations. Whether the "activities" of the joint-venture corporations are domestic or transnational, the multinationality of the arrangements puts the companies into the "transnational" category. This form of the "transnational shipping corporation" represents one of the simplest cases, because it is an instance of the commonly accepted "ownership-" based classification of corporations.

Second, vertically integrated transnational corporations at times create or acquire transnational shipping subsidiaries operated, mostly or exclusively, to service the raw material transport and semi-finished or finished product distribution needs of the parent companies. The purposes of possessing shipping subsidiaries may include: a) lowering of transportation and distribution costs; b) assuring the certain availability of carrying capacity when needed; and c) gaining or maintaining a substantial advantage over competitors through superior or exclusive access to specialized transport capabilities.

Third, conglomerate corporations at times acquire or create transnational shipping branches for investment or financial purposes rather than in order to service the transport needs of the parent company or the requirements of extraction or production oriented sister companies. Developing countries may have a special need to monitor the fate of such financially oriented companies because their assets and ownership are subject to international manipulation whose aims are not closely related to shipping needs. As a result, the availability and the costs of services normally offered by conglomerate controlled transnational shipping companies can be abruptly altered in ways adverse to the users of the services.

POLICY OPTIONS FOR HOST COUNTRIES

Policy options for host countries regarding the role that they assign to transnational shipping corporations and the degree to which they allow foreign based transnational shipping corporations to participate in their transportation sectors, will primarily depend on the intentions and capabilities of each country to be self-sufficient.

Policy Alternatives

1. Maximization of direct data ownership and control of both the domestic and transnational shipping activities of the nation. This first alternative is oriented toward a national government-owned shipping industry which hopes to derive benefits whenever possible from the many-sided activities of transnational shipping. The activities may include ship building and repair, port construction, port expansion, port upgrading, training of maritime personnel, training of managers, operation of representative and agent offices both domestically and abroad, and partially or completely financing equipment purchases and supporting facilities. Under the leadership and control of the government, this policy aims to maximize the GNP impact and employment benefits of the nation's existing and growing domestic and international transport sectors.

The emphasis of self-reliance can lead to the balance of payment benefits of import substitution. The existence of transport capabilities large enough to achieve self-sufficiency is likely to also result in the periodic presence of excess capacity which may be placed in the service of foreign accounts to generate additional foreign exchange earnings and to improve the nation's balance of payments position.

Self-sufficiency oriented policies will have considerable validity if the policy makers can comfortably assume that the large amounts of capital needed for the shipping sector can be raised domestically or that essential hard currency supplies will be available from a healthy surplus position in the country's balance of payments.

2. <u>Movement toward self-sufficiency maximization but through a mixture of private and state-owned enterprises.</u> The mixture of private and state enterprises may aim to achieve the same GNP, employment, and balance of payments benefits for which the completely government-controlled growth plans are aiming. It has the added potential benefit of taking advantage of the entrepreneurial and managerial skills that are more likely to be forthcoming in reaction to the motivating forces of private and mixed ownership. Additionally, the capital resources of the government may be supplemented by private domestic capital and by funds acquired from foreign lenders who are more willing to provide loans to profit oriented private ventures.

3. <u>Internationalization of the country's shipping through a mixture of self-reliance and the employment of foreign transnational shipping corporation offered services which can be usefully combined with evolving national shipping resources.</u> The internationalization approach is also self-sufficiency oriented but to a lesser degree than the two previous alternatives. The policy recognizes that while the country is expanding, its domestic and transnational shipping sectors, it can benefit greatly from combining forces with and partially relying on foreign services. From a transportation company orientation, this policy moves toward a more balanced approach that gives greater consideration to shippers' interests since the government is not pressed to make a success of its shipping companies even if the success is achieved at the expense of shippers.

4. <u>Gradual development of nation's shipping sector.</u> Developing countries that already have active domestic and transnational shipping sectors may be desirous of enlarging these sectors. However, shipping may not be one of the economic sectors receiving extraordinary priority status. Rather, the shipping sector is subjected to the rationales of effective scarce resource allocation procedures. Foreign transnational shipping corporations are allowed to provide services because of pragmatic operational and financial rather than ideological considerations. The government will have a dual obligation to pursue the fair treatment of the nation's shipping companies by multinational consortia such as liner conferences and bulk

shipping associations while at the same time ensuring that the members of the nation's shippers associations receive adequate quality service at fair prices. Under the gradual development policy governments are more likely to evolve even handed, nondiscriminatory treatment of domestic and foreign based shipping corporations, thus providing an environment within which both groups can prosper and benefit themselves as well as the country.

5.   Reliance on foreign-based corporations for the supply of most essential transnational shipping services. Some developing country governments may recognize the limitations of their capital and skilled worker resources and may find a lack of any overriding need to have a large degree of self-sufficiency in transnational shipping. Thus, they decide to rely heavily on foreign transnational shipping corporations. Such a policy puts the country in the shippers' rather than the transport companies' interest group. Consequently, the government is likely to monitor and regulate the freight rate charges and service quality practices of foreign shipping companies.

The government can also encourage the activities of shippers' councils so that their interests receive effective representation through dialogues with the liner and tramp service companies that provide transnational shipping services to and from the country.

There are several fundamental advantages derived from significant reliance on foreign transnational shipping companies: a) large capital investments in vessels are avoided; b) investments in port facilities are complemented by additional facilities constructed by the foreign shipping companies; c) indirectly the trained worker resources of foreign nations are utilized by the host country; d) investment risks and the risks of inefficient utilization of assets are avoided; e) there is no need to maintain shipping company representative offices in foreign countries or to deal with foreign agents; f) despite the absence of adequate nationally owned shipping capacity the country is still able to receive most needed transport services at reasonable prices.

6) Subsidization versus full exposure to competition. Governments that long for higher degrees of self-sufficiency in infrastructure sectors would usually prefer to be the owners and operators of well structured, cost efficient and internationally competitive shipping industries whose revenues are adequate to cover operating and amortization costs. These desires often are not realized because of high initial costs, lack of experience, irregularity of load factors, severe competition and unfair practices by others. It is even more difficult for shipping companies than for many infant industries to operate in the black without direct or indirect governmental support or protection. Consequently, policy alternatives chosen by governments must be preceded by and coordinated

with decisions concerning the types and magnitudes of direct and indirect subsidies the government is willing and capable of providing to the shipping sector.

The assumption that after a reasonable growth period the industry will be able to compete effectively against foreign transnational shipping corporations without significant subsidies or protective measures (which are alternate forms of subsidization) usually proves to be invalid. Numerous new or unforeseen events occur necessitating the indefinite continuation of subsidies which act as perpetual drains on national resources. Developing country policy makers, therefore, should be especially certain that the stream of benefits from self-sufficiency in transnational shipping will outweigh the virtually endless stream of costs.

7) Short-term and intermediate-term planning. Host country policy makers whose analyses lead them to rely extensively on foreign transnational shipping corporations will have to develop national transportation plans and forecasts not only for the long run but over short and intermediate time periods as well. Although short term or spot rates for shipping services fluctuate widely, both general cargo liner services and bulk cargo transport services exhibit freight rates stability or gradual rate increases if contracts are negotiated one to five years in advance. If the country's shipping requirements are appropriately coordinated with foreign suppliers of shipping, adequate services at reasonable rates can be assured. This highly desirable condition is possible to realize, because the world supplies of carrying capacity in the intermediate run are large enough or can be enlarged to meet the needs of all shippers astute enough to make advanced arrangements.

TRANSNATIONAL SHIPPING CORPORATIONS AND THE NEW ECONOMIC ORDER

In the "Declaration on the Establishment of a New International Economic Order" (Gardner and Vambery, 1975), the membership of the United Nations express their desires for progress toward a new world economic order (United Nations, 1977). Expanding industrialization and new industrial logistics are important components of the desired, new, emerging system.

The growth and restructuring of the transport infrastructure of nations is a central aim of economic development efforts to be pursued during the next decade. The movement of cargos across national boundaries and over the seas is of major concern to transportation interests.

The U.N.'s declared aim is the internationalization of shipping activities, not only to increase international trade but also to broaden participation in shipping industry activities to many nations who now only have minor or secondary roles.

Besides the crucial issues of dealing with liner conferences, shippers' councils, and port development, the importance of the present and future roles of transnational shipping
corporations needs to be examined in order to provide more
information that will be helpful in maximizing the mutual benefits generated by TNC's and to assure the appropriate distribution of these benefits among the participants in international
shipping processes.

Figure 9.2 indicates how the problem of transnational
shipping corporations fits into the general question of transportation and the new international economic order.

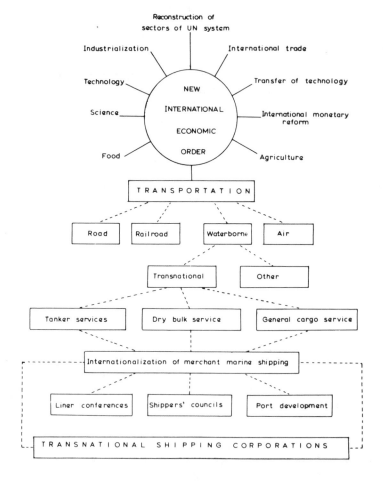

Fig. 9.2. Transnational shipping corporations and the
New International Economic Order.

HOST-COUNTRY POLICIES TOWARD INDUSTRIALIZED
COUNTRY-BASED TRANSNATIONAL SHIPPING
CORPORATIONS

Revised and new interactions between transnational shipping corporations and developing host countries often result in growth of total output. Under such circumstances, all participants in the economic cooperation are able to enlarge the benefits they receive.

In numerous cases, however, host countries may seek to increase their revenues faster than the rate of economic growth. They may also plan to transfer assets from TNC's to themselves irrespective of the presence of rises in real output and net income. Naturally, therefore, the treatment of TNC's by host countries and international agencies will be of concern to home base country governments whose task and duty it is to attempt to prevent abuses against their citizens and corporations.

Somewhat curiously, the economically and/or militarily weaker developing countries are often in a superior bargaining position when economic resources and business opportunities, such as the right to provide shipping services to and from their countries, are redistributed.

1. The host countries can claim national sovereignty which entitles their governments to the take over of all properties inside national boundaries.

2. They can claim that security and independence considerations require that complete ownership and control of the shipping sector be in the hands of domestic governmental or private concerns.

3. They can point to eminent domain rules on the basis of which national takeovers of shipping facilities and tasks would better assure that the needs of the government and the needs of domestic producers and shippers would be met.

4. They can use the infant-industry argument in support of excluding transnational shipping corporations from their transport markets under the pretense that their domestically based transport companies (whether under private or government ownerships) are too inexperienced or undercapitalized to compete effectively with seasoned and well financed, foreign based transnational companies.

5. They can turn, as many industrialized countries do also, to the use of preferential treatment in favor of their national flag shipping companies when choosing carriers for the management of export and import cargos. Thus through practice, rather than through legislation or the exercise of government power, foreign transnational shipping corporations can be excluded from or at least discriminated against in the transport market.

6. They may implement cargo reservation rules, a privilege which can hardly be denied to any country. They would then allocate cargos to their own companies up to the maximum practical carrying capacities of these companies and give other transnationals a part of the shipping business when additional carrying capacities are needed.

Figure 9.3 helps to depict the cargo-allocation process between national-flag and transnational-shipping companies under a system of cargo reservation. It indicates that occasionally demand falls below the carrying capacity of the national-flag companies. At other times, demand may substantially exceed average levels and the services of transnational shipping corporations are employed.

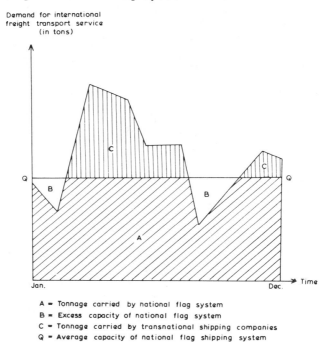

A = Tonnage carried by national flag system
B = Excess capacity of national flag system
C = Tonnage carried by transnational shipping companies
Q = Average capacity of national flag shipping system

Fig. 9.3.   Allocation of cargos between national flag
and transnational shipping companies.

The diagram, however, is a policy model. Cargos are assigned a) according to a policy decision to utilize domestically based international shipping capacity, and b) according to the need to use foreign-based transnational shipping corporations when more capacity is required than is domestically available.

The model shows behavior that may be quite independent of business, economic, and operating-efficiency considerations. Decisions are made without measuring capital equipment acquisition costs, relative operating costs and the charges for which freight services can be bought from transnational corporations.

7. The developing countries can also muster arguments based on economic development and indirect development effects.

a) If domestic companies are used to carry much of the nation's international trade then the transport business opportunities will be received by the country's own economy instead of aiding the economies of foreign countries. Since in most cases national economies suffer under utilization, especially unemployment, it is desirable to channel existing demand to the country's own companies.

b) While self-reliance may cause the need to charge freight rates that are above the ones readily available from the transnational corporations, the excess costs are in large part compensated for not only by the familiar balance of payments benefits but also

   i. the multiplier effects of new expenditures in the domestic economy which make it possible for companies and employees to buy the services and products of yet other domestic producers and

   ii. the accelerator effects on corporations that produce the capital equipment utilized by the shipping companies: a rise in the need for new transport equipment can induce a very substantial rise in the volume of new orders received by equipment and supporting facilities producers.

8. Political-economic ideology statements are also used in justifying the partial exclusion of transnational corporations from specific transport markets. Irrespective of economic merit, certain governments do not allow private ownership or control while other governments do not allow foreign ownership or control of transportation operations inside their borders regardless of the ownership nature of the foreign organizations.

Governments may choose to discriminate selectively against or co-operate extensively with transnational shipping corporations that originate from nations which are directed by governments with similar political-economic ideologies.

9. Nationalism, xenophobia in business, states of belligerence among nations, and ultimately states of war can be ranked as most powerful arguments favoring shifts away from relying on foreign based transnational shipping corporations. In the cases of strong nationalism and xenophobia in business, self-sufficiency even in international transportation may be viewed as preferable or a prerequisite irrelative of many cost considerations.

Finally, whatever the offered freight rates or service qualities may be, few could argue in support of using the services of transnational shipping companies from countries against whom a nation feels strong belligerence or with whom a nation is at war.

FUNDAMENTAL ISSUES CONCERNING TRANSNATIONAL SHIPPING CORPORATION PERFORMANCE

The fundamental economic question in evaluating the contributions of transnational shipping companies from the viewpoint of host countries is the trade-off between relying on foreign based transnational shipping corporations versus self-sufficiency in shipping.

The benefits may be 1) those accruing to a nation as a whole; 2) those accruing to the shippers of the nation including governmental accounts; or 3) those accruing to the nation's own transport companies. The benefits received by this third group may be in part at the expense of the country's shippers of commodities and products and at the expense of the nation at large.

In studying the impact of transnational shipping corporations in a country or region, it should not be assumed that the behavior of transnational shipping corporations operating in a country or a region are identical or of a similar nature. Nor are the effects of the transnationals simply proportional to the magnitude of their operations.

The origins, nationality, business goals, and philosophies of the transnationals vary greatly. Some are profit maximizers over the long run, others are primarily concerned with assuring the availability of quality service, while yet others are mostly interested in short-term or intermediate-term gains without a concern for providing mutual benefits for their host countries.

On another level, whatever the goals of various transnational shipping companies may be, their successes in achieving their aims differ substantially. A specific TNC may aim to maximize earnings in the short run, try to engage in predatory business practices, plan to minimize the utilization of host country resources and expatriate from the host countries as much hard currency as possible. It may succeed at many of these aims. Though providing some benefits to the host country through the delivery of useful shipping services, relative to other transnational shipping corporations, such a corporation is likely to be less beneficial or even harmful to the host country.

On the other hand, the malintentioned corporation of this example may largely fail to accomplish its counterproductive

aims. It may manage to attract cargos only when offering service at substantially below prevailing rates, be unable to avoid
using local employees and accumulate only a small amount or no
hard currency for expatriation from the host country. Consequently, despite its aim to pursue practices which could evoke
the disapproval of host-country governments, even this company may provide a net benefit stream for its hosts.

CONCLUSION

The transnational shipping business is not a zero sum game.
The total earnings possibilities for the industry are rising from
year to year. Often shipping companies compete aggressively
against one another. At other times they successfully divide
or share markets in a live and let live atmosphere.

As corporations of more and more countries enter into the
shipping industry and the market share of firms from developing countries increases, some redistribution of assets and
opportunities becomes inevitable. However, all present and
future participants in transnational shipping should focus their
efforts on creating gains for world shipping by enlarging their
total output (in terms of more service quantity, better service
quality and greater productivity) rather than just focus on the
redistribution of existing assets and transport markets.

Moreover, since the demand for transnational shipping
services is derived from the demand for commodities and products, shipping companies in all countries should participate
vigorously in national and international efforts to expand ra-
tional economic growth.

REFERENCES

Bejgar, Stanislaus. 1976. Polish Maritime News: 1-3.
Gdynia, Poland.

Council of European and Japanese Shipowners' Association -
European National Shippers' Councils. 1977. Symposium
on Linear Shipping: 24-44. Lausanne, Switzerland.

Gardner, Richard N., and Vambery, Robert G. 1975. "Progress Towards a New World Economic Order." Journal of
International Studies 5, no. 3: 5-14.

United Nations. 1974. United Nations General Assembly Resolution (May 9). A/RES/3201(S-VI).

---. 1977. United States Interoffice Memorandum (September 7).

IV

Managers of Multinational Corporations

10 The Man Who Manages Multinationals: A Comparative Study of the Profiles, Backgrounds, and Attitudes of Chief Executives of American, European, and Japanese MNCs

Sandra van der Merwe
Andre van der Merwe

The grooming of high-potential executives for corporate head office responsibility is occupying an increasingly prominent position in the workforce programs of multinational corporations (MNCs). These enterprises are increasingly recognizing that maintaining the highest possible standard of managerial efficiency and lines of management succession is critical to their performance.

Problems experienced by MNCs in the development of their human resources are similar to any large, diversified company operating domestically. The internationalist character of the MNC, however, makes the task a more complex one mainly because personnel destined for top managerial positions in MNCs have to cope with special factors related to doing business in more than one country.

One of the issues that needs to be resolved in the research-based data on MNCs is the type of skills, training and experience required by executives who are marked for the higher executive positions in these institutions. Information of this type has an important role to play in the human resource planning of MNCs and in their executive development and training programs.

AN INTERNATIONAL STUDY

One way to ascertain the background, training and experience that has thusfar been successful in the highest corporate echelons of multinational management is to look at the profiles of existing chief executive officers.

This kind of analysis is not only interesting in itself but can serve as "role models" for potential candidates aspiring to the top corporate ranks of MNCs. At the same time it can give direction to MNCs in the training and developing of their key employees.

An international research project conducted this year was undertaken for this purpose. Designed specifically to obtain profiles of chief executives in the leading multinational companies of the world, it set out to find answers to several crucial questions, for example: What is their background? What formal training have they had? What added training do they feel would have assisted them in their jobs? What functional experience have they had? What additional experience do they believe could have been better preparation for their jobs? Are there profiles typical of MNC chief executives or do trends differ significantly between American, European, and Japanese executives?

Another object of the study was to provide practical insight into the prevailing views held by these opinion leaders with regard to some of the more pertinent aspects involved in the development of staff for their group head-office management team. This part of the exercise is particularly significant for governments, businesses and academics intent on upgrading the level of multinational managerial skills.

Specifically then, this research project was aimed at bringing interested parties up to date with:

- An understanding of the type of background experience and training that has been successful for chief executives in the managing of MNCs.
- The types of executive training and development needed in grooming multinational executives for corporate head-office mobility.
- What can be done to tailor executive development programs specifically for MNCs.
- Possible areas of difference between MNCs in America, Europe, and Japan in their executive development requirements.
- The implication of their attitudes toward executive development on the adaptability and flexibility of their corporations to home and host environments.

METHODOLOGY

To obtain representative profiles and trends of these world executives and at the same time comparable data between America, Europe, and Japan, a stratified random sampling technique was employed. The Fortune lists, comprising the world's top 500 industrial companies and the 500 largest industrial firms in America, were used as the initial universe. From this MNCs were stratified into three groups - those with their head office in America, those in Europe, and those in Japan. A random sample was then chosen. Refusals were randomly replaced when necessary.

Questionnaires were addressed personally to the chief executive officers of these MNCs. In all, 120 questionnaires were returned and analyzed, the result of which form the essence of this paper. Participants were representatively spread across a broad spectrum of industries, operating, geographically speaking, from various countries - Belgium, Denmark, Finland, France, Holland, Italy, Japan, Norway, Spain, South America, Sweden, Switzerland, United Kingdom, United States, and West Germany.

DEMOGRAPHIC PROFILE

Their Age

The demographic diagrams in figure 10.1 show that Europeans heading MNCs tend to be younger than Americans or Japanese - Japanese are considerably older. Most of the American and European executives are between 45 and 65 years of age - 88 percent of the Americans fall into this category and 89 percent of the Europeans do. A much higher percentage of Americans however, 61 percent in all, are between 55 and 65 years of age, compared to the Europeans, where only 42 percent are in this age category. Over half the Japanese, 59 percent in total are between 65 and 75 years old - 2 percent of European executives are in this age group.

The age discrepancies between the three countries can no doubt be accounted for by differences in their organizational cultures. The trends are nonetheless significant in that they point to the fact that Europeans need to be groomed more quickly for top corporate positions than Americans or Japanese. This could influence the types of career paths designed for them and the speed at which they need to be trained. Americans on the other hand and, to a great extent, Japanese, have longer to develop and more time to be trained for key multinational responsibility.

Their Nationality

A comparison of the nationalities of chief executives suggests differences as well between European executives and those in America and Japan. From the research it is evident that there is more executive mobility from country to country in Europe than in America or Japan. In Japan everyone occupying chief executive posts in multinationals are nationals whereas 3 per-

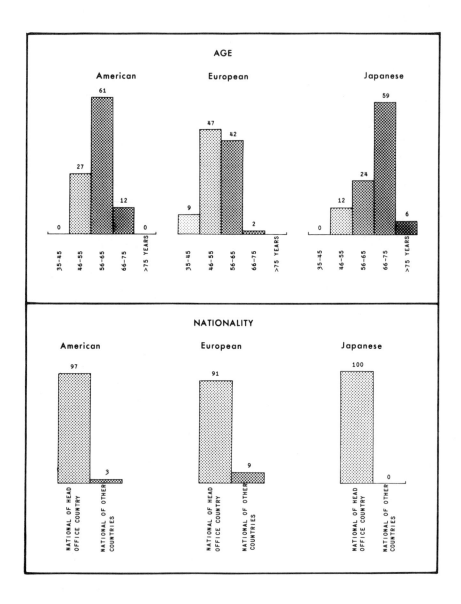

Fig. 10.1.   Demographic profile.

cent of the American and 9 percent of the European are nationals of other countries.

TRAINING PROFILES

Their Formal Training

Formal training backgrounds are the rule rather than the exception. This applies equally to executives of all countries surveyed. All Japanese executives have had some formal study - so have the majority of the Americans and Europeans. Comparative formal training profiles are presented in figure 10.2 for each of the three countries. On analysis what emerges from the data is that:

- Twelve main areas are predominantly those in which chief executives of MNCs have studied formally. These are: accounting, business administration, chemistry, economics, engineering, finance, humanities, industrial economics, commerce, law, marketing, mathematics and political science.
- In general, European executives tend to have formal training in areas spread across all of these twelve areas. Americans and especially the Japanese have more specialized backgrounds with far more formal education experienced by them in fewer areas.
- A great many respondents have formal training in more than one area - 22% of the Americans, 28% of the Europeans and 35% of the Japanese have studied in two fields, 2% of the American, 6 percent of the Japanese and 9 percent of the Europeans have had formal training in three areas, and 2 percent of European executives have had formal study in more than four fields.
- Engineering is the area where most of the Americans (43 percent) and most of the Europeans (37 percent) have had their formal training. The Japanese are relatively low in this area (12 percent).
- Finance is the area where a major portion of respondents in each of the countries have had formal training. Amongst Japanese, finance is the most popular (24 percent) and in Europe (21 percent) and America (17 percent) the second most popular.

Additional Training as Better Preparation for Them

When asked in an open-ended question what additional training they feel would have been better preparation for their jobs as chief executive officers of MNCs, 54 percent of the Japanese

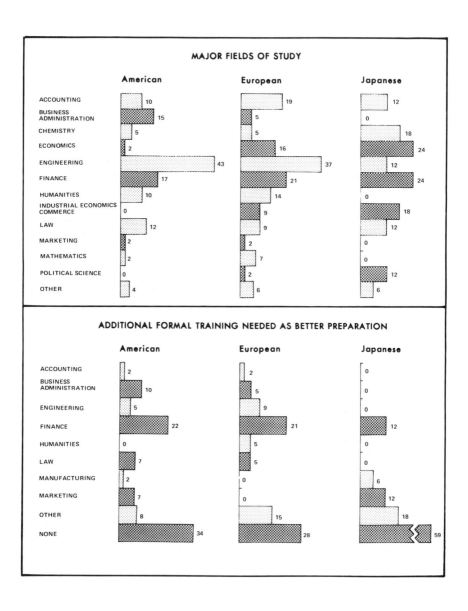

Fig. 10.2. Training profile.

replied that there were none. Thirty-four percent of American executives and 28 percent of Europeans agreed with this.

Of the areas mentioned as those which would have been useful as additional training, seven were stated most often. These are: accounting, business administration, engineering, humanities, law, manufacturing and marketing - some miscellaneous areas were also mentioned but not to any significant extent.

In all three countries finance was put forward most often as an area where executives feel they would have been better off had they had training. Twenty-two percent of the Americans, 21 percent of the Europeans and 12 percent of the Japanese expressed this opinion. This suggests a worldwide need for training in finance, a factor which should be given priority in both outside and in-company MNC training efforts.

Japanese respondents feel that apart from finance, marketing and manufacturing are areas where additional training could be useful. Twelve percent of the Japanese executives also mentioned foreign languages. European and American executives offered most of the eight areas in response to the question. They also mentioned "refresher courses" in general management.

EXPERIENCE AND MOBILITY PROFILE

Their Functional Experience

The experience and mobility profiles of the respondents are shown in figure 10.3. Basically there are eleven functional areas where they had experience prior to moving into their present positions. These are accounting, engineering, finance, general administration, law, marketing, operations, personnel, production, research and development, and sales.

Figure 10.3 confirms that in America, Europe and Japan multinational executives have had wide exposure to a variety of functional areas. The five most popular for each of the samples is illustrated below:

	America	Europe	Japan
1)	General Administration	General Administration	General Administration
2)	Operations	Operations	Operations
3)	Finance	Marketing	Sales
4)	Sales	Production	Production
5)	Marketing	Finance	Research and Development

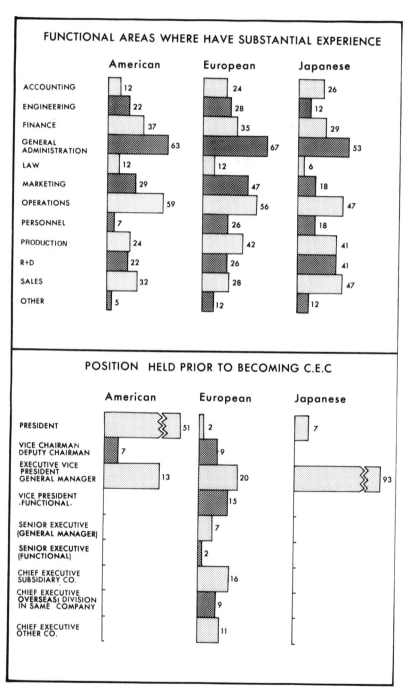

Fig. 10.3.   Experience and mobility profile.

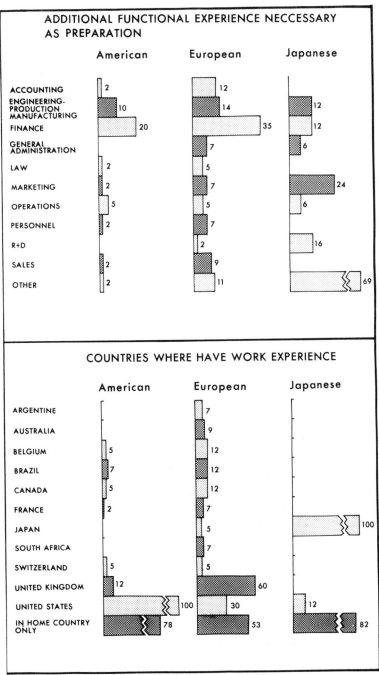

Fig. 10.3. (continued)

Many of the executives have had functional experience in more than one area, some having worked in up to eight of the eleven fields. The matrix below contains the number of American, European, and Japanese executives who have worked in more than one area in their careers. From this analysis it seems typical that chief executives of MNCs have had wide and diversified experience.

Functional Area	American	Europe	Japan
	%	%	%
2	20	7	24
3	27	11	24
4	27	6	29
5	5	9	6
6	5	8	6
7	2	1	0
8	2	0	6

Additional Functional Experience as
Better Preparation for Them

All executives agreed that some additional functional experience would have assisted them in their present jobs. Once again finance featured overall most often in their replies - 20 percent of the Americans mentioned it, 35 percent of the Europeans, and 12 percent of the Japanese. Japanese however mentioned marketing experience more often than any other functional area as the one in which, in their opinion, additional experience would have improved their performance. The fact that Japanese executives responded in this way but that marketing is an area where they have had relatively little actual experience in comparison to the Americans and Europeans, could indicate a gap in the marketing training of Japanese MNCs executives in general and a need for marketing to be introduced to a greater extent into Japanese MNC career-development programs.

Their Positions Prior to Becoming Chief Executives

The number of positions held prior to becoming chief executives vary a great deal between the countries. In Japan, for example, executives only reported to be in two positions before becoming chief officers - the one position "president" and the other "executive vice president." This highlights the rigid nature of the Japanese mobility system and should be taken into account by executives aspiring to senior positions in MNCs in

Japan and in the career-development programs designed for these institutions in that country.

In comparison, American chief executives have come from four types of positions - "president," "vice chairman/deputy chairman," "executive vice-president" and "vice-president" in functional management. European executives on the other hand, are generally more mobile, a point referred to previously. Nine different types of positions, both in and outside their countries, were held by these executives prior to their becoming chief executives of their present companies in addition to which 16 percent were chief executives of subsidiary companies, 9 percent were chief executives in overseas divisions of their present company, and 11 percent were chief executives of other companies.

Their Experience in Other Countries

Many of the executives interviewed have had experience confined to their home countries. This is particularly true of the Japanese where 80% have worked only in Japan - of the others 12 percent have worked in the United States. This again highlights the particular nature of the Japanese system as opposed to that in America and Europe.

On the whole, Americans have had more experience outside their home country than the Japanese. Whereas 78 percent have worked exclusively in companies based in America, the others have worked around the globe in Belgium, Brazil, Canada, France, Switzerland, the United Kingdom, and South American countries. About 10% have worked in one or two countries other than America, 2 percent have worked in four other countries and 7 percent in more than five countries.

European executives show more mobile characteristics than the Americans or Japanese. Their profile differs in that only 53 percent of them have had work experience confined to their home country. Countries other than those in Europe and the United Kingdom where they have had exposure are: Argentina, Australia, Brazil, Canada, Japan, South Africa and the United States. Nine percent have worked in one country in addition to their own, four percent in two, nine percent in three, nine percent in four and two percent in more than six other countries.

TRAINING AND DEVELOPMENT ATTITUDE PROFILE

Attitudes and opinions expressed by chief executives in an organization must to an extent reflect the executive training and development needs within countries. To a degree, they are bound too to influence what types of worker training and development is most likely to be accepted and implemented within MNCs.

To a large extent, these attitudes determine as well how flexible top management is in the development of the executives who succeed them. Also they indicate the extent to which the managerial talent in MNCs acquire the special abilities needed to be performed in different social, economic, technological, political, and cultural environments as well as under different business and legal conditions.

Attitudes Expressed

There is fair agreement among the American (71 percent) and European (79 percent) respondents that multinational management at group head office is complex due to the number of countries with which management has to deal. The majority of Japanese executives reinforce this view, although only 59 percent do.

To examine the current thinking in executive multinational circles regarding development of personnel for MNCs and pinpoint to what extent opinions differ from country to country, respondents were given a series of statements presented in semantic differential form. The results are shown in figure 10.4.

Most executives agreed that the most progressive companies are those who ensure that their top corporate management at group head office have as international an outlook as possible. Consensus was more evident however among Europeans with 63 percent strongly agreeing with the statement and 37 percent agreeing. Eighty-one percent of the Americans agreed - 19 percent strongly and 62 percent to a lesser extent. The remaining 19 percent disagreed. Of the Japanese 100 percent agreed, 47 percent strongly and 53 percent to a lesser extent.

In order to gauge the extent to which chief executives regard a so-called internationalist perspective as necessary for senior management operating MNCs at corporate head office, respondents were asked whether they agreed with the statement that job descriptions for top management at group head office should emphasize the individuals' ability to handle problems locally where the head office is located. Both the Japanese and American (86 percent) executives agreed - fewer European executives agreed however, 60 percent in all - 40 percent disagreed.

Fifty-three percent of the Americans indicated that they preferred nationals working in top management positions at group head office while 51 percent of the Europeans and 59 percent of the Japanese said they do. What is interesting, is that not only were the responses fairly consistent from country to country, but within each country, in each instance, executives opinion was divided on this issue - as the results show, 48 percent of the Americans disagreed, indicating that they didn't necessarily prefer nationals as did 49 percent of the European and 41 percent of the Japanese.

This trend in current thinking could mean that the policy of favoring the recruiting of local nationals for group headquarters is changing. This is particularly significant as a trend for Japanese companies where mobility and transfer across countries has been largely limited. As an overall trend, however, it could require a change in the executive development programs and techniques of MNCs from all three countries and a revaluation of training and recruitment procedures.

In response to another question, European executives once again showed that they were more in favor of a multinationalist approach to managing MNCs than do the American or Japanese respondents. Whereas 67 percent of the Americans feel that training programs for individuals with group head office executive potential should be largely designed to suit conditions where head office is located, 76 percent of the Japanese feel this way and less than half (45 percent) of the Europeans do.

Most respondents from all three countries agree that individuals who have proved themselves in countries with complex environments have an excellent chance of being successful as top managers at group head office. The trend toward this thinking is strongest among European executives - 93 percent of them agreed. Of the Americans 86 percent agreed and of the Japanese 83 percent agreed.

Here again there therefore seems to be a trend in the thinking of MNCs chief executives worldwide, with emphasis on mobility and on a global approach to business. They agree though that individuals marked for top managerial positions at group head office are best evaluated in the country in which group office is situated the Europeans (63 percent) less so though than the Americans (76 percent) and Japanese (94 percent).

American executives are more inclined than executives from the other two countries toward using females in senior positions in MNC organizations. Forty-three percent of them disagree that males necessarily make better corporate executives than females - A 100 percent of the Japanese respondents agreed with the statement though and 72 percent of the Europeans did.

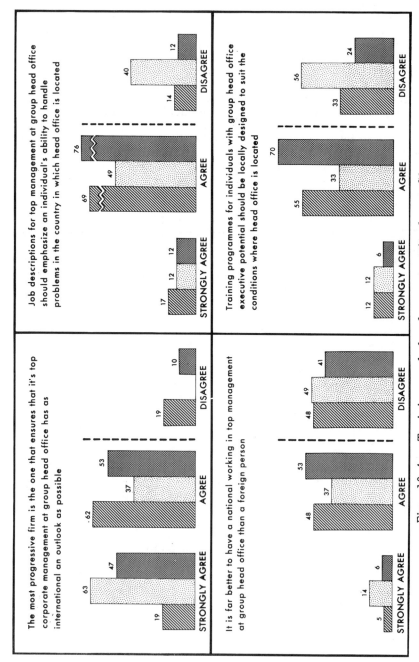

Fig. 10.4. Training and development attitude profile.

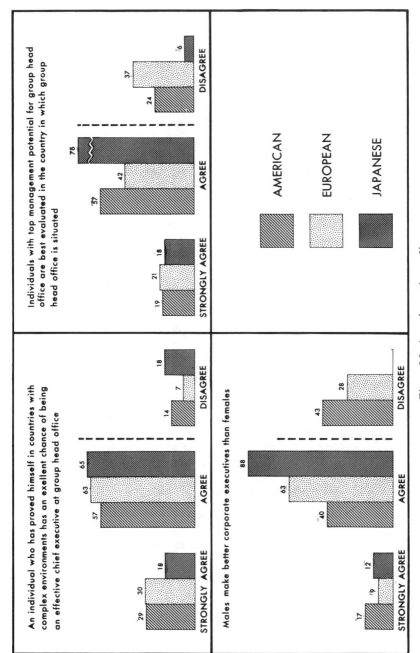

Fig. 10.4. (continued)

223

Implications of Attitudes Expressed on Host and Home-Country Adaptability

The complexity of MNCs, clearly needs high potential executives at corporate head office, developed to acquire the talent and sensitivity necessary to adapt to the host countries in which their corporations operate.

At the same time they need to work within the framework of the policies and procedures of their home country. Fostering this type of approach is important as well for the international transfer of managerial talent for foreign assignments and for the staffing of foreign operations in host countries.

The question therefore arises as to whether or not and to what extent the opinions of those interviewed reflect an adaptable approach on their part to cope with host and home countries' policies and the changing international business environments.

Responses given to questions in this regard highlight that generally attitudes expressed are not as multinationalistically inclined as might have been expected. European executives however clearly demonstrate attitudes that are more global in nature and indicate a greater inclination toward flexibility in terms of adapting to host and home country variations. For example research showed that the Europeans:

- agreed more strongly than the American or Japanese that an international outlook on the part of top corporate management is important as a success ingredient;
- don't believe to the same extent as the American or Japanese executives, that the job descriptions of MNC executives should emphasize home country (rather than host country) problems;
- don't feel to the same extent either as do the Americans and the Japanese respondents, that MNC training for corporate head office should be designed essentially to suit home (rather than host country) conditions;
- are more convinced than the American or Japanese sample that executives who have been successful in countries with complex environments make good potential candidates for the MNC chief executive job;
- are more in favor than American or Japanese executives of evaluating potential corporate executives in countries other than just the home country.

The European and American executives are both more convinced than the Japanese that corporate multinational management is more complex than domestic management due to the number of countries with which they have to deal. In fact generally, Japanese responses seem to be more home-base oriented than those expressed by executives from the other countries.

CONCLUDING NOTE

This study was designed and executed to contribute to the body of knowledge in the area of multinational business and to provide guidelines for the future training and development of multinational managers with top executive potential.

The profiles which have emerged as a result of the research highlight some facts useful as indicators of success ingredients and sound career paths for candidates who are top MNC corporate management material. As such they can act as important feedback to government business and academics intent on directing effective MNC human resource programs. From an empirical point of view the project offers an improved knowledge base for future research into MNCs in todays changing international business environment.

11
Living in a Dual World: A Comparative Study of Japanese Expatriates and Australian Local Managers
Bruce W. Stening, J.E. Everett, Glenn Boseman

INTRODUCTION

Numerous researchers have examined the attitudes of managers cross-culturally and drawn implications from the similarity and differences in those attitudes for the relations between expatriate and local personnel in subsidiaries of multinational corporations. Such implications have been derived either from studies of the respective cultural groups in their own environment (for example, Haire, Ghiselli and Porter (1966), Whitehill (1964), Whitely and England (1977)) or directly from studies of specific expatriate-local groups (for example, Negandhi and Prasad (1971), Harari and Zeira (1974; 1976)). Typically, an assumption has been made that issues about which there are differences in attitude between the managerial groups will result in misunderstandings and problems at an interpersonal level. Such an assumption may be limiting to the extent that individuals do not conform to the stereotype associated with their nationality as suggested by Bass (1971), or, as Alpander (1973) and Toyne (1976) found, have adjusted their attitudes and behaviour to suit their international circumstances.

This paper reports a study that sought to examine the attitudes of intercultural work colleagues at an interpersonal level. The concern of the paper is with developing a conceptual framework for exploring the extent to which expatriate and local personnel are able to appreciate (at the interpersonal level) differences in one another's subjective culture (as defined by Triandis (1972)), i.e., the extent to which there are misunderstandings about the similarity or dissimilarity in their viewpoints. A test of the framework is based upon empirical research into various work-related attitudes of local Australian and expatriate Japanese middle- and upper-management personnel in the Australian subsidiaries of Japanese corporations.

CONCEPTUAL FRAMEWORK

A number of alternative frameworks could be employed to probe the nature of misunderstandings between expatriates and locals. Given that a serious deficiency in cross-cultural studies has been their neglect of the interpersonal aspects of understanding, it seems logical that any new scheme should utilize the dyad as the unit of analysis. Sayles has pointed out that the dyad is the most appropriate conceptual unit for the consideration of managerial relationships:

> the contemporary manager spends a large portion of his time interacting with other managers (peers or near peers). Here he is providing the connective tissue that helps to hold together the specialised sub-parts of the organization. . . . While there are exceptions, in general these are pair relationships which the manager conducts himself; i.e. they are two-person contacts (Sayles, 1964, p. 49).

In this sense the dyad is the fundamental organizational unit, critical to the coordination and control of organizational activities (Farace, Monge and Russell, 1977).

Examination of interpersonal relationships within organizations has stemmed from a variety of research traditions. In one major review (Thomas 1967), three main streams emerged: psychodynamic approaches (where one's personality and life history are dealt with as the central determinants of relationships with others); cognitive approaches (interpretations and understandings as key elements in one's relations with others); and role theory approaches (where the relationships between persons are interpreted through the specific roles they play). The cognitive theory approach seems most appropriate and will be used for the purposes of this research.

The behavior of, and relationship between, two individuals is likely to be a complex function, not merely of each person's own attitudes but also of such factors as one's perceptions of the other's attitudes, one's perception of the other's perception of one's attitudes, and so on. Thus, there is reciprocal adaptation of behavior in relation to the perceptions of one's own and the other's attitudes on a number of levels. If the concern is with the behavior of the parties toward each other and with the overall consequences of their relationship, an understanding beyond that provided by the consensus approach (that is, an examination beyond mere agreement) is necessary. This premise has been at the base of a variety of studies spanning such subject areas as the general relationships between individuals (Goffman, 1959), international relations (Kelman, 1965), and even international

espionage (Goffman, 1971). Such studies have focused attention on reciprocally-matched comparisons of the attitudes of
parties to relationships. With considerable methodological variation (but only limited conceptual variation), these works have
all used what is fundamentally a coorientational framework in
their analysis of dyadic relationships.

The coorientational framework, as presented in figure 11.1
describes not only the level of agreement between two parties
with respect to a specific issue, but also (by assessing the
perceptions of each party with respect to the other's perception of the same issue) the degree to which each party perceives congruency between its and the other party's views,
and the degree to which the perceived congruency is accurate.
The boxes indicate measures that are taken on each individual
(say, an expatriate and a local).

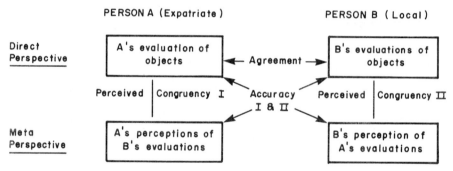

Fig. 11.1.   Component evaluative indices of a coorientation
situation: agreement, accuracy and perceived congruency.

The coorientation framework has its origins in at least
five different schools of thought (McLeod and Chaffee, 1972-
73). Foremost among these are the A-B-X communication
paradigm of Newcomb (1953) and person-perception research
(for example, Tagiuri, Bruner and Blake, 1958). The three
additional major bases are, first, the consensus approach of
Wirth (1948), second, the symbolic interactionist views of Mead
(1934), and third, the social concept of personality and psy-
chotherapy advanced by Sullivan (1953). The principal
strength of the coorientational framework is that, in examining
interpersonal relations, it moves attention from the individual
to the dyad and, as a result, it is somewhat more realistic.
Essentially, its aim is "to analyze a pair of persons as if they
were a dyadic or 'microsocial' system rather than as isolated
individuals" (Chaffee, 1972, p. 111).

The coorientational framework is based upon two key assumptions. First, that "each person in the coorientating pair
has two distinguishable sets of cognitions: he knows what he

thinks, and he has some estimate of what the other person thinks" (Chaffee and McLeod, 1968, p. 662). Second, that "a person's behavior is not based simply upon his private cognitive construction of his world; it is also a function of his perception of the orientations held by others around him and of his orientation to them" (McLeod and Chaffee, 1972-73, p. 470). On the basis of these assumptions, three concepts emerge: agreement, perceived congruency, and accuracy. Agreement reflects the actual level of cognitive overlap between the members of the dyad; perceived congruency is a measure of the degree to which each dyad member perceives cognitive overlap between himself and his partner, and accuracy is a measure of the degree to which each person is accurate in his perceptions of the extent of cognitive overlap. The concepts are assessed with respect to a specific issue, though it is possible (and usually highly desirable) to build up an overall score for each index based on a number of issues. It should be noted, too, that there is considerable interchangeability of terms for each of the concepts within the literature: for example, between agreement and objective homophily (Rogers and Bhowmik, 1970-71), accuracy and empathy (Chaffee, 1972), accuracy and understanding (Laing, Phillipson, and Lee 1966) and perceived congruency and subjective homophily (Rogers and Bhowmik, 1970-71). Though all three concepts are central to the framework, the point has been made (McLeod and Chaffee, 1972) that only one of them (accuracy) is a truly coorientational (interpersonal) variable.

Fundamental to this broad framework is an assumption that the potential for improving the level of agreement between intercultural partners who have basic attitudinal differences toward a situation is, at best, limited. Therefore, central attention should be directed toward investigating matters related to coorientational accuracy (an emphasis which the literature indicates is a dominant feature of various cross-cultural training programs). Though it is recognized that the level of agreement and the extent of perceived congruency are important factors influencing the nature of the interrelationships between the parties, from the perspective of improving interpersonal and organizational performance, accuracy is the variable that holds most promise. Without an accurate understanding between the parties of their respective viewpoints, no base exists upon which to construct effective and efficient task relationships.

Looking first at the situation in its most simple terms, there are conceivably eight possible situations of understanding or misunderstanding between expatriate and local personnel in a multinational corporation (Bass, 1971, pp. 296-299). In the first instance, one may consider a set of circumstances where the expatriate and the local are actually similar in their orientation towards a particular issue. Four situations are pos-

sible: 1) Both accurately recognize the similarity; 2) the expatriate perceives a difference, the local accurately recognizes
the similarity; 3) the expatriate accurately perceives the similarity, the local perceives a difference; or 4) Both perceive a
difference.   Conversely, one may consider a set of circumstances in which the expatriate and the local are actually different in their orientation toward a particular issue.   Again,
four situations are possible: both, or one, or the other, or
neither member of the dyad may accurately perceive that there
is a difference.   Of course, when the possible variety in the
magnitude of the difference is considered, the permutations
increase without limit.

The tendency of those researchers who have undertaken
comparisons of managerial beliefs and practices cross-culturally
has been to classify the parties being compared as either similar or different and to leave it at that.   Moreover, they have
often concluded that managers from countries with similar belief patterns (as measured through national samples) will have
few problems working together, while managers from countries
which are dissimilar in those respects will have much greater
problems (Bass and Eldridge, 1973; Kraut, 1973; Vansina,
1968).   As the coorientational framework suggests, the situation is considerably more complex than that; whether managers
are able to work together satisfactorily may depend very much
on how well their personal similarities and differences in orientation are understood by each other.

Conceptually, it is possible to go beyond this one level of
reciprocal cognition to successively higher levels (Laing, Phillipson, and Lee, 1966; Scheff, 1967).   In fact, Scheff's
definition of complete consensus assumes this:

> complete consensus on an issue exists in a group
> where there is an infinite series of reciprocating un-
> derstandings between members of the group con-
> cerning the issue (Scheff, 1967, p. 37).

It is probable that such a situation is rarely achieved.   Despite this it is worthwhile to contemplate extension of the basic
coorientational model to encompass at least the second level of
reciprocal cognition (that is, the meta-meta level) by dyadic
partners.   The outline of such an extended framework is
presented in figure 11.2.

By extending the framework to incorporate meta-meta perspectives, two additional measures are obtained for each
member of the dyad.   In the first place, one is able to assess
the degree to which each individual feels he is understood or
misunderstood by his partner.   In the second place, the meta-
meta perspective indicates the extent to which each dyad
member realizes (or fails to realize) that he is being
understood or misunderstood.   The framework of fig. 11.2 is

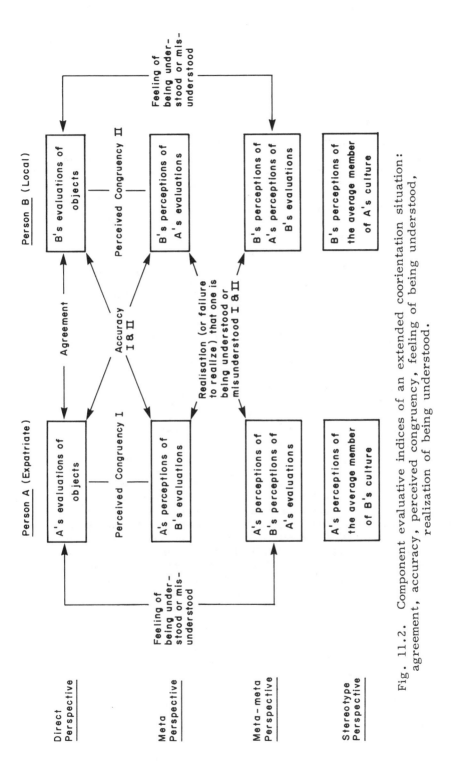

Fig. 11.2. Component evaluative indices of an extended coorientation situation: agreement, accuracy, perceived congruency, feeling of being understood, realization of being understood.

231

completed by the stereotype perspective of the "average" member of the other person's culture.

Awareness of a dyad member regarding whether he is understood or misunderstood by his partner is particularly important. It suggests that there are substantial grounds for advocating that the analysis should be extended to incorporate the meta-meta perspectives of the dyad members. By so doing it would be possible to examine the meta-accuracy of the pair, that is, the extent to which each realizes or fails to realize that he is understood or misunderstood by his dyad partner. Clearly the principal benefit to be derived from this extension is a more sophisticated appreciation of the manner in which the accuracy of perceptions is associated with various measures of the effectiveness of their relations.

If the coorientational framework is so extended and if only the accuracy dimensions are considered (that is, first, accuracy and second, realization or failure to realize accuracy or inaccuracy of the other) the number of possible situations that may be derived increases dramatically (16 each for situations restricted to the dichotomy of agreement and disagreement).

Though the discussion thus far places greater emphasis upon accuracy than upon perceived congruency or the feeling of being understood or misunderstood, this does not negate the importance of the latter two variables. It must be acknowledged that in the short term it may actually be desirable that the parties believe they are similar (that is, perceive a high level of congruency) when in fact they are not (in other words, be inaccurate in terms of their assessment of the other's attitude) (Feather, 1976; Nwankwo, 1973). Perceived incongruency (whether accurate or not) may be an important source of discontent.

Though a comparison of the direct perspectives of the dyad members (that is, the agreement that exists between them) will be of considerable interest in itself, it is the relationship between each of the three levels (direct, meta, and meta-meta) which will provide the basis for analysis. It should be recognized that a stable, long-term relationship between the members of a dyad does not necessarily depend upon agreement (though for some people it may) as much as upon an understanding of the other's viewpoint and a realization that one is being understood or misunderstood by one's partner. If, for example, the parties fail to agree but recognize this and each knows that the other recognizes this, they can either undertake measures to resolve their differences or reach a compromise or, alternatively, agree to disagree and work from that basis. On the other hand, where misunderstandings and failures to realize occur (whether they arise out of situations of agreement or disagreement), there is a communication breakdown which is a potential source of conflict for the parties involved and dysfunctional for the organization in which they work.

Several writers (Laing, Phillipson, and Lee, 1966, pp. 131-140; Thomas, 1967, p. 186) have acknowledged the potential usefulness of such a general framework in an intercultural context (one in which there are, it has been suggested, greater than "normal" possibilities for misunderstandings). To date, no empirical investigation has been reported, perhaps due to the possibility of increasing the complexity of what is already recognized as a quite complex model. Despite the conceptual difficulties, it is considered to be the most suitable framework for use in achieving the objectives of this study.

METHOD AND SAMPLE

The research described in this paper was based on a sample of 96 Australian-Japanese dyads of middle- and upper-management personnel in Australian subsidiaries of twenty major Japanese trading and manufacturing corporations.

Japanese (rather than, say, American, British or German) multinationals were selected for study in the belief that Australian and Japanese cultures were more disparate than others. Also, on a more pragmatic basis, there are considerably more expatriate Japanese executives in Australia than any other single expatriate group.

Several criteria were established for the selection of companies. Firstly, it was financially feasible to include only firms in the Sydney area (most of the trading companies and a large proportion of the manufacturing companies have their headquarters in Sydney, so this was not considered a major limitation). Secondly, both trading and manufacturing companies were included in the sample to make it representative. Thirdly, in the interests of effort economy, the firms asked to participate were those with the largest number of Japanese personnel working for them in Australia. Twenty firms were asked to participate and all agreed.

Ideally, the selection of specific individuals and the pairing of them to form dyads should be made on a purely random basis within the limits of the available population and in line with other established criteria (for example, they must be members of middle- or upper-management). However, the very nature of the coorientational basis used in this study required that persons be paired who were involved in at least some task communication. It was resolved that the researcher and a member of top management in each of the companies concerned would pair individuals on the basis of the task communication criterion and organization rank; such non-random sampling is often unavoidable (Brislin and Baumgardner, 1971).

Using this process, 108 dyads were formed within the twenty companies and requested to cooperate. Ninety-six pairs of Australians and Japanese agreed to participate, which represented a response rate of 89 percent.

Research Instrument

Separate questionnaires (using the same questions) were developed for the Australians and Japanese. Each questionnaire was divided into three major parts: Part A, which incorporated questions on the work history and other matters related to the background of the respondents; Part B, in which the attitude of respondents toward the coorientational issues was examined; and Part C, which comprised questions designed to measure the level of dyadic satisfaction and performance of respondents. Only Part B of the questionnaires (the coorientational issues) will be used for purposes of this paper. Part B was divided into four sections, each comprised of the same 26 attitudinal items, using 5-point Likert scales. (Given a previously noted tendency for Japanese respondents to use a neutral response category in Likert scales to a greater extent than certain other national groups – for example, Zax and Takahashi, 1967 – a four-item scale was used: Strongly Agree/Agree/Disagree/Strongly Disagree. The values 5, 4, 2 and 1 were assigned, respectively, to the categories, a value of 3 being assigned to non-responses to particular items. The appropriateness of this method has been noted by Kerlinger, 1973, p. 497.) The 26 items appear in this chapter's appendix. These four subsections assessed the direct perspective, meta perspective, meta-meta perspective and stereotype perspective of respondents, as illustrated in figure 11.2. With the exception of questions 2 and 12, which were identical to two items used by Haire et al. (1966), item seven, which was adapted from the Haire et al. study, and question eight, which was adapted from a study by Schein (1966-67), the questions were original to this study. The 26 items were designed to tap important differences in attitude between the two groups regarding matters which the literature suggested would impinge upon their interpersonal work relationships. The items covered five broad areas of potential difference in attitude relating to: the relationship between headquarters and the subsidiary; group versus individual decision making; differentiation of work and private life; leadership preferences and superior-subordinate relationships, and specific relationships between Australians and Japanese.

Given the requirement that the research instruments be directly comparable, a sequence of translation and back-translation was undertaken, resulting in minor changes in both the English and Japanese questionnaires. Minor adjustments also resulted from a pretest conducted among a small sample of Australian and Japanese managers.

ANALYSIS OF RESULTS

Summary

The procedure for analysis is presented in figure 11.3. For most of the 26 attitudinal items, the Australian and Japanese self-evaluations differ significantly. From the 26 items, a linear composite is formed which best discriminates between the two group self-evaluations. This discriminant function is used to define an intercultural dimension along which the direct, meta, meta-meta and stereotype perspectives of figure 11.2 can be calculated. The relationships between the three levels of perspectives for the dyad pairs are then investigated by Pearson correlation and by principal components analysis. It is shown that, although the direct, meta, meta-meta and stereotype perspectives of the same respondents are significantly correlated, the responses of the two members of a dyad are virtually independent. The results are interpreted in the light of a combined projection/stereotype regression model.

Establishing the Discriminant Function

Table 11.1 shows the means and standard deviations for the Australians and Japanese self-evaluations of their own attitudes on the 26 items. A t-test on individual items shows that, for most of the items, the two groups have significantly different means. However, a suitable linear composite of the items will have more power to discriminate between the two groups than will any one item on its own. To search for the best discriminant function, a stepwise discriminant analysis was carried out on all 26 items, using Rao's V method (Nie et al., 1975, p. 477). The results are tabulated in table 11.1, with the items being listed in the order of their inclusion into the discriminant function. It can be seen that the inclusion of the first 17 items is significant at the one percent level. But to be conservative, the discriminant analysis was re-run using only the 15 most significant items ($\alpha < 0.1\%$). The resulting understandardized score coefficients are reported in table 11.1, and can be used to calculate the discriminant function from the 15 included items. The discriminant function obtained by this procedure would have correctly classified 93 percent of the individual Japanese and Australians.

It will be noted that many of the items not included in the discriminant function have significantly different means for

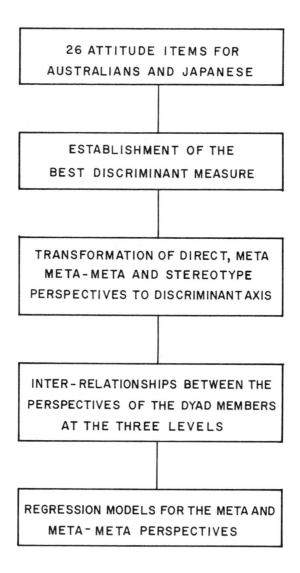

Fig. 11.3. Analysis procedure.

Table 11.1. Discriminant Analysis Based on Australian
and Japanese Self-evaluations (direct perspective)

Item	Difference in Means						Discriminant Function D			
	Australian		Japanese		t	Sig α	Change in Rao's V	Sig. α	Score coeff	ρ between D & Item
	m	s	m	s						
07	3.85	1.00	2.24	0.99	11.4	.000	131.8	.000	.486	.742
21	3.16	1.30	1.88	0.91	8.1	.000	73.9	.000	.255	.547
12	2.40	1.15	3.41	1.11	6.3	.000	52.3	.000	-.360	-.485
04	3.54	1.25	2.39	0.99	7.2	.000	35.6	.000	.320	.536
23	3.42	1.07	2.74	1.08	4.5	.000	23.1	.000	.208	.356
01	3.41	1.13	3.93	0.75	3.8	.001	23.0	.000	-.425	-.309
10	3.93	0.83	4.36	0.73	3.9	.001	21.4	.000	-.518	-.313
26	3.69	1.04	3.36	1.04	2.2	.028	22.1	.000	.257	.183
14	4.15	0.84	3.97	0.91	1.5	.134	24.4	.000	.339	.118
06	3.60	1.07	2.66	1.16	6.0	.000	23.1	.000	.259	.461
19	3.29	1.35	2.34	1.02	5.6	.000	29.6	.000	.209	.433
20	3.17	1.26	3.10	1.16	0.4	.689	14.0	.000	-.155	.036
13	3.52	1.14	3.86	0.93	2.3	.021	14.9	.000	-.199	-.187
15	2.82	1.18	2.75	1.15	0.4	.689	14.5	.000	-.163	.034
02	3.20	1.27	2.17	0.95	6.5	.000	14.5	.000	.164	.493
22	3.02	1.16	3.55	1.13	3.3	.002	8.6	.003	-	-.204
17	2.22	1.15	2.09	0.89	0.9	.368	8.1	.004	-	.131
03	2.36	1.10	2.80	1.18	2.7	.007	5.6	.018	-	-.173
25	4.22	0.69	3.77	1.00	3.7	.001	3.9	.048	-	.259
05	3.54	1.08	3.34	1.13	1.3	.194	4.1	.042	-	.076
08	2.82	1.27	3.11	1.19	1.7	.089	1.4	.235	-	-.109
09	2.61	1.29	2.99	1.22	2.1	.036	1.1	.289	-	-.151
16	3.51	1.24	3.59	1.12	0.5	.617	1.0	.320	-	-.028
11	3.38	1.18	3.56	1.10	1.1	.271	0.6	.445	-	-.068
18	3.50	1.12	3.51	1.04	0.1	.920	0.1	.669	-	.012
24	3.01	1.18	2.67	1.12	2.1	.036	-	-	-	.168

the two groups. This occurs because of the intercorrelations between the items: that is, if an item is strongly correlated with another item already included in the discriminant function, the item may have no further significant discriminating power. Accordingly, it can be seen from the last column in table 11.1 that some of the items not included in the evaluation of the discriminant function (D) are strongly correlated with it.

Reliability of the Discriminant Function

To verify that the discriminant function was stable, the sample of dyads was split into two halves. The discriminant function score coefficients for the 15 items were recomputed for the first 48 dyads, and again for the last 48 dyads, to define two other estimates (D1 and D2) of the discriminant function. For the entire sample, three discriminant function scores (D, D1 and D2) were calculated. The two independent estimates (D1 and D2) of the discriminant function had a Pearson correlation coefficient of 0.894 and their correlations with the overall discriminant function (D) were 0.964 and 0.978 respectively.

This validation of the discriminant function can be considered very satisfactory, especially in view of the fact that all the respondents from the largest firms were concentrated in the first part-sample (D1). Splitting the sample so that alternate dyads were assigned to the two part-samples gave even more satisfactory results: the discriminant functions from the part-samples had a Pearson correlation of 0.935 with each other, and of 0.980 and 0.985 respectively with the overall discriminant function (D).

Direct, Meta and Meta-meta Perspectives

The discriminant function defines the one dimension that best distinguishes between Australian and Japanese self-evaluations of their own attitudes. It therefore provides an appropriate measure of "Australianess" or "Japaneseness" and will be used as a measurement scale for intercultural distance. Furthermore, since the dimension is formed as a linear composite of the individual items, measurements along this dimension have the added virtue that they can be assumed to be normally distributed on an interval scale. This permits later analysis to be carried out with less reservations than would be called for using the original Likert-scaled items.

Using the item score coefficients of table 11.1, the direct, meta and meta-meta perspectives can all be collapsed onto the intercultural axis to provide a single measure for each member of the dyad at each perspective level. Six measurements along the intercultural dimension are thus calculable for each dyad, as follows:

Direct Perspective:
    DA = Australian's own evaluation of his attitude
    DJ = Japanese's own evaluation of his attitude
Meta Perspective:
    DAJ = Australian's perception of Japanese's evaluation
    DJA = Japanese's perception of Australian's evaluation
Meta-Meta Perspective:
    DAA = Australian's perception of Japanese's perception of Australian's evaluation
    DJJ = Japanese's perception of Australian's perception of Japanese's evaluation.

Having calculated the six measurements for each dyad, the interrelationships between them can be investigated.

Two further measurements along the intercultural dimension are also calculated, representing each member's perception of the members of the other culture as a group (that is, the member's stereotype perspective):

    DAJS = Australian's perception of the stereotype Japanese
    DJAS = Japanese's perception of the stereotype Australian.

Interrelationships between Dyad Perspectives

Pearson correlation coefficients between the six dyad measurements are shown in table 11.2. About 96 dyads were usable for each correlation. It was found that all the intrapersonal correlations were significant at an α of less than one percent whereas none of the interpersonal correlations were significant even for an α of ten percent.

Table 11.2. Relationships between Dyad Perspectives
(Pearson Correlation Coefficients)*

	DA	DAJ	DAA	DJ	DJA	DJJ
DA	1.00					
DAJ	.24	1.00				
DAA	.47	.26	1.00			
DJ	-.01	.04	.01	1.00		
DJA	-.01	-.11	-.09	.24	1.00	
DJJ	.02	-.08	.00	.24	.35	1.00

*For α = 1%, r = .23; for α = 10%, r = .13.

The dichotomy between the Japanese and Australian perspectives can also be seen in figure 11.4, where the mean values of the six measurements are plotted on the discriminant axis. To greatly simplify the matter, it appears that the Australians do not realize the Japaneseness of the Japanese, and vice versa. In fact, the mean Australian perception of the Japanese attitude is more Australian that the mean Japanese perception of the Australian attitude. Furthermore, while one recognizes that the other's perception of him or her is likely to be distorted toward the other's culture, the distortion is underestimated by at least 50 percent.

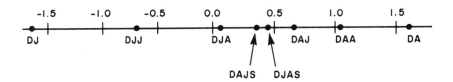

Fig. 11.4.   Mean values on discriminant axis.

Referring to figure 11.2, the following relations between the dyad pairs can be associated with the corresponding pairs of measurements:

Agreement: DA with DJ
Accuracy: DA with DJA; DJ with DAJ
Realization of whether one is understood: DAA with DJA;
               DJJ with DAJ.

Since table 11.2 shows that the correlations between all these pairs of measurements are insignificant, we are forced to conclude that, at least along the intercultural dimension, there is no evidence of any agreement, accuracy or realization of whether one is understood.

Principal Component Analysis of the Dyad Perspectives

The conclusions regarding the lack of interrelationships between the perspectives of each individual in the dyads can be illustrated graphically through principal component analysis.
The principal components of the six measurements DA, DJ, DAJ, DJA, DAA and DJJ were extracted. The first two principal components had eigenvalues of 1.71 and 1.53, while the remaining eigenvalues were 0.88 and less. Applying a varimax rotation of the first two principal components produced

principal component loadings that are mapped in figure 11.5. It can be seen that the Australian direct, meta and meta-meta perspectives (DA, DAJ and DAA) load clearly onto one axis, while the Japanese direct meta and meta-meta perspectives (DJ, DJA and DJJ) load clearly onto the other axis.

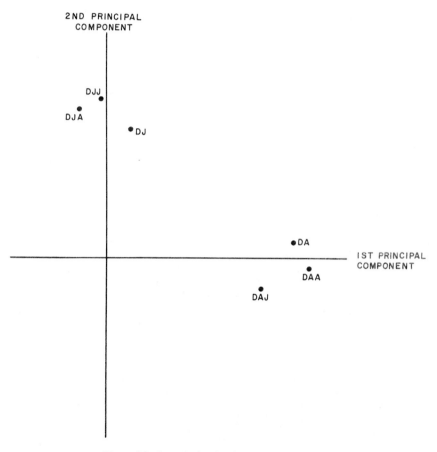

Fig. 11.5.   Principal components.

The same picture arises if an oblique rotation, instead of varimax, is applied to the first two principal components. The pattern matrix is given in table 11.3.   Again DA, DAJ and DAA load clearly onto one component, while DJ, DJA and DJJ load clearly onto the other.   After oblique rotation, the Pearson correlation coefficient between the two factors is -.050, showing that the two factors are virtually independent of each other.

Table 11.3.   Oblique Factor Pattern Matrix
(After Rotation with Kaiser Normalization)

Construct	Factor 1	Factor 2
DA	.797	.087
DAJ	.608	-.087
DAA	.808	.018
DJ	.072	.648
DJA	-.089	.747
DJJ	.010	.754

Interpretation: The Stereotype

The intercorrelation and principal components analysis of the six dyadic perspectives indicate that, at least along the intercultural dimension, the Japanese and Australian perspectives are unrelated.

The findings are consistent with a model under which each member of the dyad's perception of the other member's perspectives are projections of her or his own. It has been shown that the projection is not correlated with the dyad partner's perspectives, though it is biased in the correct direction. This bias of the projection can be ascribed to the respondent's perception of a stereotype of the other culture.

The mean Australian and Japanese perceptions of the stereotype of the other culture are plotted on figure 11.4. DAJS is the Australian perception of the stereotype Japanese, and DJAS the Japanese perception of the stereotype Australian. It can be seen that the stereotypes lie in the correct direction, but still underestimate the intercultural differences (though not by as much as do the dyadic interpersonal perceptions).

The projection plus stereotype model is supported by correlations of DAJS and DJAS with the six dyadic perspectives as shown in table 11.4. It is seen that each member's meta-perspective correlates significantly ($\alpha < 1\%$) with her or his

Table 11.4.   Stereotype Perceptions (Pearson Correlations of the Stereotype Perceptions with the Dyadic Perspectives)*

	DA	DAJ	DAA	DJ	DJA	DJJ
DAJS	.11	.32	.35	-.13	-.14	-.02
DJAS	-.01	-.03	-.14	-.04	.29	.13

*For $\alpha = 1\%$, r = .23; for $\alpha = 10\%$, r = .13.

stereotype of the other culture, though (as we have already seen in table 11.2) the meta-perspective does not correlate significantly with the partner's direct perspective. In the case of the Australian, the meta-meta perspective also correlates with his stereotype of the Japanese, although the Japanese meta-meta perspective does not appear to correlate so strongly with his stereotype of the Australian.

Regression Models

As further validation of the projection/stereotype model, each member of the dyad's meta and meta-meta perspectives were regressed against both members' direct and stereo perspectives.

The results for the Australian and Japanese respondents are reported in tables 11.5 and 11.6, for the meta and meta-meta regression models. In each case, it can be seen that there is no significant difference between the model coefficients for the Australian and Japanese respondents. Accordingly, it is reasonable to combine the cultural groups and obtain overall regressions of the meta and meta-meta perspectives of each respondent against his own and the other member of the dyad's direct and stereo perspectives.

The overall regression models are also reported in table 11.5 and 11.6. Each coefficient is tested to see if it differs significantly from zero. At a one percent significance level it is seen that the respondent's meta and meta-meta perspective depend directly upon their own direct and stereo perspectives, but that there is no evidence of any dependence upon the dyad partner's direct or stereo perspectives. Furthermore, the constant term in each regression model does not differ significantly from zero.

The results support the hypothesis that the bias of a respondent's meta and meta-meta perspectives away from his direct perspective can be ascribed to his stereotype of the other's culture and is not related to the actual perspectives of his dyad partner.

Thus the results agree with a combined projection and stereotype model. Under this model a respondent is unaware of his dyad partner's individual attitude. His perception of his partner's attitudes is a projection of his own attitudes combined with a partially accurate stereotype of his partner's culture.

Table 11.5. Regression Models for Meta Perspectives (Coefficients of the Regression of Meta Perspectives against Direct and Stereo-Perspectives)

Respondents	Constant Term	Direct Perspectives		Stereo Perspectives		Adjusted R^2
		Own	Other	Own	Other	
Australian	.21±.30	.27±.11	.13±.13	.30±.10	-.01±.10	15%
Japanese	.39±.29	.31±.13	.01±.11	.33±.10	-.09±.10	13%
All (Significance)*	.19±.09 (4.1%)	.26±.06 (0.0%)	.07±.06 (26.5%)	.30±.07 (0.0%)	-.05±.07 (44.2%)	18%

*Significance test of null hypothesis that coefficient is zero.

Table 11.6. Regression Models for Meta-Meta Perspectives (Coefficients of the Regression of Meta-Meta Perspectives against Direct and Stereo-Perspectives)

Respondents	Constant Term	Direct Perspectives		Stereo Perspectives		Adjusted R^2
		Own	Other	Own	Other	
Australian	.35±.29	.51±.11	.08±.13	.28±.10	-.13±.10	26%
Japanese	-.24±.32	.31±.14	.00±.12	.14±.11	.04±.10	2%
All (Significance)*	.12±.10 (21.3%)	.50±.07 (0.0%)	-.03±.07 (51.8%)	.21±.07 (0.0%)	-.01±.07 (84.2%)	42%

*Significance test of null hypothesis that coefficient is zero.

DISCUSSION OF FINDINGS

This study sought to examine the extent to which parties to an intercultural work relationship were able to appreciate differences in one another's subjective cultures. The results illustrated conclusively that, along a dimension of intercultural differences, there was no evidence that the members of the Australian-Japanese dyads studied could accurately assess either the attitudes of their partner or their partner's view of their attitude.

Though both Australian and Japanese respondents were able to predict the direction in which their dyad partner's attitudes would differ from their own, neither was even remotely aware of the magnitude of these differences. A clear tendency was demonstrated for individuals to project their own attitudes on to their partner in a way that substantially underestimated the degree of difference between the two. This finding is consistent with certain previous studies into the relationship between interpersonal agreement and perceived congruency (Rogers and Bhowmik, 1970-71). The results do not accord, however, with the assimilation-contrast hypothesis (Sherif and Hovland, 1961) which suggests that parties to interpersonal relationships will tend to exaggerate both differences and similarities; that is, on attributes where the parties are fairly similar they will tend to perceive greater similarity than exists in fact, while on attributes where they are fairly different they will perceive the differences as even greater than they really are. Had the assimilation-contrast phenomenon been operating, it would have then, been expected that each party would have seen the other in more extreme terms than was actually the case. That one party's evaluation of the other was even directionally correct was shown to be related to the stereotype held regarding the other's cultural group. Though the stereotype perspectives of both Australians and Japanese were closer to the actual view of each partner, even here the degree of disagreement was substantially underestimated. These findings support the view (expressed by, among others, Bowes (1977) and Triandis (1977)) that stereotyping is not necessarily a negative process disruptive of interpersonal understanding but, rather, may provide the basis for greater interpersonal accuracy than would otherwise be the case.

The importance of the stereotype perspectives was also shown in the meta-meta perspectives of the respondents, that is, in the way they believed their partner would perceive they had evaluated the various issues. The meta-meta perspective of both was related largely to their stereotype perspective of the other rather than the actual views of their partner. In accordance with various intracultural studies (for a review of several, see Norman (1969)), both Australians and Japanese expected a difference between their own evaluations and their partner's perceptions of their evaluations and were accurate in assessing its direction. However, each group felt understood to a considerably greater extent than was actually the case.

The findings of the study have important implications for the management and training of personnel within multinational corporations. The importance of the stereotype perspectives in providing a directional reference point (albeit, still an inadequate one) for the perceptions of expatriates and locals with respect to one another's attitudes lends considerable support to stereotype-based training programs. Foremost in developing such programs have been Bass and his colleagues (Bass, 1969) who have built up an enormous data bank of the managerial philosophies and practices of different cultures, and Fiedler and his colleagues (Fiedler, Mitchell and Triandis, 1971) who have worked on developing assimilators for various cultures. Though, as Bass himself has commented, "to rely alone on stereotypes would be folly when dealing with individuals" (Bass, 1971, p. 289), it would appear that (particularly in instances where there are wide differences between the cultures concerned) a reasonably "accurate" stereotype may actually enhance interpersonal understanding.

On a broader level, the findings provide considerable food for thought regarding the relationships between a multinational corporation and the host country. The model could usefully be extended to examine such issues, perhaps using senior management in multinational corporations and politicians in host countries as the subjects.

APPENDIX: THE COORIENTATIONAL ISSUES(1)

1. The head office of a multinational corporation must reserve the right to have the final say on any policy decision made in its subsidiaries.
2. A good leader should give detailed and complete instructions to his subordinates, rather than giving them merely general directions and depending upon their initiative to work out the details.
3. Determination and driving ambition are more important qualities for a businessman than an ability to work well with colleagues.
4. Australian employees are inadequately paid compared with their Japanese counterparts in this company.
5. On the whole, groups make better decisions than individuals.
6. It is quite reasonable to reserve certain key positions in the overseas subsidiary of a multinational corporation for executives of the parent company.

7. The average Australian employee seeks responsibility and is capable of exercising self-control with respect to that responsibility.

8. The private life of an employee is properly a matter of direct concern to his company for the two can never be entirely separated.

9. Sometimes in the operation of a subsidiary a matter can be decided only by the Japanese personnel acting alone, without involving the Australian personnel.

10. Open expression of disagreement with a superior by his subordinates is often a healthy means of ensuring that anxieties are released and that a better working environment is created.

11. A multinational corporation operating in Australia has a right to make public comment on any Australian political issues that affect it directly or indirectly.

12. Leadership skills can be acquired by most people regardless of their particular inborn traits or abilities.

13. There is no such thing as an eight-hour work day; one must be prepared to be on call at all times to attend to matters relating to one's job responsibilities.

14. Advancement for Australian employees within a Japanese subsidiary should be based on his job performance and should take little or no account of the number of years he has been with the company.

15. The head office of this company has too much say in the management and administration of this subsidiary.

16. The responsibility for an inappropriate business decision should be borne not by any single individual but, rather, by all persons consulted about or involved in deciding on that particular matter.

17. If a Japanese manager believes that the directives given by an Australian superior are not in the best interests of the corporation, he should bring the matter to the attention of his Japanese superiors and, if they agree, ignore the directives of the Australian.

18. Job definitions and job responsibilities should be as broad as possible in scope.

19. Australians employed by multinational corporations with branches in Australia have just as much loyalty to the corporation as their colleagues from head office.

20. No employee of this subsidiary should be fired because of circumstances he played no direct part in bringing about (for example, as a result of a downturn in the economy).

21. It is more important for young employees to learn to respect authority than it is for them to become independent decision makers.

22. When decisions are made in the Australian subsidiary of a multinational corporation, the welfare of the whole worldwide corporation should be considered, not just the welfare of the Australian subsidiary.

23. Compromise results in inappropriate decisions; an executive should hold out for what he believes is right.
24. Australian employees are generally more motivated to work well as a result of an atmosphere of group harmony and cooperation than as a result of generous financial incentives.
25. Any member of middle- or upper-management should be willing to work overtime, irrespective of whether he is paid for this or not, whenever circumstances in the company require this.
26. In the case of most business decisions it is more important that a consensus is reached between the personnel concerned regarding the best course of action than that a decision is made quickly.

NOTE

(1) The instructions to respondents for the four parts of Section B were as follows:

Direct Perspective:	"Please state your opinion with respect to each of the following statements."
Meta Perspective:	"How do you think Mr . . . would respond to each of the following statements?"
Meta-meta Perspective:	"How would Mr . . . think you would respond to each of the following statements?"
Australian's Stereotype Perspective:	"How do you think the average Japanese businessman in Australia would respond to each of the following statements?"
Japanese's Stereotype Perspective:	"How do you think the average Australian employed by a Japanese company would respond to each of the following statements?"

REFERENCES

Alpander, Guvenc C. 1973. "Drift to Authoritarianism: The Changing Managerial Styles of the U.S. Executives Overseas." Journal of International Business Studies 4:1-14.

Bass, Bernard M. 1971. "The American Advisor Abroad." Journal of Applied Behavioral Science 7:285-308.

Bass, Bernard M. 1969. "Combining Management Training and Research: Management Analysis Exercises to Build International Data Bank." In Comparative Management and Marketing: Text and Readings, ed. J. Boddewyn, Glenview, Ill.: Scott, Foresman.

Bass, Bernard M., and Eldridge, Larry D. 1973. "Accelerated Managers' Objectives in Twelve Countries." Industrial Relations 12:158-171.

Bowes, John E. 1977. "Stereotyping and Communication Accuracy." Journalism Quarterly 54:70-76.

Brislin, Richard W., and Baumgardner, Steven R. 1971. "Non-Random Sampling of Individuals in Cross-Cultural Research." Journal of Cross-Cultural Psychology 2:397-400.

Chaffee, Steven H. 1972. "The Interpersonal Context of Mass Communication." In Current Perspectives in Mass Communication Research, ed. F. Gerald Kline and Phillip J. Tichenor, Beverly Hills: Sage Publications.

Chaffee, Steven H. and McLeod, Jack M. 1968. "Sensitization in Panel Design: A Coorientational Experiment." Journalism Quarterly 45:661-669.

Farace, Richard V., Monge, Peter R., and Russell, Hamish M. 1977. Communicating and Organizing. Reading, Mass.: Addison-Wesley.

Feather, Norman T. 1976. "Value Systems of Self and Other Australian Expatriates as Perceived by Indigenous Students in Papua New Guinea." International Journal of Psychology 11:101-110.

Goffman, Erving. 1971. Strategic Interaction. Philadelphia: University of Pennsylvania Press.

---. 1959. The Presentation of Self in Everyday Life. Garden City, N.Y.: Doubleday.

Haire, Mason, Ghiselli, Edward E., and Porter, Lyman W. 1966. Managerial Thinking: An International Study. New York: John Wiley.

Harari, Ehud, and Zeira, Yoram. 1976. "Limitations and Prospects of Planned Change in Multinational Corporations." Human Relations 29:659-676.

Harari, Ehud, and Zeira, Yoram. 1974. "Morale Problems in Non-American Multinational Corporations in the United States." Management International Review 14, no. 6: 43-53.

Kelman, Herbert C. 1965. "Social-Psychological Approaches to the Study of International Relations: Definition of Scope." In International Behavior: A Social-Psychological Analysis, ed. Herbert C. Kelman, New York: Holt, Rinehart and Winston.

Kraut, Allen I. 1973. "Management Assessment in International Organizations." Industrial Relations 12:172-182.

Laing, R.D., Phillipson, H., and Lee, A.R. 1966. Interpersonal Perception: A Theory and a Method of Research. London: Tavistock Publications.

McLeod, Jack M., and Chaffee, Steven H. 1972-73. "Interpersonal Approaches to Communication Research." American Behavioral Scientist 16:469-499.

---. 1972. The Construction of Social Reality." In The Social Influence Process, ed. James T. Tedeschi, Chicago: Aldine.

Mead, George Herbert, ed. 1934. Mind, Self and Society. Chicago: University of Chicago Press.

Negandhi, Anant, R., and Prasad, S. Benjamin. 1971. Comparative Management. New York: Appleton-Century-Crofts.

Newcomb, Theodore, M. 1953. "An Approach to the Study of Communicative Acts. Psychological Review 60:393-404.

Nie, N.H., Hull, C.H., Jenkins, J.G., Steinbrenner, K., and Bent, D.H. 1975. Statistical Package for the Social Sciences. 2nd ed. New York: McGraw-Hill.

Norman, Warren T. 1969. "To See Ourselves as Others See Us!: Relations Among Self-Perceptions, Peer Perceptions and Expected Peer Perceptions of Personality Attributes." Multivariate Behavioral Research 4:417-443.

Nwankwo, Robert L. 1973. "Communication as Symbolic Interaction: A Synthesis." Journal of Communication 23: 195-215.

Rogers, Everett M., and Bhowmik, Dilip K. 1970-71. "Homophily-Heterophily: Relation Concepts for Communication Research." Public Opinion Quarterly 34:523-538.

Sayles, Leonard. 1964. Managerial Behavior. New York: McGraw-Hill.

Scheff, Thomas J. 1967. "Toward A Sociological Model of Consensus." American Sociological Review 32:32-46.

Schein, Edgar A. 1966-67. "Attitude Change During Management Education." Administrative Science Quarterly 11:601-628.

Sherif, Muzafer, and Hovland, Carl I. 1961. Social Judgment: Assimilation and Contrast Effects in Communication and Attitude Change. New Haven: Yale University Press.

Sullivan, Harry Stack. 1953. The Interpersonal Theory of Psychiatry. New York: W.W. Norton.

Tagiuri, R., Bruner, J.S., and Blake, R.R. 1958. "On the Relation Between Feelings and Perceptions of Feelings Among Members of Small Groups." In Readings in Social Psychology, ed. E. Maccoby et al., New York: Henry Holt.

Thomas, John M. 1967. "Role and Self in Organizational Behavior: An Interpersonal Perspective." In Behavioral Sciences in Management, ed. Suresh Srivastva, London: Asia Publishing House.

Toyne, Brian. 1976. "Host Country Managers of Multinational Firms: An Evaluation of Variables Affecting Their Managerial Thinking Patterns." Journal of International Business Studies 7, no. 2:39-55.

Triandis, Harry C. 1977. Interpersonal Behavior. Monterey, Calif.: Brooks/Cole.

Triandis, Harry C. 1972. The Analysis of Subjective Culture. New York: John Wiley.

Vansina, L.S. 1968. "Cultural Issues Within Multinational Organizations." In Proceedings of the XVIth International Congress of Applied Psychology, Amsterdam: Swets and Zeitlinger.

Whitehill, Arthur M. 1969. "Cultural Values and Employee Attitudes: United States and Japan." Journal of Applied Psychology 48:69-72.

Whitely, William, and England, George W. 1977. "Managerial Values as a Reflection of Culture and the Process of Industrialization." Academy of Management Journal 20: 439-453.

Wirth, Louis. 1948. "Consensus and Mass Communication." American Sociological Review 13:1-15.

12 Japanese Managers and Management in the Western World: A Canadian Experience
Hiro Matsusaki

UNIQUENESS OF JAPANESE MANAGEMENT

Since the basic principles of Japanese management were initially outlined as quite different from American principles but
nonetheless very efficient (Abegglen, 1958), the nature of the
unique Japanese management style has been studied from a
variety of disciplinary viewpoints. For example, they range
from an anthropological perspective (Vogel 1963, 1979; Nakane,
1967, 1970, 1972) to managerial perspectives (Yoshino, 1968;
Adams and Kobayashi, 1969; Gibney, 1975).

Interests in Japanese management reached a peak, so to
speak, when it was regarded as providing useful suggestions
or models to be emulated in North America. The competitive
advantage of Japanese business, then, had been attributed to
high employee morale, institutional loyalty and individual
motivation - the very aspect of American management that
appeared to be lacking In American industrial relations and
management practices. The management literature had been
laced with such catchy titles as "How We Can Learn From
Japanese Management" (Drucker, 1971) and "Made in America
(Under Japanese Management)" (Johnson and Ouchi, 1974).
Although some critical voices were also heard (Sethi, 1973),
the general tenets of the discussion were favorable to Japanese
style of management (Robinson, 1971; Diebold, 1973).

Recently, the very success of the Japanese business in
major world markets had inspired a strong sense of rivalry and
resentment, and it has become unfashionable to tout the vir-
tues of Japanese management. But, scholarly interests in
Japanese management continue.

As the activities of Japan-based multinational corporations
have grown in relative importance, there seems to exist a sort

of revival of academic investigation on the effectiveness of
Japanese management in different cultural settings or environments. The Japanese ways of doing business, for one thing,
present sharp contrasts to the Western practices, providing an
interesting material for cross-cultural studies. The increased
foreign direct investment on the part of Japanese business,
moreover, have expanded an empirical data base, offering suitable research opportunities to management scholars.

APPLICABILITY OF JAPANESE MANAGEMENT PRACTICES

The seeming uniqueness and the apparent business success
enjoyed by Japanese "ways" of conducting business have inspired a search for probable "reasons" or possible "causes" for
effective performance. The effort has taken a variety of
forms.

In the United States, the advantages of Japanese style of
management have been discussed, with special reference to its
applicability to the North American context. The argument has
centered around the notion that if Japanese business is successful, its management practices must have something going
for it. Generally, journalism includes most of the advocates
(Business Week, 1977, 1978) who imply that the principles of
Japanese management can and should be applied successfully in
America to boost efficiency.

However, management and organization scholars or researchers have tended to approach the topic by focusing on
the relative efficiency of respective management in comparable,
controlled settings. Often, empirical and experimental measures have been taken concerning the functioning of the
organizations. A comparative analysis can be taken of
performance proxy variables or surrogates including
productivity, communication, employee turnover or morale, and
related measures on various ratios of material inputs versus
tangible outputs. According to a recent study (Pascale,
1978), after carefully accounting for the environmental differences in governmental policy, technological condition, and
so on, it was found that there were practically no differences
in productivity under respective management in the United
States and in Japan.

Compared to this somewhat "micro" point of view in
America, where a rigorous comparison is made to discover the
different impacts of the management practices, the general
European writings about Japanese business approach the subject from typically a "macro" point of view. Europeans seem to
ascribe the nature of business success enjoyed by the Japanese organizations to the general environmental factors.
Rather than the strength of management, the reference is often

made to the unique Japanese history, industrial structure, comparative environmental advantages, political stability, external and internal economies of scale, and so on.

The different approaches adopted to study the reasons for business success should be noticed here. The U.S. approach is predominantly analytical, and thus credits or discredits the internal organizational factors. The European approach is to note the external factors of the environment as the root cause of Japanese business success and negate the traditional variables of organization design, functional structures, work flows or arrangement, and others. Put differently, the European approach can be summarized as being philosophically reasoned, and the American as being empirically scientific. This rough observation can be corroborated by the popularity of the contingency theory in the U.S. (Lawrence and Lorsch 1962), and the organization research tradition with various behavioral science tools of analysis.

Interestingly, until recently the Japanese writers on the subject have been critical of their own "ways" of doing business, advocating more westernized "ways" of American management principles - including human relations, sensitivity training, project teams, merit pay, profit centers and so on - within the Japanese environment. Thus, very few have advocated the use of Japanese style management outside of Japan. They have argued that the Japanese style management must be modified for application in different cultures.

In reality, however, few business executives have been so adept or resourceful as to switch over, suddenly, to what they perceive as the American way of doing things in their overseas assignments, even in their U.S. ventures. Failures and successes have followed. Then, with an increase of direct foreign investment in South East Asia, the needs for adaptation have increased but the degree of adaptation to the western ways has generally declined. And again, both failures and successes have resulted.

On the other hand, Japanese management researchers, once very critical of their own style of management, have started to reappraise its applicability in different foreign environments. A systematic effort has been made, for example, to discover both the strength and weakness of Japanese management in foreign ventures (Sakamoto et al., 1973; Nihon Keizai Chosa Kogyo Kai, 1976). Meantime, empirical data about actual Japanese experiences have increased to provide valuable clues to practicing business executives. Journalistic reports give general backgrounds (Nakagawa, 1974; Kaminogo, 1975; Asahi Shinbun Keizaibu, 1977), while case histories recounted by practitioners can be illuminating (Shioda, 1976; Mistubishi Shoji Koho Shitsu, 1977) reflecting a variety of viewpoints and international settings (Hattori, 1972; Watanabe, 1973).

THE JAPANESE STYLE OF DOING BUSINESS:
THE MANAGERIAL DIFFERENCES

The Development of Management Thought in Japan

Modern management terms and jargons are a well-established concept in daily business parlance for business executives in Japan. For example, many of the latest marketing techniques find ready acceptance, wide diffusion, and selected applications in Japan - with little time lag from their advocated use in America. The applicability of newer management techniques will at least be tested by leading practitioners in Japan. The situation resembles that in the United States.

The terminologies or the concepts of modern management techniques are, however, quite foreign to the Japanese language. Often, they are introduced in the original phoneticized form, since there are no suitable Japanese counterparts available. Many marketing terms fall under this category, even today.

When Peter Drucker's Practice of Management (1954) was being translated toward the end of the 1950s, many new terms and phrases had to be coined: the ideas in the book had no equivalent expressions in the Japanese - they were totally novel. Thus many expressions had been invented, sounding quite awkward at the time, sometimes reviving somewhat archaic classical Chinese and traditional Japanese terms. For all the pioneering efforts, however, the book was very well received, selling over a million copies in three installment versions over a few years. The translation was a voluntary work by a group of young executives who had organized themselves under the banner of gendai keiei kenkyu kai (modern management research group), which had used the original work by Drucker as a text for their regular weekly study sessions.

This episode underscores the newness of "modern" management concepts, including marketing concepts and techniques, in Japan. The ideas and tools of "modern" management have been new to the language, and consequently new to the psyche of the people as well. In the two decades since then, however, Japanese executives seem to have learned to accept the ideas, techniques, and concepts of "modern" management - judging from the nature of the literature available on the subject.

The Japanese have also developed what may be aptly called their own unique and somewhat indigenous set of management techniques, by extending the initial conceptualization on problem solving and creativity stimulation (Kawakita, 1967, 1970; Nakayama, 1968, 1970). The adaptations have been made to maximize the impact use of the language, group decision-making practices, and the psyche of the people - far beyond the initial development - to suit the managerial climate of Japan. And they have been well accepted.

Japanese Perception of Japanese Style of Management

If there is a strictly traditional style of management in Japan, and if the existing practices reflect it, then the dominant characteristic is yet to evolve: it cannot be separated from the background culture and the surrounding milieu. In my view, it is still evolving on a trial-and-error basis. It operates from day to day, adopting what seems to work best as situations warrant. It is an existential experiment - very elastic in principles. And history and tradition have dictated its current course of development.

If this observation holds, the rapid diffusion of modern American managerial techniques can be understood as a Japanese attempt to improve the practices. For example, performance review and merit evaluation systems have been widely accepted, but they seldom serve the same purpose in terms of reward and salary determination. Likewise, the idea of profit as the business objective has been accepted without reservation, but its manifestation in organization structures or functions can be radically different.

Customs reinforce the management practices, but changes are built into the Japanese system, perhaps for this reason. It also explains why some American ideas or techniques have never caught on, despite repeated attempts at introduction, and appears as if the Japanese practices are incompatible with the Western notions of management. For example, the human relations approach was never popular, despite ardent advocates. Everyone seems to agree that the techniques associated with detailed job descriptions and operating manuals of procedures as a valuable managerial tool, but they are seldom utilized to the extent they are in the United States. The product-division system was adopted by many large companies, but subsequently dropped for lack of tangible results, while some firms had insisted that they had had the system for quite some time with good results and that they had found no need to "adopt" it.

Moreover, the economic outlook at this juncture of 1980 is that of retrenchment. Many large firms have already retrenched considerably by forcibly trimming off the "extra" workforce geared to the growth and prosperity of the pre-oil crisis days. They have responded to the need for retrenchment by asking older employees to retire earlier than the stipulated age limit (which in many cases has been about 55) and by removing unwritten rules to offer reemployment after the formal retirement age. The move has been tantamount to a de facto firing of the middle-aged and older employees.

In view of the traditional custom of a lifetime employment and the seniority system in Japan, the recent trend is doubly significant for is severity and social repercussions. Apparently the move to "rationalize" has met little opposition from those most affected by it. Many seemingly profitable companies have also resorted to it and as a result, the employment problem for the less mobile middle- and older-aged has become a social issue, which has inspired a special governmental action to mitigate its impacts.

From the vantage point of the Japanese business, therefore, it appears that there are no traditional ways of management, nor a uniquely Japanese style of management. Perhaps the practice currently in use is best for Japanese management - subject to future modification and improvements, as the need may arise.

American Perception of Japanese Style of Management

As an originator of modern management techniques, the American executives seem to be puzzled by the Japanese response to modern management. For despite the apparent disregard of the basic management principles, Japanese were highly efficient (Abegglen, 1958) and have continued to be so even in the United States (Johnson and Ouchi, 1974). The general consensus is that of a difference resulting in more effective performance.

While this notion may be in error and contrary to rigorous analytical findings (Pascale, 1978, p. 153), the difference is real. Those who have had an opportunity to deal with Japanese businessmen in Japan do attest to the salient difference in management practices - sometimes on a very humorous note - from a variety of vantage points (Maloney, 1975, 1977; Gibney, 1975).

The problem in understanding what makes Japanese management different is compounded by a relative neglect on the part of U.S. business to understand foreign management cultures. In contrast, the Japanese have attempted to explain the major managerial differences foreign businesspeople are likely to encounter when doing business in Japan through various seminars and production of 16mm films (Council for International Understanding, 1977). Japan External Trade Organization (JETRO), for example, has been active in promoting export sales to Japan through its U.S. offices, rather than promoting export sales from Japan, supported by a series of well-planned pamphlets and documents outlining the nature of the Japanese market and managerial practices.

Study of Japanese management by research scholars, in the meantime, has been marked by a variety of different approaches, mirroring their disciplinary background and training.

Their findings, therefore, do not constitute a definitive, integrated body of knowledge about Japanese management either. For these reasons, there seems to exist no firm comprehension of what actually constitutes the Japanese "style" of management, or what differences in management practices exist between Japan and the United States.

Despite limitations, however, a large body of knowledge has accumulated relative to the workings of business and management practices in Japan, from a variety of viewpoints and different vantage points of allied academic disciplines. It is not the purpose to present here an integrated body of knowledge on the subject, synthesizing the diverse materials from different perspectives. Only the major differences between the two will be outlined by way of introduction to the subject and the main body of the research findings to be presented. It is best to remember that not only the frames of reference but also the levels of abstraction can differ considerably when discussing the Japanese style of management practices, depending on study approaches.

THE JAPANESE PERCEPTION OF THE JAPANESE MANAGEMENT "STYLE"

From actual case histories and joint-venture experiences in overseas direct investment, the Japanese seem to have learned that almost everything they do can be different from the local practice, but that it can also be acceptable - at a cost - until learning and mutual accommodation take place. Thus, in overseas ventures they will consciously attempt to adopt to the Western ways of doing business. According to a series of field research works, almost all the respondent executives in Japanese overseas ventures have modified or changed their managerial practices (Shishido et al., 1977). Apparently, on a trial-and-error basis, a direct application of Japanese "ways" of management have been avoided outside of Japan. For example, employee relations will be altered to conform to the local practices, as much as possible and practicable.

Interestingly, these executives have not been able to point out the major features of "Japanese" management. Generally they have vaguely referred to certain techniques and concepts in management, which have not amounted to a set of well-defined features under an overall conceptual framework. The respondents have had different observations and ideas in this regard.

In my view, the Japanese management practices mirror Japanese language, culture, and environment to such an extent that most of the frames of reference in management practices cannot be articulated. They can be reached by a process of

elimination, by discounting anything not included in the reference frames. Whatever the reference points the Japanese
executives may have about their own management, therefore,
have originated with American management scholars or authors.
The Japanese have learned from Americans what makes their
system unique and different from the Western management
practices.

THE AMERICAN PERCEPTION OF THE JAPANESE MANAGEMENT "STYLE"

Normally, the custom of a lifetime commitment (shushin koyo)
strikes the Westerner as the most Japanese feature and perhaps the most salient characteristic, followed by the seniority
rule (nenko seido) and the group decision practices (shudan
ishi kettei or gogi sei, consensus system), although no clear
agreement exists among management scholars (Abegglen, 1958;
Yoshino, 1968; Gibney, 1975, pp. 169-219). The idea of a
lifetime employment by one company would sound rather far-
fetched to the American pysche, if not to the European
psyche, and therefore this is one of the major differences
often quoted.

Similarly, the seniority and the consensus system strike
the Westerner as contrary to the accepted practices. The
former runs counter to technological progress, industrial efficiency, and general worker morale, while the latter suggests
an opposite stance of democracy in action. Furthermore, many
Japanese firms operating in the American environment have
apparently retained many traditional features in their management practices, either by design or by default, and performed
well - for better or for worse. Thus, there has evolved a
myth that the management style is very different, but defi-
nitely better (Business Week, 1978). (Perhaps, facts are
stranger than fiction, and myths and realities can be so far
apart!)

Every business executive with some Japanese experience
seems to assert that there are sharp, contrasting differences
in the management practices. But they are often limited to
isolated observations, incidents, scenarios, and general im-
pressions including hearsay. On the other hand, the researchers tend to reflect their disciplinary backgrounds and
training in interpreting the empirical evidence, often leading to
analytical but fragmented results. They can see the trees
clearly, but not the forest.

THE "MACRO" LEVEL CONTRASTS IN THE
BUSINESS PRACTICES

With occasional help of a research assistant with North American cultural background, I spent nearly a year in Japan to
observe and record those unique features and special characteristics that seem to be in sharp contrast to the Western
business and management practices. The process included
literature study, interviews, news reportings, and a limited
number of personal contacts.
    Only those observations or the phenomena that appeared
to be "contrary" or "opposite" to the American perception were
noted. Minor differences were disregarded. Since there had
been no fixed reference, or anchor point, to indicate what
constituted American management practices at that time, a
great deal of liberty was taken in that respect. The purpose
of the research was to understand the Japanese style of management, and not to generalize the prevalent managerial patterns in actual practices in North America.
    Since personal experience, observations and intuitions
played a significant role in generating the original data, the
basic methodology employed to arrive at the listing of the contrasts was that of a method of abduction from available data.
This method is often advocated in anthropological field investigation. It is also applied for problem solving and creativity
stimulation in business, government, educational institutions
and the like in Japan, and has enjoyed a good reputation and
wide acceptance (Kawakita, 1970).
    Initially, the observed contrasts were summarized at the
three levels of individual, organization, and industry.   And
for expositional purposes, the listed contrasts were somewhat
exaggerated. As generalizations went, there were many exceptions to the rule, so to speak, of contrasts.
    A summary of the contrasts are given, in a highly con-
densed manner, on table 12.1, which follows.
    The observations as the basis for table 12.1 are drawn at
a societal level. They are a "large picture" in a sense that
they have been inferred from the contrasting phenomena as
practiced in respective cultural settings, more or less in a
"pure" form. They can provide a theoretical underpinning for
studying the adaptation in management practices which may
take place in a cross-cultural management situation in joint
venture firms, at the "micro" level.
    Also to be noted is the fact that they are not assigned to
any particular classification by a predetermined conceptual
design, as with the case of a majority of cross-cultural research data. No central theoretical frameworks have been
used to collect the data. Instead, the empirical observations
of the salient contrasts have been compiled. Then, no arbi-

Table 12.1.   A Macro Level Comparison of Business
and Organizational Practices: Between Japan and North America

Practices	Japan	North America
(Jobs to be Done)		
Work assignments	Fits jobs to workers	Fits workers to jobs
Worker specification	General qualities	Specific skill qualities
Job description	Assigned to groups	Assigned to individual posts
Task responsibility	Broadly defined	Narrowly and sharply defined
Task orientation	Elastic, multi-roles	Rigid, highly specialized
Accountability	Minimum performance expectations and levels	Maximum limits indicated demarcation for disclaimers
(Modus Operandi)		
Functions of the boss and manager	Liaison things and people: coordinate tasks	Order people and things around: see that the job's done
Use of assistant or executive secretary	Rare	Common
In-house training job rotation	Widely used Generally welcomed	Used on a limited scale Not necessarily a welcome thing
Attitudes toward flow of work: new tasks, etc.	Very willing to tackle any outside works, if they belong to the group	Seldom willing to take up the duties not within one's purview, even if left undone
(Work Habits)		
Office hours	Start at the same time	Ends at the same time
Use of company time	Elastic, tends to stretch for personal usage	Exact, measured rigorously to exclude personal use
Flow of information	Multi-channeled, group basis	Limited-channel, individually
Communications	Circular, two-ways, redundant	Uni-directional, one-way
Colleagueship	Cooperation: harmony	Confrontation: competence
People skills	Group conscious	Individual conscious
(Mobility)		
Executives	Intracompany, vertically	Intercompany, horizontal
Social	Through business activities	Through community involvement
Promotion	On seniority/judgement	On achievement/drive/ability
Merit base	Generalized norms	Specific norms
Loyalty	To the company - the group	To the profession - the boss

trary categorization or assignment of the data to an established classificatory scheme has been made to process the data. Rather, meanings have been assigned to the observed empirical data, only after the collection of the data has finished, by a successive exercise of concept formulation and idea generation. The concepts created in this way, as per table 12.1 under practices, are therefore neither mutually exclusive nor distinct. They are formed as a result of the researcher's judgment as to how close the observation is associated with other "like" observations, more or less on an intuitive basis. No preconceived drawers or boxes have been used to sort out and assign the observation to a particular slot.

IMPLICATIONS OF THE MACRO-LEVEL FINDINGS

The major features for respective management styles and practices in table 12.1 are highly interrelated. For each culture, the observations are functionally interdependent and congruent among themselves. This tentative conclusion applied to the initial set of more detailed contrasts at the three levels of individual, organization, and industry. The condensed data in table 12.1 suggest that the functional interrelationships can be reduced to a relatively simple set of concepts, as the data contained there have been more exaggerated to permit this exercise.

From the macro-level contrasts, therefore, I have chosen a term "generalist orientation" to denote the most salient organizational features of Japanese management, and a contrasting term "specialist orientation" to denote the common element for American management practices. This conceptualization extends, hopefully, beyond the original meanings attached to the term generalist and specialist, or generalization and specialization, which would be at the micro level of individual executives. The new concepts, then, can be applied to the macro level of the management practices in Japan and in America, so that the major features can be labelled under them in a convenient, abbreviated fashion.

If the above analyses hold, the findings can be applied to many of the cross-cultural management conflict situations or problems involving Japanese managers and management in North America. It can be shown that the conflicts are inevitable, that the conflict resolution must involve more than token adaptations or adjustments in operational specifics, and that mutual accommodation and learning must eventually take place from both sides to understand the "other" system. These are the tangible, direct benefits of practical nature which can be derived from the study.

At a theoretical plane, the notion of the generalist versus specialist orientation can be constructed to denote the basic management principle of organization design. It is possible to argue that at any given "micro" level of specific business, a proper mix of the two polar constructs must exist, and that the mix has to be functionally viable to be effective. And therefore, as a matter of policy, the orientation can be a useful "ideal type" construct to understand the functioning of a multinational firm. It can be employed to understand the functioning of the multinational firms with various national origins. This, then, would be the task left to future research and scholarly investigation. Tentatively, the policy implications are outlined on table 12.2, which follows.

THE CANADIAN EXPERIENCE AT THE "MICRO" LEVEL: AN EMPIRICAL TEST

A series of field research trips were conducted in order to interview the top executives at the major Japanese joint ventures in manufacturing or in direct sales in Canada, mostly concentrated in and around Vancouver, Manitoba, Toronto, and Montreal. Excluding those in the export, import or service industries, there were about 30 firms. All the executives in managerial, decision-making capacities in these firms were asked to fill out an 80-item, self-administered questionnaire on an anonymous basis. About eighty usable returns were eventually obtained, roughly half being Canadian executives with Canadian cultural background and the rest being European or Japanese in origin.

One of the chief objectives of the questionnaire was to discover the predictor variables that can differentiate the two groups of the executives from Canada and from Japan. Contrary to the initial expectations, however, the discriminant variables have not surfaced among the perception measures on the self-image, achievement motivation, self actualization, etcetera, nor among the situational measures. At best the interest patterns differed between the two groups, as were the property measures of the culture, language, training and so on. The full details of the research design cannot be outlined here, due to space limitation. But, the results indicated an almost identical response pattern between the two groups, with one exception: the composition of the self-image.

An examination of the measures on the self-image of the respondents revealed that the Japanese executives demonstrated a very high intercorrelations of the component dimensions, whereas the Canadian executives did exhibit the opposite tendency of low component intercorrelations. The component image patterns showed similarities on an item by item compo-

Table 12.2. The Policy Implications of Generalist versus Specialist Orientation Construct

	Generalist Orientation (Japan)	Specialist Orientation (North America)
Organizational Pattern (Business Needs)		
Effective adaptation to changing environment	Flexible, can adjust by internal development for new skills	Rigid, must adapt by an inflow of new blood from outside
Efficiency (input/output)	Redundancies: ambiguity	Straightforward: maximum
Performance norms	Longer-run . . . general	Shorter-run . . . specific
Executive growth	Situational general to the milieu	Skill acquisition specific to chosen skills
Basic philosophy (jobs to be done)	Workers exist and come first (fits jobs to workers)	Jobs exist and come first (fits workers to jobs)
Talent use (modus operandi)	Coordination and liaison: planning	Performance and results: execution: not the process
Task environment (work habits)	Whole person involved group, harmony, togetherness, cooperation	Segmented skills involved individual, competence, confront and compete
Aspiration (mobility)	Generalized norms long timeframe intangible	Specialized norms short timeframe tangible

nent basis. But, they reflected an entirely different set of one's own image vis-a-vis the ego-involving reference groups of respective peers.

Put differently, the two groups reacted differently in composing an overall reference image of themselves, when pitted against the "competing" peers. There existed in the minds of the Canadian executives a clearly separable "specialized" talent component. If they were good on one dimension, it did not necessarily mean that they were equally as good on other dimensions, or vice versa. On the other hand, the Japanese executives regarded themselves as sort of "generalists," balancing the talent components rather evenly.

In terms of the ratings scores on each dimension, regardless of the cultural groups used as a reference, the Canadian executives had a strong inclination to differentiate each component dimension separately and independently of the others. The self-ratings of the Japanese executive on one dimension was highly dependent on other ratings. They linked their ratings together without distinguishing one dimension from the others.

DISCUSSION

While there may be some structural factors unique to the surveyed firms in Canada, which could partly account for the sharp differences noted, the findings agree with the macro level contrasts given in table 12.1. Many of the listed features about Japanese management style or practices reflect a predominance of the generalist philosophy, tendency, and advantages, while the opposite tendency of specialist leanings can be discerned in the Canadian practices. As far as the Japanese-Canadian joint ventures went, the respective groups of executives have retained their basic orientations in this regard.

Generally, the Japanese expected their Canadian counterparts to be more versatile and perform "other," related duties. On the other hand, the Canadians expressed doubts about the ambiguity and lack of responsibility or authority in the Japanese ways of doing business. Clearly, the Japanese management style runs a direct collision course against the local, specialist performance norms.

The questionnaire returns seem to have endorsed our theoretical postulate. They provided the data base to point out the prominence of the generalist orientation in Japan and the specialist orientation in Canada. A replication in the United States of a similar study may provide an additional data base, despite the learning and adaptation occurring there, as the Japanese ventures in Canada were at a formative stage when the investigation was made.

This line of research follows the traditional methods in natural sciences of experimentation, hypotheses testing, and controlled replication of the phenomena for measurement and analysis. The field data are used either to confirm or refute statistically, (accept or reject) the postulated arguments, as in processing the laboratory data.

This approach - a highly analytical one - cannot be extended to cross-cultural research without reservation. For the cross-cultural management situation is essentially a learning situation. Most problems encountered there are unexpected, quite often, unpredictable and cover a wide range of phenomena. Hypothesis testing in the traditional sense requires stability of the phenomena under study, or the latent cause of conflicts.

The problem becomes compounded by the essentially very soft nature of the data involved. Artificial stimuli are introduced to solicit artificial responses and behavioral reactions, which are measured by "proven" instruments. How can we continue to break a slice of the pie into smaller and smaller pieces to understand it? There seems to be a limit in our typically analytical approach.

For example, when technology and governmental factors are equal, the Japanese companies' U.S. subsidiaries do not outperform their American counterparts, despite what has been widely reported in the U.S. press to the contrary (Pascale, 1978, p. 153). Moreover, the administrative process of communication, the quality of decision making, and the tools and actual organization processes of management, however different they may be between Japan and the U.S., do not seem to affect their relative performance (Pascale, 1978, p. 154).

This line of reasoning and discussion suggests that there are specific differences in management practices, but they are not a major determinant of effective performance. A logical extension of this argument would be that an application of American ways of doing business in Japan, or of Japanese style of management in America, may do just fine - as a matter of fact, as well as any other styles of management. A further consequence of this logic would lead us to conclude that, for overseas ventures, any management style may succeed as long as the user is familiar with it and produces results - regardless of the environment.

As a corollary to the above discussion, I have encountered a variety of approaches among the Canadian ventures by Japanese multinational firms. They ranged from a very traditional, Japanese style to a very localized, adaptive pattern of doing business. From my own observations, there were no recognizable, "set" patterns of adaptation. Radically different adaptive management styles were noted, despite their seemingly successful or mediocre performance. And the Japanese themselves did not seem to have any clear idea as to what could be the best approach.

CONCLUDING REMARKS

The macro-level contrasts suggest that the nature and type of conflicts in cross-cultural management, such as would be encountered in joint ventures, can be explained by the notions of the generalist versus specialist orientation. Also, the conceptual findings from the micro level research tend to reinforce and endorse the macro level contrasts. Thus the root causes of conflicts can perhaps be traced to the fundamental orientations and their differences.

The Japanese orientation is consistent with the formal education, training, professional experience, interpersonal relationships and others noted for the Japanese society, which are basically geared to some sort of involvement of the entire person with the business career. On the contrary, the Canadian orientation is not compatible with these Japanese patterns, but it does conform to the corresponding dimensions of the Canadian social fabric.

Therefore, it is possible to obtain a higher order set of concepts out of the interrelationship patterns explainable by these two concepts. In any joint venture situation at the "micro" level, a proper mix of the two polar ideal-type orientations could be found at a stable, equilibrium state. Further, cross-cultural conflicts and problems can be predictable and avoidable, if the theoretical constructs can be known in advance by both parties, as learning or mutual accommodation take place.

From a theoretical perspective, this position can be articulated. A hypothetical argument has emerged from this study: the generalist and the specialist orientations are at the core in understanding the cross-cultural management conflict problems between Japan and North America, and that this hypothesis can be extended to apply to general cross-cultural management situations, and further that the argument can be expanded to cover an important portion of the general organization behavior theory and research pertaining to the multinational firms and their operations.

REFERENCES

Abegglen, James C. 1958. The Japanese Factory. Glencoe, Ill.: Free Press.

Adams, T. F. M., and Kobayashi, N. 1969. The World of Japanese Business. Tokyo, New York, and San Francisco: Kodansha International.

Anonymous. 1977. "Japan's Ways Thrive in the U.S." Business Week (December 12), pp. 156-160.

---. 1978. "Texas Instrument Shows U.S. Business How To
Survive in the 1980s: Special Report." Business Week
(September 18), pp. 66-92.

Asahi Shinbun Keizaibu. 1977. Sogoshosha. Tokyo: Asahi
Shinbun Sha.

Council for International Understanding. 1977. "How to Do
Business in Japan - Negotiating a Contract." Los Angeles: Committee for International Business (A 16mm
color film, approx. 30 minutes).

De Mente, Boye. 1972. How To Do Business in Japan: A
Guide for International Businessmen. Los Angeles,
Calif.: Center for International Business.

Diebold, John. 1973. "Ideas and Trends: Management Can
Learn From Japan." Business Week (September 29), p.
14.

Drucker, Peter F. 1954. The Practice of Management. New
York: Harper and Row.

--- 1971. "What We Can Learn From Japanese Management."
Harvard Business Review 49 (March - April): pp. 110-
122.

Gibney, Frank. 1975. Japan: The Fragile Super Power.
Tokyo: Charles E. Tuttle.

Hattori, Masaya. 1972. Ruwanda Chuo Ginko Sosai Nikki (A
Diary of the President of Rwanda Central Bank). Tokyo:
Chuo Koron Sha.

Johnson, Richard Tanner, and Ouchi, William G. 1974. "Made
in America (Under Japanese Management)." Harvard
Business Review 52 (September-October): pp. 61-69.

Kaminogo, Toshiaki. 1975. Naze Kaigaini Shinshutsu Suruka
(Why Venture Out to Overseas?). Tokyo: Daiyamondo
Sha.

Kawakita, Jiro. 1967. Hassoho (Method of Idea Creation).
Tokyo: Chuokoron Sha.

--- 1970. Soku Hassoho (Sequel to Method of Idea Creation).
Tokyo: Chuokoron Sha.

Lawrence, Paul P., and Lorsch, Jay W. 1967. Organization and Environment. Boston: Harvard Graduate School of Business, Division of Research.

Maloney, Don. 1975. Japan: It's Not All Raw Fish. Tokyo: The Japan Times.

--- 1977. Son of Raw Fish. Tokyo: The Japan Times.

Mitsubishi Shoji Koho Shitsu (External Affairs, Mitsubishi Corporation). 1977. Jisa Wa Kane Nari (Time Lag is Money). Tokyo: The Simul Press.

Nakagawa, Yasuzo. 1974. Ujiminasu Monogatari (A Case History of Joint Steel Mill in Brazil). Tokyo: Sangyo Noritsu Tandai Shuppan Bu.

Nakayama, Masakazu. 1968. Kan no Kozo (Structure of the Sixth Sense Inspiration). Tokyo: Chuokoron Sha.

--- 1970. Hasso no Ronri (The Logic of Idea Generation). Tokyo: Chuokoron Sha.

Nakane, Chie. 1967. Tateshakai No Ningen Kankei (Human Relations in a Vertical Society). Tokyo: Kodan Sha.

Nakane, Chie. 1972. Tekio No Joken (Conditions for Adaptation). Tokyo: Kodan Sha.

Nakane, Chie. 1970. Japanese Society. Los Angeles, Calif.: University of California Press.

Nihon Keizai Chosa Kyogi Kai (Japan Economic Research Council). eds. 1976. Takokuseki Kigyo No Keiei: Nihon Kigyo Eno Shishin (Management of Multinational Firms: Pointers for Japanese Business). Tokyo Daiya Mondo Sha.

Pascale, Richard Tanner. 1978. "Zen and the Art of Management." Harvard Business Review 56 (March-April): 153-162.

Robinson, Richard D. 1971. "The Future of International Management." Journal of Business Studies, Spring.

Sakamoto, Yasumi, Sakurai, Tooru, Setou, Reiji, and Miura, Ikuya. 1973. Nihon Kigyo No Kaigai Shinshutsu: Keiei Kankyo To Sono Mondaiten (The Overseas Ventures of Japanese Enterprise: The Problems and Its Managerial Environment). Tokyo: Toyo Keizai Shinpo Sha.

Sethi, S. Prakash. 1973. "Drawbacks of Japanese Management." Business Week (November 24), pp. 12-14.

Shioda, Nagahide. 1976. Sogo Shosha (The Central Trading House). Tokyo: Nihon Keizai Shinbun Sha.

Vogel, Ezra F. 1963. Japan's New Middle Class: The Salary Man and His Family in a Tokyo Suburb. Calif.: University of California Press.

---. 1979. Japan As Number One. Cambridge: Harvard University Press.

Watanabe, Takeshi. 1973. Azia Kaigin Sosai Nikki (A Diary of the President of the Asian Development Bank). Tokyo: Nippon Keizai Shinbun Sha.

Yoshino, M.Y. 1968. Japan's Managerial System. Cambridge, Mass.: MIT Press.

13 Unresolved Issues: Agenda for Research

Anant R. Negandhi

In this volume, we outlined some of the critical issues confronting the multinational corporations and the home and host countries of the MNCs. The fast-changing international economic and political conditions, resulting in a two-digit inflation, unemployment, energy shortages, and slowdown in economic and industrial activities in the industrially-advanced countries as well as the developing countries, are the major problems facing the political leaders around the world.

The changing economic and political realities have resulted in the so-called North-South Dialogue and a debate on establishing a New International Economic Order. Gone are the days when industrially developed countries were the "givers" and the less-developed or developing countries were the salient "receivers" of the wealth, technology, and know-how of the rich countries. Although the disparities between the "have" and "have not" countries have not changed much as yet, what has changed are politically-charged overtones of the developing and the oil-rich Arab countries, demanding fundamental changes through the New International Economic Order. At the same time, while still enjoying a high standard of living, the industrially developed countries themselves are no longer rich enough to give away what they possess. They are experiencing difficulty in holding on to what they have. The developed world itself is confronted with serious problems of inflation, unemployment, and a stagnant economy, not to mention the socio-political upheaval which generally accompanies when the economic machine is moving too slow.

In the first section of this volume, we attempted to capture this changing economic and political scene, and pinpointed some obvious implications of these changes for the survival and growth of the multinational corporations.

273

In the same section, we also examined the impact of the multinational corporations at the socio-cultural levels in host countries.

Caught between the changing economic and political situations, restrictive and hostile environments, and the increasing social consciousness for preserving and improving the ecological systems, the multinationals are hard-put to balance the requirements of efficiency through their global rationalization of production and marketing processes and to adjust to each country's special demands and idiosyncracies. In Part II, we probed into some of these balancing acts of the multinational companies by examining their strategies, policy-making apparatus, organizational structures, and adaptive processes.

Lastly, in Part III, we took a brief look at the individual who ultimately manages or mismanages the operations of the MNCs by reviewing the manager's background, education, training, and outlook.

Although the research-based papers presented here provide useful insight into various problems discussed above, the gap between knowledge and ignorance is still vast and challenging.

We still do not know exactly where the present debate and dialogue on the New International Economic Order will lead us, and what the implications of these changes will be for the developed and developing countries as well as for the multinationals. Will the establishment of the New International Economic Order make the poor a little bit richer, and the rich a little bit poorer? Or will it make everybody wealthier and happier? And how will change be accomplished, by force or through peaceful and civilized means? Will change occur through governmental and international agencies, or through the private-enterprise system? And how will the multinationals be figured in this drama of world-wide change?

With respect to the multinational corporations' strategies, policies, organizational structures, and adaptive processes, we are unsure whether these attributes are rationally determined and implemented, or whether they are mainly ad-hoc procedures, shots-in-the-dark phenomena disguised under scientific jargon.

These and other unknowns were the concerns that prompted us to organize the conference at the International Institute of Management, Science Center, Berlin, where we gathered some 30 academicians, thoughtful businesspeople, and governmental officials to probe into these important questions.

As one would expect, academicians, businesspeople, and governmental officials have had different views, insights, and responses to many of the issues discussed. In the following few pages, we will outline some of their views and perspectives, since they do provide a challenging agenda for future research.

THE CHANGING ECONOMIC AND POLITICAL SCENE
AND THE ROLE OF THE MULTINATIONALS

The genesis of the current discussion, and hue and cry for establishing a New International Economic Order, is the failure of, and disappointment with, the result of the Development Decade, which hopelessly failed to generate needed industrial and economic growth in many of the developing countries. And whatever few economic gains were made during this time, they were swallowed up by an expanding population in these countries. Governments and political leaders lacked the will to create social legislation, (such as land reforms), to provide a conducive business environment, and to redistribute wealth for industrial and economic growth to become a reality – so declared the thoughtful businesspeople. They also argued that the multinationals can only create wealth, but bear no special responsibilities to redistribute the wealth throughout the country. Doing so would be nothing less than direct interference with the governmental policies and affairs, and would thereby jeopardize the nation-states' sovereignty.

They also argued that the MNCs have no way of resolving socio-economic and political problems of a country when the government is tightening their hands by imposing all sorts of imaginable restrictions on their operations. Our job is to produce goods and services at a price the consumer is willing to pay, they say. Our concern is to maintain and improve the efficiency of our operations. In this regard, we can help the government and society and uplift the well-being of the people through increased productivity of the work-force.

This is not so, argued the governmental decision-makers. International trade and investment, international division of labor, transfer of technology and management know-how, reduction of inequalities, redistribution of wealth,and creation of a large middle-class to generate and sustain growth are all interrelated phenomena, and the MNCs, for their own self-interest, must address these problems systematically and collectively. Business is part of the social fabric, and it must act that way, demanded the governmental officials. You cannot eat your cake alone – you must share with the people and be responsible in what you produce, how you produce, and for whom you produce the goods and services. The MNCs cannot thrive by just satisfying the needs of a handful of rich and middle-class urban dwellers. Attention must be paid to the needs of the large and poor rural population in those countries.

These arguments and counter-arguments are based on emotions rather than on scientific inquiry, lamented the academic crowd. They argued that we do not yet know enough about developmental and growth models. Yet growth itself may not be enough. What is needed is growth plus distribution policies, which could form a large middle class to sustain growth and prosperity in a given country. There may be many different roads to arrive at the same destination. Multinationals, governmental, political, and local business leaders need to work together to find the most suitable means for achieving the desired results. In this regard, the MNCs must assume the responsibilities to share their resources and knowledge in a more enlightening manner, rather than concentrating on achieving higher operational efficiency and return on their investments.

Whatever the merits and demerits of the above arguments and counter-arguments advanced by governmental and business leaders, one fact seems rather clear: the bargaining position between nation-states seems to be gaining. Only a few years ago, the multinationals were regarded as potentially a new world power. Vernon, for example, wrote in 1971, "Suddenly, it seems, the sovereign states are feeling naked. Concepts such as national sovereignty and national economic strength appear curiously drained of meaning" (Vernon, 1971, p. 3). In 1977 Vernon wrote, thereby reflecting this change in the bargaining power of the nation-states, "national leaders . . . have sensed that their own bargaining power has actually been increasing in their dealings with such enterprises" (Vernon, 1977, p. 194). Vernon attributes this shift in the bargaining position to a shrinkage of the international space, the improvement of communication, appearance of rival sources for the supply of needed capital and technology, and access to the international markets. Others have pinpointed the increased world demand for certain essential raw materials, such as oil and iron ore, as well as increasing political cohesion among developing countries at international levels (for example, the Group of 77 at the U.N.).

Whatever the reasons for this shift, as Bergsten has observed, "sovereignty is no longer at bay in host countries. To be sure, the degree of this shift in power differs from country to country and from industry to industry. It is virtually complete in most industrial host countries and some developing countries . . . only in a few countries . . . policies on foreign investment have not yet begun to emerge" (Bergsten, 1974, pp. 138-139).

It thus seems clear that the MNCs, whether they like it or not, will be obligated to adjust their strategies and policies to satisfy the host as well as the home countries' needs, demands, and policies. In other words, MNCs, in order to survive and grow, will have to perfect their act of balancing the requirements of efficiency through global rationalization of production and marketing processes, and at the same time adjust their operations to satisfy the special needs of the country in which they are operating. To say the least, it is a difficult act to master, but there seems to be no alternatives.

Nation-states also, for their part, must learn to balance their policies to secure obvious economic contributions made by the multinational enterprises against their own needs for maintaining national sovereign rights and self-respect. Particularly, the developing countries, in order to achieve stated industrial and economic growth, will still have to rely on one or another form of large-scale enterprises for the supply of advanced technology, capital, and management and marketing know-how.

To understand this process of accommodation between MNCs and nation-states, academic researchers could help a great deal by closing the gap between what we know and what we need to know about the functioning of MNCs, their strategies, policies, structures, and adaptative processes, as well as precise contributions of the MNCs to the host and home countries, especially to the developing countries where tension and conflict seem to be the most intensive.

THE MNCS' CONTRIBUTIONS TO THE HOST COUNTRIES

Although the claims of positive contributions by the MNCs to the host countries, in terms of supplying needed capital, technological and managerial know-how, improving the balance of payments position, increasing exports and reducing imports, developing human resources, and generating higher industrial and economic growth, and the counter-arguments by the critics over the negative impact of the MNCs abound in the public debate, the empirical evidence to substantiate these claims and arguments is largely lacking, while the little and scattered evidence that does exist is largely being ignored by policy makers and researchers alike (see Negandhi and Baliga, 1979, pp. 64-84.) For example, the available data on the impact of MNCs' investments on the balance of payments does suggest that more than often the developing countries seem to be the losers in this zero-sum game. A U.N. report on multinational corporations provides substantial evidence to pinpoint the negative impact of foreign investments on the balance of payments position of developing countries. For example, the report shows that between 1965 and 1970, the net direct foreign investment inflow of the investment into 43 developing countries was only 30% of the outflow of the investment's income in terms of remitted profit and royalty payments (United Nations, 1973). After reviewing a number of case studies on the impact of the MNCs' investments on the balance of payments' position, the U.N. reports concluded that in developing countries, where the availability of foreign exchange is often a problem, the excess of the investment's outflow over inflow has been a serious source of tension between the host countries and the multinational enterprises.

Strangely enough, the data generated by the U.S. Department of Commerce (1972), Business International (1972, 1974), National Foreign Trade Council (1971), the National Association of Manufacturers (1972), and the Emergency Committee for American Trade (1972), in the process of proving a positive impact of the American MNCs' investments on the U.S. balance of payment position, could be interpreted to show a negative impact on such investments on the host countries' balance of payment position.

However, as with most questions raised by multinational investment, that of the impact on the balance of payment is not so simple as the statistics really indicate. For example, it could be argued that foreign private investors, besides establishing "growth industries," which stimulate other businesses in the host countries, also generate considerable exports, earned foreign exchange, and decrease imports.

Case studies on the so-called multiplier effects of the MNCs' investments in the host countries are largely lacking and awaiting serious attention by the international business scholars.

Similarly, the impact of the MNCs' investments on employment, transfer of technology, management know-how, and so forth, is too sketchy to arrive at reasonable conclusions. We, indeed, need some concentrated efforts towards these directions (see Negandhi and Baliga, 1979, pp. 64-84).

THE MULTINATIONALS' STRATEGIES AND
THEIR POLICY MAKING

Turning to the operational aspects of the multinational corporations, we observed considerable controversies and disagreements among academic scholars, businesspeople, and government officials. It was argued, for example, that such concepts as global rationalization of production and marketing processes, global strategy, and even transnational enterprises are merely academic concepts without much practical meaning.

Multinational corporations may not differ from comparable large, local companies in terms of their strategies, policies, and adaptative processes. They all are embedded in their environments, and their responses to environmental demands are a function of the whims, wishes, and skills of those managing them.

The global strategy, and holy or unholy collusion between the MNCs' headquarters and subsidiaries, may be nothing more than myth, while the strategy formulation process and the policy making may be ad-hoc and largely counterproductive. Although the research studies on multinational corporations, generated during the last 15 years or so by the Harvard

Business School (Vernon, 1977; Stopford and Wells, 1972; and Negandhi and Baliga, 1979; and other scholars), provide some insight into the workings of American, European, and Japanese multinational corporations, we still have a long way to travel to provide satisfactory answers to the questions, such as:

1. In what manner and for what reason are the American, European, and Japanese multinationals different in terms of their strategies, policies, structures, and adaptive processes?   And what are the consequences of these differences for their survival and growth?
2. Why do American MNCs follow the so-called global strategy, while Europeans and Japanese are seemingly adjusting to the local conditions?   Does this behavior on the part of U.S. MNCs reflect ignorance or arrogance or some schema of a master plan?   Regarding European and Japanese MNCs, do their strategies of adapting to local conditions reflect lack of self-confidence and/or less bargaining power on their part?
3. Who is usually responsible for formulating and implementing corporate strategies and policies?   Are these rationally and logically determined, as claimed by some, or are they largely unsystematic, ad-hoc phenomena?
4. What will be the consequences of the emergence of multinational corporations from the developing countries (such as India, South Korea and Brazil) for the MNCs originating from the developed countries, as well as the developing countries' present policies on multinational investment?

Questions of global consequences, as well as the operational-level problems outlined above, await our attention as we move into the 1980s.

REFERENCES

Bergsten, Fred C. 1974. "Coming Investment Wars?" Foreign Affairs 53, no. 135.

---. 1972. The Effects of U.S. Corporate Foreign Investment 1960-1972. (Second in a series.) New York: Business International.

Emergency Committee for American Trade. 1972. The Role of the Multinational Corporation in the United States and World Economies. Washington, D.C.: Emergency Committee for American Trade.

National Association of Manufacturers. 1972. U.S. Stake in World Trade and Investment: The Role of Multinational Companies. New York: National Association of Manufacturers.

National Foreign Trade Council, Inc. 1971. The Impact of U.S. Foreign Direct Investment on U.S. Employment and Trade: An Assessment of Critical Claims and Legislative Proposals. New York: National Foreign Trade Council.

Negandhi, Anant R., and Baliga, B. R. 1979. Quest for Survival and Growth: A Comparative Study of American, European, and Japanese Multinationals. West Germany: Athenaum Verlag Konigstein. New York: Praeger.

Stopford, John and Wells, Louis T. Managing the Multinational Enterprise: Organization of the Firm and Ownership of the Subsidiaries. New York: Basic Books, Inc. 1972.

United Nations. 1973. Multinational Corporations in World Development. ST/ECA/190. New York: United Nations Publications.

United States Department of Commerce. 1972. Policy Aspects of Foreign Investment by U.S. Multinational Corporations. Washington, D.C.: U.S. Department of Commerce.

Vernon, Raymond. 1971. Sovereignty at Bay: The Multinational Spread of U.S. Enterprises. New York: Basic Books.

---. 1977. Storm over the Multinationals. Cambridge, Mass.: Harvard University Press.

Conference Participants

Michael Z. Brooke
The University of Manchester
Institute of Science and Technology
P.O. Box 88
Manchester M60 1QD
England

Mrs. P.A. Denham
Department of Industry
1 Victoria Street
London SW1H OET
England

Yves L. Doz
Graduate School of
Business Administration
Harvard University
Soldiers Field Road
Boston, Massachusetts 02163
USA

John H. Dunning
Faculty of Letters and Social Sciences
Department of Economics
University of Reading
Whiteknights
Reading RG6 2AA
England

Michel Ghertman
Centre d'Enseignement Superieur
des Affaires
78350 Jouy-en-Josas
France

Robert Grosse
Department of Finance
School of Business and
Organization Sciences
Florida International University
Tamiami Campus
Miami, Florida 33199
USA

Walter Goldberg
International Institute of Management
Platz der Luftbrucke 1-3
1000 Berlin 42
Germany

Gunnar Hedlund
Stockholm School of Economics
Institute of International Business
Stockholm
Sweden

Helmut Hoss
Honeywell GmbH
Kaiserleistr. 55
6050 Offenbach/Main
Germany

V.B. Kadam
Reserve Bank of India
Economic Department
Post Box No. 1036
Bombay 400 001
India

Hiro Matsusaki
Institute of Int'l Business
Georgia State Univ.
University Plaza
Atlanta, Georgia 30303
USA

Sandra and Andre van der Merwe
University of Witwaterstand
Graduate School of Business Admin.
2 St. David's Place
Parktown, Johannesburg
South Africa

Jean A. Millar
London Graduate School of
Business Studies
Sussex Place, Regents Park
London NW
England

Joseph Miller
Graduate School of Business Administration
Indiana University
Bloomington, Indiana 47401
USA

Sisir Mitra, President
Organization of Pharmaceutical
Producers of India
Thomas Cook's Building
Dr. Dadubhoy N. Road
Bombay 400 001,
India

Anant R. Negandhi
Department of Business Admin.
University of Illionois at
Urbana-Champaign
219 Commerce West
Urbana, Illinois 61801
USA

Lars Otterbeck
Stockholm School of Economics
Institute of International Business
Stockholm
Sweden

C.K. Prahalad
Graduate School of Business Admin.
University of Michigan
Ann Arbor, Michigan 48106
USA

H. Lee Remmers
I N S E A D
Boulevard de Constance
F-77305 Fontainebleau
Cedex, France

Alan M. Rugman
Assoc. Professor of Finance
Concordia University
1455 De Maisonneuve Blvd. West
Montreal, Quebec H3G 1M8
Canada

Karl P. Sauvant, Director
Center on Transnational Corporations
United Nations
New York, New York 10017
USA

Achim Sura
University of Konstanz
Postfach
7550 Konstanz
Germany

Bruce Stening
Department of Management
University of Western Australia
Nedlands
Western Australia 6009

John Stopford
London Graduate School of
Business Management
Sussex Place, Regent's Park
London NW1 4SA
England

Robert G. Vamberry
Baruch College
City University of New York
46 East 26th Street
New York, New York
USA

Name Index

Subject Index

About the
Contributors

ANANT R. NEGANDHI is a Professor of International Business at the University of Illinois at Urbana - Champaign. He earned his B.A. (Hons) B. Com degrees from the University of Bombay, India; his M.B.A from Texas Christian University; and his Ph.D. from Michigan State University. Prior to coming to the University of Illinois, he taught at the University of California in Los Angeles and Kent State University. During 1976-78, he served as Senior Research Fellow at the International Institute of Management Science Center Berlin in West Berlin, Germany. In 1977 he was appointed as Fellow of the Academy of Management and, in 1971, as Outstanding Educators of America. Dr. Negandhi has published over sixty scholarly articles in such journals as Human Relations, Academy of Management Journal, California Management Review, Business Topics, and Economic Records (Australia). He is the author of Quest for Survival and Growth: A Comparative Study of American, European and Japanese Multinationals (New York: Praeger Publishers, West Germany: Anthenaum, 1979). He was founder-editor of the quarterly journal Organization and Administrative Sciences.

B. RAJARAM BALIGA, D.B.A., Kent State University, is an Assistant Professor of International Business and Business Policy at Texas Technological University. He is the author of two research books and several articles. His latest book is Quest for Survival and Growth: A Comparative Study of

American, European and Japanese Multinationals (with A.R. Negandhi).

G. BOSEMAN, D.B.A., Kent State University, is an Associate Professor of Management at Temple University in Philadelphia, Pennsylvania. He is the author of several books and articles. His latest book Decision Making in Administration: Text, Critical Incidents and Cases (with J. Gatza and J.S. Milutinovich) was published by Saunders Publishing Company in 1979.

YVES L. DOZ, D.B.A., Harvard University, is an Assistant Professor of Business Administration at Harvard. He is the author of several articles and a book, Government Control and Multinational Strategic Management: Power Systems and Telecommunication Equipment (New York: Praeger Special Studies, 1979)

JAMES E. EVERETT, Ph.D., Cambridge University, is a lecturer in Management Science at the University of Western Australia. He is the author of several articles and has published in such journals as Financial Management.

KRISHNA KUMAR, Ph.D., Michigan State University, is a Research Associate and Project Coordinator of Transnational Impact Project. He is the author of several books and articles. His latest book TNEs: Their Impact on Societies and Cultures, was published by Westview Press in 1980.

JOSEPH C. MILLER, Ph.D., the University of Wisconsin-Madison and J.D. from the University of Chicago, is an Associate Professor at the Indiana University School of Business. He is the author of several articles.

HIRO MATSUSAKI, Ph.D., Michigan State University, is a Visiting Associate Professor at the Institute of International Business at Georgia State University. He is the author of several articles.

C.K. PRAHALAD, D.B.A., Harvard University, is an Associate Professor of Policy and Control at the University of Michigan in Ann Arbor. He is the author of several articles and his forthcoming book entitled Power within the Multinational (with J.L. Bower).

ALAN M. RUGMAN, Ph.D., Simon Fraser University, is a Visiting Associate Professor in the Graduate School of Business, Columbia University, and Associate Professor of Finance at Concordia University, Montreal. He is the author of International Diversification and the Multinational Enterprise (Lexington Books, 1979) and many other publications in the areas of international finance and international business.

KARL P. SAUVANT, Ph.D., University of Pennsylvania, is the Transnational Corporations Affairs Officer at the United Nations' Centre on Transnational Corporations in New York. He is the author of several books and articles. He is the editor of Changing Priorities on the International Agenda: The New International Economic Order (Elmsford, New York: Pergamon, forthcoming).

BRUCE W. STENING, Ph.D., University of New South Wales, is a Lecturer in Organizational Behavior at the University of Western Australia. He has published articles in such journals as Journal of Cross-Cultural Psychology, Journal of Social Psychology, and International Journal of Intercultural Relations.

ROBERT G. VAMBERY, Ph.D., Columbia University. He is the author of scholarly articles on international business and transportation, and of the book Capital Investment Control in the Air Transport Industry. (Oceana Publications, Inc. 1977)

ANDRE VAN DER MERWE, D Com, University of Stellenbosch, South Africa. His current research topic is on chief executives in both national and multinational companies.

SANDRA VAN DER MERWE, D.B.A., University of Stellenbosch, South Africa, is an author of several articles. Her current research interest is factors influencing foreign investment decisions by multinationals.